FRANCE - A JOURNEY
Recollections And Reflections

Part Two
From 2011 to 2015

Michael Clark

Grosvenor House
Publishing Limited

All rights reserved
Copyright © Michael Clark, 2021

The right of Michael Clark to be identified as the author of this
work has been asserted in accordance with Section 78
of the Copyright, Designs and Patents Act 1988

The book cover is copyright to Michael Clark

This book is published by
Grosvenor House Publishing Ltd
Link House
140 The Broadway, Tolworth, Surrey, KT6 7HT.
www.grosvenorhousepublishing.co.uk

This book is sold subject to the conditions that it shall not, by way of
trade or otherwise, be lent, resold, hired out or otherwise circulated
without the author's or publisher's prior consent in any form of binding or
cover other than that in which it is published and
without a similar condition including this condition being imposed
on the subsequent purchaser.

A CIP record for this book
is available from the British Library

ISBN 978-1-83975-625-2

Contents

An Introduction   v

Gizeux – Le Grand-Pressigny – Cajarc – Margon – Cassan – Méditerranéen – St-Thibery – Causse du Larzac – Vaylats – St Savin-sur-Gartempe – Le Lude – Montsûrs – Bayeux.
May/July 2011   1

Chinon – Richelieu – Chenonceau – Sologne – Chambord – Orléans – Saint-Amand-en-Puisaye – Vézelay – Noyers-sur-Serein – Château-de-Malaisy – Abbaye-de-Fontenay – Alesia – Flavigny-sur-Ozerain – Source de la Seine – Chateauneuf-en-Auxois – Abbaye de Cîteaux – Nolay – Château de Sully – Cluny – La Chaise-Dieu – Conques – La Taillade – Cahors – Cènevières – Albussac – Beaulieu – Argentat – Moussais-la-Bataille – Fresnay-sur-Sarthe – St-Evroult-Notre-Dame-du-Bois – Cerisy-la-Forêt – Arromanches – Formigny
August/October 2011   45

TGV to l'Herault   *June 2013*   207

Lille and Arras   *October 2014*   257

Farewell to Normandy   *September/October 2015*   301

An Epilogue   397

An Introduction

In Part 1 of *France – A Journey* I referred to events and experiences which contributed to my awareness of France – our nearest neighbour just across the Channel. My father's service in France during the Great War, day trips to France in the 1930s by family members, also in that same decade sitting on the beach at Weymouth and realising that beyond the horizon lies France and somehow relating that to the numerous young men in naval uniform. Then, of course, came 1939 and the Second World War, France became an enemy territory, accommodating the aircraft which frequently attacked our towns and cities, and constituting a real prospect of a German invasion.

Following the end of the war, my first venture into France was in the early 1950s – a visit to one of the launching sites of the V1 and V2 Rockets (Flying Bombs). A guided visit to Paris followed in August 1952.

However, my planned journey across France and into other countries in July 1956 ended on the outward crossing with a broken leg. Being incapacitated I was driven home to Camerton in my own car. What a blessing it was that, just a few weeks before, I had met and got to know, Margaret. She visited me regularly during my convalescence and our relationship was cemented for the next 60 years or so.

Cometh July 1970 and, as a family of four, from our camp site in Kent, we made a day visit to Boulogne. It was the first visit to France for Margaret, Paul and Ian. However, our first family holiday in France was not until July 1979. Then, in July 1980, the four of us completed a journey incorporating France, Italy, Switzerland, Germany and France which was very similar to that which I had planned, but was aborted, in 1956. Thereafter, we visited France every year at least once, often twice and occasionally three times until 2015, except that we had to abandon plans for 2012 because of Margaret's deteriorating health.

Margaret contributed so much to our journeys, not only reliable navigating, but particularly in meticulously maintaining a detailed daily diary. It was indeed her hope and wish that I should prepare a narrative of her diary records. Unfortunately, I fear that my life will simply not be long enough to record all our journeys in a meaningful way, but it has been an immense pleasure to compile these two parts of *France – A Journey*.

I hope you will find interest in the journeys described in this part.

Gizeux – Le Grand-Pressigny – Cajarc – Margon – Cassan – Méditerranéen – St-Thibery – Causse du Larzac – Vaylats – St Savin-sur-Gartempe – Le Lude – Montsûrs – Bayeux

MAY/JULY 2011

For many years we have much enjoyed the character and atmosphere, the 'southern sun' and the pattern of life of the southern regions of France, the Herault Department, in particular. As this year could well be our last opportunity to do so, we felt we would like to spend a longer period in our 'summer retreat' and for the tenth year in succession. Acknowledging that, having reached the age of eighty and, as I might not enjoy the long drive to the Mediterranean so much as in past years, we considered travelling by train to Agde.

However, when we discovered that *Barfleur* was returning to provide a convenient ferry service from Poole and, in view of the fact that we would very much like to visit our friend Ginette, at Cénevières in the Lot Department, following the death of Maurice and also, that it would be impossible to take with us all that we like to have, we made the decision to once again make the journey by car in comfortable stages.

Day 1 – Friday, 27 May 2011

We left home at 08.50; it was a pleasant journey with only moderate traffic and no hold-ups, reaching Poole Harbour at 10.15. Fortunately, we were allowed to board almost immediately and without being asked any ridiculous questions as in previous years, such as, "Have you any knives, guns, or weapons with you". Unfortunately, because of weather conditions, the crossing was not one of the most enjoyable, but we docked at Cherbourg at 16.30. Being on the upper car deck it was some 20 minutes before we were able to drive off. However, we were allowed to drive through the French border controls with little more than a salute without really stopping and we were quickly on to the N13 (E46) and driving down the familiar route of the Cotentin peninsula. Because of road works in connection with the construction of the new N174 and its link with the N13 we missed the existing turning for St-Jean-de-Daye and had to continue until the next junction then taking the D5, D11, D6, passing through Moon-sur-Elle (the only information I can offer about this commune in the Manche Department is that in 2006 it had a population of 838) and eventually finding our way through St-Lô before joining our intended route, the N174, to the west of the town. Invariably, and this was no exception, we spend half an hour or so at Torigni-sur-Vire for refreshments before continuing to VIRE which we reached at 19.30. We had driven 134 miles so far and it is 14°C. Finding somewhere to park near the Hôtel de France was always difficult and we had to wait some while for a space to become available. We have sojourned at this hotel on many occasions in the past but not for some years and it was strange not to recognise anyone and not to be recognised as, of course, it has changed hands. As it was a pleasant evening we walked around the quiet and peaceful town of Vire; we noted that we did not see any unoccupied shop premises and neither did we see any charity shops. We could not help thinking of the town we had left in the morning!

(134 miles)

Day 2 – Saturday, 28 May 2011

After a good night in a very comfortable room and a satisfactory breakfast we left Hôtel de France and Vire at 10.40 for Chinon. We drove non-stop to La Fleche a distance of just about 100 miles – D524 – Tinchebray – D22 – Domfront – D962 – Ceauce – Ambrières-les-Vallées – Mayenne – N162 – D24 – Montsûrs – D24- Vaiges – Ballée – D21 – Sable-s-Sarthe – La Flèche at 13.24. As always it was a most enjoyable drive and, once again parking under the plane trees between the Loir and the road, we had a welcome meal of sandwiches, etc., while sitting in the car. As usual we had some food for the ducks which, not being content to be fed in the river, flew up over the wall and gathered around the car. This is always a very pleasant place for a refreshment stop and, indeed, to linger for a couple of hours for, in addition to its convenient location, it has very attractive views along the river. However, at 15.25 we felt we must continue our journey taking the D306 for Le Lude and then the D307.

When we were driving along the D767 between Le Lude and Noyant on 31 August of last year we discovered the ancient Abbey of LA BOISSIERE. Fortunately, we had found the chapel open and we were able to go inside. However, we did not have time to explore any of the other buildings, therefore, we made another diversion today, at 16.30. On this occasion we walked along the road leading to Dénezé-sous-le-Lude and towards the other buildings of the convent where we were greeted by a rather large and vociferous chien. It was not long before a lady came to our rescue and we had a very interesting conversation during which it emerged that the other buildings, including the former dormitory of the monks, are in private occupation and not open to the public. Also, we found that on this occasion the chapel itself was closed.

We then continued on the D767 through Noyant – D141 – Breil and Parcay-les-Pins – D86 to GIZEUX where we decided to, at least, find the château. The Château de Gizeux is a very impressive edifice and is a fully furnished residence where three generations of the de Laffon family live together. There is a record of a wooden fortress built in the 11th century on the actual site. However, it completely disappeared, and the oldest parts of the existing buildings are the entry tower, the right wing and the enclosure which go back to 1334. From 1315 to 1660 the Château belonged to the du Bellay family; during the Renaissance Period they enlarged it by building the main building in a 'U' shape. Joachim du Bellay, the writer and poet, was born in 1522 and died on 1 January 1560. During the 18th and into the 19th century the Château was in the ownership of the Contades dynasty. This château is open to the public from April to November. As we had parked in front of l'église we spent 10 minutes inside; it contains splendid tombs of the du Bellay family. We also photographed the nearby war memorial. In 2008 the population of Gizeux was 451.

We proceeded via Bourgueil – D749 – to Avoine, where, in view of the fact that tomorrow was Sunday, we felt it advisable to fill the tank. Unfortunately, the station was closed but, for the first time anywhere, we made use of the automatic facility – 43 litres, €67.47. We duly arrived at CHINON at 18.00 where the temperature was 23°C. The distance from Vire to Chinon was 159 miles – a wholly enjoyable journey. Having parked in front of the hotel we were soon very warmly welcomed at the Hotel Le Plantagenet by Martine and Barbara. We were taken again to the very comfortable room which is equipped for the use of disabled persons (perhaps it was the obviously advancing years that prompted them to provide us with this facility!) and Barbara ensured that all our likely needs were provided for before leaving for home. It was a very pleasant evening and we walked through the centre of the town and to the Rabelais statue before returning alongside the river Vienne. Back at the hotel there was time enough to see the last part of the European Cup Final between Barcelona and Manchester United (I will not mention the result) before l'heure du coucher.

(159 miles)

Day 3 – Sunday, 29 May 2011

Petit déjeuner at Le Plantagenet always includes a wide variety of food not least the range of lovely jams made by Martine. We left the hotel at 11.20 looking forward to returning at the end of August.

Our first destination today is Le Grand-Pressigny. From Chinon the D8 took us along the north side of the Vienne with vineyards on our left; continuing on the D760 with the vast cereal lands of Touraine to our right before bypassing Ste Maure-de-Touraine; then taking the D59 for Sepmes and Liguel; the D50 and D60 brings us to Le GRAND-PRESSIGNY. Once again, we left the D60 and drove the few hundred yards to the elevated site of the Château. It was 12.40 and 23°C.

Prehistoric man lived in this area of Touraine 400,000 years ago, attracted by an abundance of high-quality flint which could be fashioned into superb tools and weapons. From the evidence of much excavation work carried out around the Château there was a human presence in this area from the Neolithic Age. The Château is a major monument in southern Touraine; it was a mighty defensive fortress. Construction of the donjon of the Château was begun by Guillaume de Pressigny in about 1193. It was later enhanced by a strong defensive enclosure with towers and was restored in about 1560. It was the scene of numerous combats and it had many owners during the course of its history. In time it was gradually abandoned and was taken apart stone by stone during the Revolution.

During the past few years we have often spent some time here, viewing the progress being made in the extensive work of preservation and restoration of the Château and the construction of the integrated Musée de la Prehistoire. Fortunately, and wisely, in the early stages of the work the adjacent grassed car park was laid out and young trees planted to mark the parking places.

Today we planned to spend as much time as possible inside the Musée, a contemporary building designed by the German architect Bernd Hoge, which was completed in 2009. However, we found that two hours was simply not long enough; as Margaret wrote, one could spend days looking, listening and reading about the remarkable displays. There is a fascinating illustrated version of the history of the Château. Flint from Le Grand-Pressigny has a place of honour in this museum and is described in all its different aspects; the way in which mankind understood and took advantage of its qualities and uses 100,000 years ago is well demonstrated. There are exhibits relating to the different civilizations found in Touraine from the middle of the Palaeolithic Age, about 100,000 years ago, until the use of flint disappeared and was replaced by bronze about 3,000 years ago. This is an excellently presented exhibition in a very spacious setting, an amazing place and well worth a visit.

Eventually we had to leave this village which proudly possesses, not only this wonderful historical feature but also, it seems, all the necessary shops, services, etc., to meet the everyday needs of its 1,029 inhabitants (2008) and visitors. We hope we shall return. At 16.00 and the temperature having fallen from 39°C to 31°C, we left for St Junien.

Our route was:- D42 – Preuilly-s-Claise – D14 – Tournon-St-Pierre – D950 – Le Blanc – D975 – La Trimouille – D675 – Le Dorat – Bellac – Montemorte – St JUNIEN.

The route from Le Blanc to Le Dorat of about 30 miles is a glorious straight road and rarely have we met more than half a dozen cars. However, it was a tiring day and shortly before reaching Le Dorat we stopped for a 20-minute rest.

We arrived at Hôtel Le Bœuf Rouge at 18.50; it was still 27°C. We have always found this excellent hotel very convenient for an overnight (and longer) séjour. It has a private car park and is just a few yards from the centre of the town. It had been a hard day and very hot. We bought a quiche from the nearby pâtisserie, which we ate in the car park opposite the hotel, and enjoyed a very pleasant walk in the evening sun.

(127 miles)

Prehistory – Period from the first humans (5 million years ago) to the invention of writing.

Paleolithic Age (Old Stone Age) – Period extends from the earliest known use of stone tools about 2.6 million years ago to about 10,000 years ago.

Neolithic Age (New Stone Age) – Period from about 4000 BC to about 2000 BC

Day 4 – Monday, 30 May 2011

I have written about the history of St Junien in the record of our August/September 2002 journey in *France – A Journey Part 1*.

After petit déjeuner, provided as usual in the foyer of the hotel, we walked into the town and bought some postcards and *Le Monde* before leaving St. Junien, sadly for the last time, for Cajarc, at 10.50. It was 23°C.

Continuing on the D675 to Rochechouart, still in the Department of Haute Vienne, where we passed again the Garage Mounier which came to our rescue with a new battery in St Junien a few years ago. Then the D901 is a picturesque route and long stretches are particularly attractive where the road is profusely lined with wild ferns. Next to Oradour-sur-Vayres and Châlus, where Richard Cœur de Lion was mortally wounded outside the Château in 1199. Still the D901 to Bussière-Galant and St-Yrieix-la-Perche. Shortly after Glandon on the D18 we crossed, at noon, into the Department of Corrèze which is Anne and Jim country and also that of former President of France, Jacques Chirac! On the D6, we headed once again for one of 'Les Plus Beaux Villages de France' – Ségur-le-Château – which we reached at 12.20. This is a gem of a village where one can park under the trees alongside the gentle little river l'Auvézère and at the small cafe just a few yards away Monsieur is always ready to provide an excellent and welcome plate of frites. We had an excellent 'lunch' of frites et jus d'orange (and bananas) for €8.50. Although it was a beautiful day at that time Monsieur mentioned that they were expecting rain later in the afternoon! It was a very welcome break, but at 14.00 we returned to our route.

Our route then was – D6 – D31 – Arnac-Pompadour – D7 – Vigeois – D7 – Le Bariolet to Junction 46 of Autoroute A20 in the direction of Toulouse. Immediately after joining the Autoroute, we made a brief stop at the Aire de Pay du Grace for refreshments – it was 27°C. We resumed the journey at 14.40.

This was a very convenient way of by-passing Brive and we covered the next 82 miles in 85 minutes. However, as we passed Cahors and approached the junction 58 for Lalbenque (Cahors South) where we would leave the Autoroute, there were extensive and very threatening storm clouds to our left. Just at the moment that we identified the arrows directing us to the exit we entered the 'orage'. Traffic slowed and we edged forward slowly moving to the right and stopped where we hoped we were in a safe position as by then water simply poured over us and I could see nothing; the weight of water stopped the windscreen wipers. After some while we were able to see sufficiently to make our way to the péage and to formally leave the Autoroute. We were then able to enter a parking area where we waited while the thunder, lightning and rain took its course. It was a very severe storm and I have never been travelling in the car in such torrential 'rain'. In all it was 40 minutes before we could sensibly attempt to continue our journey to Lalbenque. We were now on the familiar D19 to Bach and Varaire. We have bought petrol at the Total Station at Limogne-en-Quercy in the past and we did so again and once more using the automatic facility. 46 litres, €73.14.

At 18.00, by the D59, we arrived at Hôtel La Ségalière in CAJARC where we had spent a night last year. As the car park is some distance from the entrance we took as much of our luggage with us as we could, but when we met Madame at the reception, we could not believe her response. It was a little unconvincing, but she had to tell us that there was no reservation and, in fact, no available room. We were very displeased, and we were able to produce our formal 'confirmation of reservation'. She clearly blamed the Logis Central Booking and made a copy of our document. She suggested that we might continue to Figeac, some 25 kilometres further on, for the night. It was only when we insisted that we wished to stay in Cajarc in order to visit a friend in Cénevières in the morning that Madame contacted, perhaps reluctantly, Hôtel La Peyrade in Cajarc and discovered that they could accommodate us. We found this alternative – apartment 4, with its view overlooking the village nestling in the Valley of the Lot, to be very satisfactory, comfortable and less expensive. I should record that on returning home we found that, after leaving on 27 May, we had been advised that we could not make the reservation and we had also received a letter of apology from Christine Bonay of La Ségalière.

We do not know Cajarc very well, but it is on the pilgrimage route from Le Puy to Santiago de Compostela. Also, it was the birthplace in 1935 of the playwright and novelist Françoise Sagan who died in 2004.

(180 miles)

Day 5 – Tuesday, 31 May 2011

We had had a good night at La Peyrade. However, it was a wet and misty morning and only 15°C, but we did some shopping and bought 12 souvenir cartes postale and the day's *Le Monde*.

At 10.15 we took the narrow and twisting D6 road south of the Lot to Cénevières and, as we had arranged during the previous evening, we visited Ginette; she was extremely pleased to see us and is looking forward to doing so again in September. After spending an interesting and much appreciated one hour and 25 minutes with her, we left at 12.05 to re-join our planned route at Limogne-en-Quercy.

We had not travelled very far along the D911 towards Villefranche-de-Rouergue when we reached the little village of Martiel where we know a patisserie which displays two remarkably realistic and lifelike ancient figures in a typical domestic setting. We could not resist stopping here again to buy some nourishment – €8.50 – for later in the day. As we continued south of Rodez, through Rieupeyroux, Baraqueville and Pont-de-Salars towards the A75 the weather was remarkably like it was on the same route last year – wet and misty, indeed at times, with very poor visibility. However, as we reached the A75 it became much clearer. We have found that the Aire de Garrigue, immediately after joining the auto-route at junction 44.1 in the direction of Millau, provides a very convenient rest area. We had a very good 'meal' of patisseries, etc; the weather had much improved and after about 85 minutes we left at 16.10 for the last part of today's journey.

This is a wonderful section of motorway, first crossing the spectacular Viaduc de Millau, which, at 343 metres, is still the highest bridge in the world, then across the Causse du Larzac before descending the Pas de l'Escalette which provides wonderful views. We left at junction 59 for Pézenas and continued on the D13 and D33 for Alignan-du-Vent and MARGON.

We arrived at the Auberge du Château at 18.02 when the temperature was 22°C, but we were disappointed not to find Fabienne and Florent there. We were very courteously welcomed by a lady we had not met before and we soon discovered that it was un jour de repos pour les propriétaires. However, before the end of the day we were welcomed again by Fabienne and Florent.

(171 miles)

Day 6 – Wednesday, 1 June 2011

We had read about the CHATEAU ABBAYE de CASSAN near Roujan and of concerts held there but had never visited it. It was a cold and very windy morning and only 14°C and nothing like the kind of weather one expects at this time of year in Southern France. Nevertheless, at 11.10, we decided to drive the short distance via the D30 and D13 to the Château only to find that it would open at 14.00.

At 12.00 we were in Pézenas where it was beginning to rain; we parked (free) under the trees and made for the nearest cup of coffee. We did not have to go very far to Le Moliere where we were able to have not only coffee but also crêpes with confiture des fraises. It was delicious! After buying some postcards we returned to Casson at 14.30.

Before entering the Château we made a note of the inscription above the door "Prieure Royal N D de CASSAN. En 805 Charlemagne fonde ce prieuré que allait etre, durant mille ans, le plus illustre monastère du Bitterôis. Eglise Romane XIIc – Palais conventuel XVIIIc". We spent much time inside visiting rooms containing displays depicting life in past times and a number of rooms that are lightly furnished in the style of earlier centuries. We also saw the church which has no windows, and which is devoid of all furnishings other than a stage for concerts.

Afterwards we walked around the whole of the rear 'gardens'; it was windy but invigorating! Since returning home we have seen aerial views of the Château and also views of the rooms we had visited on French Television during the course of the coverage of this year's Tour de France which passed nearby. The Château has been built, razed, rebuilt, burnt down and is still being rebuilt and the present owners hope to restore it to its former glory.

Cassan is likely to have been of Celtic origin; the Gallo-Romans took it over; after the fall of Rome in 410 came the Wisogoths; when the Goths were defeated by Clovis in 480 Cassan became occupied as part of the Frankish Kingdom under the Merovingiens followed by the Carolingiens. There is no doubt that a church belonging to the family of Guilhem Alquier a descendant of the Carolingien Counts existed at Cassan. Was the church founded by Charlemagne or earlier at the time of Clovis or even in the early days of Christianity? Studies are still being carried out with a view to determining when Christianity first came to Cassan.

Saint Giraud constructed the present Priory Church, which was consecrated on 6 October 1115, the same year that St Bernard founded Clairvaux. The Church has a 45-metre-long single nave which spans more than 12 metres and is 15 metres high. The lateral forces pushing the walls apart are enormous and the architects of the period decided to counteract this by placing massive weight on the walls, which are themselves two to three metres thick. There is no wooden frame above the Romanesque vault but an infill of masonry under a stone roof, to which more infill was subsequently added and then covered with tiles; the total weight is some 2,400 tons.

The Château has had many owners, and many uses in its time including housing wine vats in the church, being a transit centre for young workers from the Overseas Territories and, in future, it is to become a European Centre for Disease Prevention and Research. It now hosts cultural events, concerts, receptions, study days, etc. This is a most interesting building.

We returned to the car at 17.15 and were pleased to be able to sit down. At 17.40 we were back at the Auberge du Château; it was still only 15°C and we were looking forward to a meal in the restaurant. Other than petit déjeuner we had not had a formal meal since leaving home and so the repas prepared by Florent and served by Fabienne was much enjoyed and appreciated in the usual friendly atmosphere.

It was an excellent meal:- "M – Agneau. M E – Porc and lovely Aveyron Red for both. Both had a small piece of asparagus – first taste – very nice. Also, first cups of mint tea! – liked that too! Several tasty morsels for afters! Then café décaféiné."

(23 miles)

<u>Days 7 to 33 – Thursday 2 June to Tuesday 28 June 2011</u>

We have always enjoyed our sojourns at this welcoming and friendly Auberge du Château at Margon where les propriétaires work so hard; knowing that we will not visit Fabienne and Florent again does not make it easy to say farewell. It was still raining with the temperature at only 13°C when we left at 11.00 and, as it is only a short distance of about 30 miles to le Cap, we decided to stop in Pézenas for another cup of coffee – €7 – at Le Moliere. At 13.00 and still raining we continued this last section of our journey.

(27 miles)

We arrived at Le CAP d'AGDE at 13.35; it was now dry, 15°C and our mileage from home – 821. We were pleased to see familiar faces again at the reception office and completing the formalities and collecting our keys was a very straightforward matter after so many years. Unfortunately, when we reached our secure parking place, we simply could not unlock the barrier. On returning to the office we were advised that the key no longer works and it was only necessary to press the button! That was true. Then, when we entered the apartment, we found that it was in darkness with the blind closed and the electricity switched off. We were prepared for this and we had a torch to enable us to find the switch. Next, we realised that we had no water, but a quick telephone call brought a response within minutes, we were reconnected and "All was well!!". In all probability the flat had not been used for some while and these services had been switched off.

This is the 10th year in succession that we have occupied this apartment, which we understood was privately owned. When we came here first in 2002 it was in excellent condition, the decoration, the furnishings, the accessories, the equipment, the facilities, etc., were all very satisfactory; it was very welcoming and so it has been every year since; always the privacy and quietude has been all that we have wished. Year after year we have returned 'home' and seemingly found it just as we had left it. How nice it has been to find the same cups, plates, cutlery, etc., ready for our use every year. The building itself is now perhaps 30–40 years old and it is not a luxury flat, but it is very practical, functional and very well equipped. It is very adequate for two persons, roomy and comfortable. In fact, it has long felt like a second home; to enhance the feeling of familiarity, comfort and warmth we tend to take with us much more in the way of personal possessions than is necessary.

It was very helpful to have access to the apartment in the afternoon, although it may have explained why the electricity and water were still disconnected! It gave us time to carry from the car most of what we would like to have for the next four weeks, to get established and, particularly, to do some shopping, before the end of the day. We soon renewed our acquaintance with, and were welcomed by, Madame at the Pâtisserie and staff at the Spar. We quickly sensed a great disappointment in the current poor weather, particularly, as it was the beginning of the main holiday season and also as it had been an exceptional spring for much of France. We had already heard stories of extremely hot days with temperatures as high as 40°C. However, we felt that during the coming weeks we would at least have a variety of weather and so it happened, but there were perhaps too many days when the forecast was described as 'maussade' (gloomy).

How often does one enter upon a new day hoping, wishing, or even longing to be able to devote one's hours to a particular task, a project, an interest, an idea, but which has no degree of priority? Then suddenly one is awakened to all the routines of daily life and the seemingly endless domestic chores of home.

Here in this apartment for the tenth successive year, with virtually all the facilities and attributes of our Trowbridge home, we also feel at home.

So, how did we spend our holiday at home by the sea? Importantly, we did not use the car during our four-week stay and we lived much as we do at home except that we are conveniently able to do shopping as and when we need to. We did not eat or drink (apart from one ice-cream) other than in the flat and we had our main meal in the evening.

Although it was not always particularly inviting, I went out every morning at about 7.00 or soon after – unfortunately after sunrise – with one exception when it was thundering in the vicinity, for a walk/run of about three to four kilometres along the shore. This is a wonderful time of the day when, as the beach is virtually deserted, one observes the many different moods of the sea, varying from calm, to agitated and sometimes to disturbed; sometimes the wind blows in from the sea and sometimes it is the Tramontane which is evident. This strong, dry cold north wind funnels down the corridor between the Pyrénées and the Massif Central and often seems to be the precursor of clearer weather. Another pleasing feature of the early morning is that of often meeting the same people and exchanging a greeting; I recall one or two fishermen, one gentleman who regularly touched his cap and an elderly lady who, even with the aid of a walking stick had difficulty in walking, always greeted me with a meaningful "Bonjour, Monsieur". Often the drivers of tractors and other vehicles in the process of preparing the beach area for the coming day gave a friendly wave. It was particularly gratifying to be able to run the two kilometres on mon anniversaire – this time the 81st – as I have done for the past five years.

Afterwards and before having our petit déjeuner we both usually went out to buy a pain complet (wholemeal loaf), croissants and often a delicious pain-au-raisin for our lunch; then if the weather permitted, walked around the harbour. Later in the day, we did shopping when it was required, and when the weather was appropriate, we sometimes walked along by the sea and spent time sitting on the beach; on one particularly beautiful evening we stayed until nearly 9pm. There was further physical exercise in accepting the annual challenge of running up the flight of 16 steps to our apartment level almost every time we returned.

Every morning without fail we purchased a copy of the local regional paper, the *Midi Libre*. This contains much news about the area from the large towns such as Beziers and Pézenas as well as many small villages quite a lot of which we know. There are reports of cultural, sporting and social activities in very small communities as well as personal news items. It makes us feel in touch with and part of the local area.

There are two recorded events which stand out in our memory. On Monday 20 June a 13-year-old girl called Carla was killed outside her school, the Collège Voltaire, at Florensac near Pézenas. The background to this terrible event was the rivalry between her and another girl of the same age regarding, mainly it seems, their relationship with a boy at another school. This rivalry had become so intense that the local Maire had become involved and that the second girl had not attended school for several weeks. When finally she returned to her classes her brother of 14 years came to meet her at the end of the day. Apparently, he was mocked by Carla and her friends and he was unable to restrain himself from applying one or two blows to her head. These proved to be fatal. There was "immense émotion" in the village and much speculation as to how such a situation could develop in this village. Apparently, there had been a "violent échange sur Facebook" and there is much concern regarding the ease with which ill-conceived messages can be instantly transmitted by Facebook and mobile phones. We understand that the Maire is so concerned about the unhealthy role of the internet and of mobile phones that he has written to the President of France. Some 1,000 people attended Carla's funeral. Unfortunately, back in England, we do not know more of the consequences (trial of the accused, etc.) of this tragedy.

The second event related to a supermarket near Beziers where concerned customers had noticed a little girl of three years left in a car with the windows closed and the temperature outside was about 30°C; the vehicle bore a German registration. The manager of the supermarket broadcast three messages, one in German, but they brought no response. He contacted the security services and was advised to do something immediately. Without delay he smashed the window of the car and released the girl; just in time it seems. When, eventually, her parents were located, the mother continued to do her shopping and the father has since threatened to make a claim against the company in respect of the damage done to his 4 x 4!!!

It is, of course, helpful and important to understand as much of the structure of the French language as is possible and we are always keen to improve our knowledge and experience by reading and understanding. In addition to the regular reading material provided by *Midi Libre*, particularly the very descriptive 'météo' for the day, we completed several crosswords (with a little cheating). We listened again to the eight CDs of the course *French with Michel Thomas*, the emphasis of which is on speaking the language.

Many years ago, I prepared a series of notes – some basic principles – on some aspects of French grammar, the parts of speech, etc., with the notable exception of the verb. However, to master speaking and writing French it is essential to understand its verb system.

During our four weeks 'holiday' I spent much time studying verbs with the help of *French Verb Drills* by R. de Roussy de Sales and preparing a chart of the various forms of the most commonly used verbs. At that time, I felt that I had a better understanding of the 'subjunctive', the verb form which is used much more in French than in English!!

On an earlier journey, in the shop of the Abbey Church of Saint-Savin-sur-Gartempe, which we frequented often, we bought an excellent book by Patrick Huchet, *Les Templiers – de la gloire à la tragédie*. We are interested in the history of Les Templiers and, as shortly we would once again be crossing the Larzac which holds much evidence of Templier activity, now would be an appropriate time to begin to read it. I made quite a lot of progress in reading, translating and preparing a summary in English and I hoped to find the time to continue this task in Trowbridge.

We did not purchase a single English language newspaper during those four weeks, but we kept in touch with national (French) and international affairs by watching *Le Journal* on television almost every evening. Of course, we watched a number of television programmes which have become favourites at home in England.

I feel that this summary gives a fairly full account of how we spent our 'holiday' by the sea. It was relaxing, enjoyable, satisfying, rewarding and fulfilling. We left with a feeling of accomplishment.

<u>Day 34 – Wednesday, 29 June 2011</u>

It was an early visit to the pâtisserie for a pain complet and croissants for petit déjeuner.

Although I had returned some of our possessions to the car on previous days there was still the unenviable task of gathering together everything that was still spread around our apartment, as well as food, etc., which we would be taking home, and making many journeys to the car. Eventually, at 11.50, we were ready to vacate the flat and, fortunately, we had not been prompted to do so. It was sunny but very windy as we drove to the reception office to return our keys where the friendly young lady expressed the hope that we would return next year. Then, before leaving Le Cap, we walked the short distance to the pâtisserie to buy two quiches lorraine for our 'lunch' later in the day and to say a final 'au revoir'. We lingered in the office, not anxious to leave, and had refreshing drinks of water. It was 13.40 when we actually started our journey to Le Caylar and the temperature was 28°C.

We had not far to go and so we decided to make a stop at St-THIBERY. We had visited this village some 30 years earlier, but we would like to see again the remains of the Pont Romain which crossed the river Hérault. This bridge is dated to the reign of Augustus (30 BC – AD 14); its missing spans were destroyed by flood some time before 1536. It was on the Via Domitia which was the first Roman road built in Gaul and linked Italy and Hispania. Nearby is a water mill – the 'Moulin A Bled du XIII C'. Also nearby is the former railway which is now in use as a 'Pedalorail'. While we were there a gentleman arrived on a bicycle with his cat standing on his shoulders; we could see that the cat was wearing a collar and lead which was linked to the man's waist. A strange sight! This was a very interesting visit which ended with a conversation with two English couples who were staying at Montagnac.

As it was only a short distance along the same road, we continued to FLORENSAC where we saw the Collège Voltaire where Carla was murdered. It is a very modern attractive looking establishment unlike schools as we know them.

Our next stop was at 16.05 in Pézenas for petrol – 44 litres, €1.53 per litre = €67.32 – 35°C – before joining the A75; this part of the journey northwards towards the Pas de Escalette provides spectacular views of the southern edge of the Massif Central. Leaving the A75 at junction 49 for Le CAYLAR on the Larzac, it is only few hundred yards to Hôtel du Rocher and we arrived at 17.25; the temperature here was only 16°C. We were met by a lady we had not seen before, but we were given the key to the same room (21) that we have occupied in past years. Très bon!

(64 miles)

Day 35 – Thursday, 30 June 2011

The CAUSSE du LARZAC is the largest and most southern of the Grands Causses and covers a vast area of 1,000 square kilometres. The plateau is uneven with deep hollows of up to 150 metres. It is often rugged and barren, but its differing soils provide pastureland for sheep and cultivated plains for producing cereals and fodder for animal raising. The area has an annual rainfall of nearly one metre. For many centuries the Larzac has had military associations, beginning with Les Templiers from the XIIth century to the beginning of the XIVth century. They were followed by the Hospitalliers from 1312 to 1789. Since the beginning of the XXth century a military camp has been based at La Cavalerie.

A large part of the Larzac was under the control of Les Templiers for some 200 years and was an important commanderie of the Order. Les Templiers grouped the scattered populations together at Sainte-Eulalie de Cernon, La Cavalerie and La Couvertoirade. This land contributed much to the Order and thus to the Crusades of the XIIth and XIIIth centuries. Following the purchase of the church at Sainte-Eulalie from the Abbey of Saint-Guilhem-le-Désert and additional purchases with the aid of donations, etc., Les Templiers became established as the main owner of the Larzac. However, they were not soldiers, but mainly agricultural producers; their role was to supply the soldiers of the Holy Land. During the past three years we have visited successively La Couvertoirade, Sainte-Eulalie and La Cavalerie and there are two other sites of historic significance.

It was a lovely morning but with a cool breeze on the Larzac and the temperature was 18°C when we left the hotel at 11.15. We drove along the D609, pausing again alongside the site of the Le Pezade graves and memorial of resistants, then by the D7 through Cornus to Fondamonte where we joined the minor road, D93, for St-Beaulize, St-Jean-et-St-Paul and finally to St-JEAN d'ALCAS which is situated far from any major road. It was 12.30 and warmer here – 22°C. In 1356 the first signs of a defence system appeared at the beginning of the Hundred Years War; the church was raised and fortified so as to serve as a refuge for the population. However, it soon became insufficient and the need to have a fortified site became very real. St-Jean d'Alcas is neither of Templier nor Hospitallier origin, but this enclosed rectangular fortified village defended by four little corner towers is contemporary to the XVth century work of the Hospitalliers; the parallel streets are lined with almost identical houses, reminiscent of monk's cells. It owes its construction in 1439 to the generosity of an abbess of the neighbouring Cistercian abbey of Nonenque, to whom the place belonged. Above a window of the courtroom the arms of the founding Abbess can be seen.

At 15.30 – the temperature was now 27°C – we left to make our way to Viala-du-Pas-de-Jaux following the excellent direction signs of the D559 and D23. Before climbing up onto the plateau we could see high above us a very prominent cross; unfortunately, when we reached the Aire de la Croix de Crepounac at 16.00, although we could see the cross through the trees, we were still some distance from it. As we continued, we passed, then stopped to photograph, an artificial dewpond which contained goldfish!

When we reached VIALA-du-PAS-de-JAUX we were able to park in a nearby field from where it was only a short walk to the tower. This village already existed at the time of Les Templiers but it was Les Hospitalliers who developed it, installing a farm which was managed by one of the brothers of the Order and building a church there in 1315. In about 1430 during the Hundred Years War, due to the very insecure climate and the long distance from the commanderie of Sainte-Eulalie, an enormous tower was built adjacent to the dwellings so that the villagers, together with their goods and animals, could take refuge there in times of danger. The tower is 27 metres high with five levels; for security reasons the ground floor was vaulted, and the door was put on the first floor. About 40 years ago the XVIIth century vault collapsed; it has just been restored and it is now possible to reach the terrace built on the top of the tower. However, the XIVth century logis leaning against the tower is in an advanced state of ruin, but it is being restored to its previous state. We did not ascend the tower, but we visited the shop, etc., and saw some of the restoration work being carried out in the dwelling. In the surrounding area are ancient transhumance routes which cross the Causse.

At 17.53 we left this very interesting site to return to Le Caylar. Along the D23, before joining the D2009, we passed the road for Ste-Eulalie-de-Cernon (D56) and the sign for the 6th century Chapelle St-Amans. We have not visited this building as we have not discovered how far it is along a track from the road. A little further on we stopped briefly at the Pic-de-Cougouille, where, at 912 metres, one has a view of Ste-Eulalie. We have had a pique-nique at this viewpoint!

It was 18.30 when, back at Le Caylar, we had to park in an adjoining car park; the temperature was 24°C. As we had not, so far, met 'Madame' we had come to the conclusion that the hotel had changed hands. However, as we had decided to have our second and last restaurant meal of our journey here, we were extremely pleased to be greeted by the lady we had known from all our previous visits. We had an enjoyable meal – although we were too late for lamb – which we followed with a short walk to see again the 'sculptured tree' – the fascinating carved elm tree.

(51 miles)

Day 36 – Friday, 1 July 2011

Today, entering into our third consecutive month in France, we leave Hotel du Rocher for the last time – time for more final farewells, but retaining many wonderful memories of the fascinating historic and physical features of this area. It was a pleasant morning and 21°C as we purchased our last possible copy of *Midi Libre* and a postcard and left Le Caylar at 10.50 for Frayssinet.

We have crossed the Causse du Larzac before construction of the Autoroute A75 commenced, using the N9 with its difficult ascents and descents. We have driven along the D992 from St-Affrique, along the valley of the Cernon, towards Millau to visit the splendid Visitor Centre and to view the progress of the work during construction of Le VIADUC de MILLAU – "A structure of great technical complexity". We have spent time in the viewing area at the northern end of the Viaduc, admiring this spectacular construction; standing in amazement that those slender pillars can support such incredible weights and we have been thrilled to drive across this highest bridge in the world a number of times – sometimes from the north and sometimes from the south when the steelwork glistens in the early morning sun.

It is not very far from Le Caylar along the A75 before crossing, for the last time, the Viaduc de Millau; it was 11.05 and the altitude 780m; the visibility was good and suitable for yet more photographs. I have no doubt that Margaret had alerted Inge that we were approaching this 'wonder of the world', as she has taken a great interest in its construction.

At 11.25 we left the autoroute at Junction 44.1 to join the D911 for Pont-de-Salars and Baraqueville in the Department of Aveyron; there is a very extensive wind farm (ferme d'éoliennes) along this section of the D911 with five turbines near the roadside. Near La Primaube, between Pont-de-Salars and Baraqueville, our progress was slowed by a large farm tractor which was transporting and, unfortunately, discharging a very smelly substance. After Rieupeyreux we stopped for a ten-minute rest; then it was Villefranche-de-Rouergue. Again, we visited the pâtisserie at Martiel to buy some food (€12.40) for lunch. In fact, the D911 continues all the way to Limogne-en-Quercy, a distance of 129 km. Here we knew we could park in the car park which serves the local doctor's surgery as well as other establishments. Arriving at 14.05, we made use of the public seat in the shade of the trees to enjoy our quiches, chocolate biscuits and drinks. etc., while observing the comings and goings at the cabinet de médecin. We think it was an infirmière who wished us "bon appetit!" This park also provides a convenient toilet.

We left Limogne on the familiar D19 at 15.55, but at 16.23 we parked at Vaylats to explore some memorials we had spotted. In fact, there was much more to see. VAYLATS is a very small commune with a population of only 150 at the last census, whereas there were 900 inhabitants at the end of the 19th century. The land here has been worked since distant times, perhaps since two or three centuries BC. The church of St Peter is very interesting; it stands on the site of a previous church dating from the 16th century and which had become too small for the population of the village. The convent of the Daughters of Jesus was constructed at the beginning of the 19th century on land sold by a descendant of the Goddaille family to a priest born in the family of Vaylats. He founded a community that became a school in 1820. Vaylats, if not the memorials, was a very interesting discovery. It was very hot – 30°C – when we returned to the car at 17.35 to continue our journey.

After Lalbenque, at 18.00, we joined the A20 autoroute at junction 58 as the short section to junction 57 offers some excellent scenery and is a very convenient bypass of Cahors. After the autoroute, the D820 is about 15 miles to PONT de RHODES just beyond Frayssinet, and at 18.40 we were welcomed at Le Relais by Madame Leveaux in the usual warm and friendly manner and directed to our familiar room, No. 3. It was a beautiful warm evening and after a cup of coffee we went for a short walk.

We have sojourned at Le Relais in the past to enable us to visit friends Beatrice, Marc and Tristan at their home in the nearby little commune of Beaumat. Beaumat had a population of about 80, but in 2016 was merged into the new commune of Cœur-de-Causse. Beatrice and family formerly lived next door to us during our annual visits to La Taillade!

(159 miles)

Day 37 – Saturday, 2 July 2011

We had read that as this was the first weekend of the holiday season a 100% increase in the volume of traffic on the roads was anticipated. In fact, on most of our journey of 185 miles to Saint Savin we could hardly have encountered less traffic.

After a short conversation with Monsieur Leveaux, particularly about the very hot weather they had endured earlier in the year, we said au revoir and left Le Relais at 10.50; it was 25°C. We joined the D704 at Pont de Rhodes stopping at the Total Garage in

Gourdon for petrol – €1.61 per litre, 45 litres, €72.45. At Groléjac (11.35) we entered the Department of DORDOGNE and after crossing the River Dordogne passed through Sarlat-la-Canéda which was busy as usual, but we did not get delayed. The D704 took us through Montignac (near Lascaux) and along the course of the Vézère to Le Lardin-St-Lazare and then to Hautefort.

We have passed the village of HAUTEFORT (population in 2008 was 1,100) on a number of occasions and observed its imposing château on the skyline. Today, we decided we would have time to find the actual entrance and take some photographs, Indeed, at 13.00 we parked near the entrance and had our lunch of bars and a drink. This ancient fortress dates back to the early Middle Ages; the first document quoting its existence as early as 987. It is certainly worth a visit.

Still on the D704 to Lanouaille, then approaching St Yrieix-la-Perche, at 14.00, we left Dordogne and were in the Department of HAUTE-VIENNE in the Region of Limousin. Most of this part of our journey was particularly delightful, cruising comfortably along quiet peaceful roads passing pleasant scenery with occasional small villages or hamlets and interesting-looking buildings. Through the north of Périgord there are vast areas of fruit trees, most of them covered with what would appear to be polythene sheeting! PERIGORD is a former province of France, which corresponds roughly to the current Dordogne Department. It is one of the most unspoiled regions of Europe. Due to its wealth of prehistoric sites the area is known as the 'cradle of mankind'; the painted cave of Lascaux, whose depictions of animals date back some 17,000 years, is the most famous site. The Périgord was one of the main battlegrounds of the Hundred Years' War.

From St Yrieix-la-Perche it was a very familiar route on the D901 – Bussière-Galant, Châlus, Oradour-s-Vayres, Rochéchouart and the D675 to St. Junien where, at 15.30, we stopped for refreshments, and a welcome cup of tea – €4.60 – at Le Boeuf Rouge where the temperature was 29°C. It's still the D675 to Bellac, le Dorat, and la Trimouille, but then the D32 for Béthines and, finally, St. SAVIN-sur-GARTEMPE. It was 19.00 and 27°C.

We have a special attachment to Hôtel de France and, particularly, to Chambre 20 with its view of the Spire of the Abbey; it is one of our 'special places'. We are always warmly welcomed by Bruno and we feel very comfortable here. While having a cup of coffee (and after) we had a long and interesting conversation with a lady (perhaps of the 40s age group) who now lives nearby and who formerly lived in London. She was very emphatic about the superior quality of life in France compared with England and made it clear that she considers that she had not left London, but that London had left her.

There was still time to take a stroll along the side of the river where we had another conversation. Our path coincided with another on the right from which a very elderly lady cautiously emerged for a little exercise in the cool of the day. We felt she would like to speak, and it only required a comment about the weather, "il fait beau ce soir" to begin quite a long conversation. She was interested to know where we had been and where we were going in France but, as we often find when talking to French people, had not heard of some of the place names. She was a charming lady to whom we eventually said "bonne nuit". As we were walking away from her, her mobile phone began to ring – no doubt she had exceeded her expected period of absence and someone was concerned for her well-being; we shall never know. It was then time for us to return to our hotel for the night.

(185 miles)

<u>Day 38 – Sunday, 3 July 2011</u>

First, we had another 'chat' with Bruno during which he told us that he has a target to cycle 3,000 kilometres this year; we have arranged to return for a longer visit in September when we will check Bruno's progress. We then visited le tabac opposite where we were able to buy an excellent magazine *Planète Cyclisme* which included *Le Guide du Tour 2011* for €5, but no *Le Monde* today! We also bought food for the day at the patisserie. At 11.20 we drove from the Hôtel and St Savin, to the Elan Garage (again) in St Germain on the other side of the river Gartempe, and purchased as much petrol as we could accommodate – 25 litres, €1.53 per litre = €38.25.

It was another beautiful day and, at 11.35 we set off for Chinon. We took the D5 for the lovely old village of Angles-sur-l'Anglin – a Plus Beaux Village de France, then by the D6 on to Tournon-St-Martin and briefly slipping into La Brenne country – the land of a thousand lakes, D14 – Preuilly-sur-Claise – D50 – Le Petit-Pressigny – Ligueil – D59 – Sepmes – Noyant-de-Touraine – D760 – L'Ile-Bouchard and along the D8 to Chinon. We passed many fields of tournesol (sunflowers) and observed the extensively cultivated areas across the vast open plains of Touraine until, as we approached Chinon, vineyards predominate.

We had only driven 71 miles but, at 13.40, Chinon was a suitable place for a rest and something to eat and drink from our larder. It was 24°C. Supplies are getting low; we salvaged what we could and threw some food away, but keeping stale bread for the ducks at La Flèche tomorrow. At 15.30 we left this pleasant car park amidst the trees by the river Vienne and with the view of the magnificent statue of Jeanne d'Arc on horseback.

From Chinon it was only 41 miles via Beaumont-en-Véron – D749 – Bourgueil – Gizeux – D86 – D141 – Noyant and D767 to Le Lude and we arrived at Hôtel La Renaissance at 17.00. The temperature was 26°C.

We knew that the hotel would be closed today (Sunday) but we followed the instructions on the door and went to the door of the restaurant on the other side of the road. We were greeted by a most polite and courteous gentleman who took us back to the hotel and to our room (No. 3) on the ground floor. He gave us a note of the code to open the door and gain access to our room, a basic but comfortable room on the ground floor and we parked the car in the hotel's private park.

We have passed through LE LUDE many times without being able to see the Château and we had decided to spend one night here with a view to, at least, locating it. We set off from the hotel following the signs for 'le château', but, of course, these signs were for the benefit of motorists and we realised that it was a rather long way round. However, eventually we were there and we knew that, as it was late in the day, we would not be able to visit the inside of the building. The 'shop' was still open and we enquired if it would be worthwhile paying to visit the grounds and gardens. We were told that it would be closing in quite a short while, but the lady at the counter very kindly told us that if we purchased the necessary tickets we could stay within the grounds for as long as we wished and she showed us how to open the large heavy door to let ourselves out. We did have time to collect some leaflets, purchase a book for €7 and a thimble for Judith, etc. before the official closing time.

We spent some considerable time walking around the grounds and viewing the majestic château in its splendid setting alongside the River Loir, after reading some of the information about it, and enjoying the scenery of the surrounding countryside. It was a strange sensation being the only persons in this wonderful and, as we realised when we saw a couple of young ladies return with some 'shopping', private place, at this time. Yes, it is, or part of it is, occupied by a family. Eventually, and somewhat reluctantly, we 'released' ourselves from this enclosed haven of peace and tranquillity. We found that there was, of course, a fairly direct route back to our hotel, but we did not hurry. We strolled along the streets of the centre of the town noting, in particular, the town hall; it was a very quiet and pleasant place. Back at the hotel it was certainly time for bed.

Situated at the crossroads of three regions, Maine, Anjou and Touraine, in the valley of the Loir, Le Lude was a strategic place in Roman times, and it was named 'castellum lusdii' due to its position near the river. The origins of the CHÄTEAU du LUDE go back to the 10th century. Built on an outcrop on the banks of the Loir and flanked by six towers, it was well-suited to defend Anjou against incursions by the Normands and then by the English during the Hundred Years War. It was occupied by the English in 1425 and two years later it was liberated by the legendary Gilles de Rais also known as 'Bluebeard' who then joined Jeanne d'Arc at Orléans. In 1457, Jehan de Daillon, then chamberlain to Louis XI, acquired the château; it had been uninhabited for three decades following the Hundred Years War and was in ruins. He immediately undertook to renovate the building and his descendants converted the grim fortress into a comfortable residence. Henri IV and Louis XIII are known to have visited Le Lude. It was here in 1685 that Henri, Duc du Lude and the last member of the Daillon family, died leaving no descendant. Joseph Duvelaer, a member of the East India Company, acquired Le Lude in 1751 and subsequently restored the edifice considerably. When he died, he left it to his niece, the Marquise de la Vieuville who, at the end of the 18th century and before the Revolution, built the west wing which faces the Loir; this is an example of Classical French architecture at its best. The Marquise de la Vieuville let the château to her daughter, wife of Louis Celeste de Talhouet and when the Marquise died the château became the property of the Talhouet family who made many alterations, especially to the North façade, during the 19th century. Le Lude is now owned by Count Louis Jean de Nicolay, a descendant of the Talhouets, who lives there with his wife and their four children. Behind the façade of the château the elegant apartments which can be visited include the dining room, the drawing rooms and the library.

(112 miles)

Day 39 – Monday, 4 July 2011

We can only describe the Hôtel La Renaissance as excellent. Our rooms left nothing to be desired and the service and attention at petit déjeuner was exceptional. In fact, the gentleman, Dany, who greeted us when we arrived and was the only person we saw, was the owner and (we believe) the chef; he was most polite, courteous and helpful. We would be very happy to return and we told him so. We left the hotel at 10.30 and a short distance along the road we were able to buy bread, etc., and also a journal; not *Midi Libre* now, but another excellent regional paper, *Ouest-France*.

We left Le Lude at 11.00, but after travelling a mere 14 miles on the D306 we stopped at 11.30, by the River Loir again, at La Fleche to spend "10 mins avec les canards" – they were waiting. We fed them the stale bread we had reserved for them. It was 23°C. At 11.40 we continued by the D306 over the Sarthe at Sablé-sur-Sarthe then taking the D24 for Ballée, around Vaiges to

MONTSURS. We could not resist pausing at this village which reminds us of Somerset as it has been twinned with Chilcompton since 1992. It was 13.00 when we arrived, 25°C and we stayed for 40 minutes; this is a delightful spot by the little River Jouanne.

Passing through the departments of Mayenne, Orne and Calvados one observes that the scenery is now of trees, hedges, fields with cows grazing and some sheltering from the hot midday sun, as well as cultivated areas; this is Northern France. After Montsûrs by the D24 we skirt Mayenne, then to admire the floral decoration on the bridge at Ambrières-les-Vallées – D23 and D962 – Ceauce – Domfront – D22 – a view of Lonlay-l'Abbaye – Tinchebray and D924 to VIRE at 15.40.

This Norman town of 12,000 inhabitants in the Department of Calvados suffered greatly during the Second World War. On 6 June 1944 at around 20.00 hours it was subjected to heavy British bombing and was largely destroyed; it was a distressing night for the people of Vire when many died. However, from the 1960s it was reconstructed and is now an attractive and pleasant town. We could not park near the church as we had planned as the area was reserved for some festive event, but eventually we were able to park near the Hôtel de France as on our outward journey. It was very busy and hot (26°C) in the town; we bought some bread and two pains au raisin for €3.85, for the evening and enjoyed une tasse de thé (€5.40) while sitting outside at the Central Café; we photographed the beautifully decorated nearby traffic island which included a wonderful display depicting a Viking boat. While in the town large notices reminded us that this year, 2011, is the 1,100th anniversary of the founding of Normandie. It was in 911 that the Treaty of Saint-Clair-sur-Epte was signed between Charles III of France and Rollo, the Norwegian or Danish Vikings leader, allowing the Normans to settle in Neustria and thus to protect Charles' kingdom from any new invasion by the 'northmen'. We shall probably hear more of this in September.

Returning to the car, which was very hot inside, we resumed our journey at 17.05. We left Vire on the D55 and D26 to Aunay-s-Odon – D6 – Villers-Bocage – Tilly-s-Seulles, where the clock was striking 18.00, and to BAYEUX at 18.30. At the Campanile Hotel we found that Room 9 had been reserved for us. As this room was looking inwards towards the restaurant and not, as where we have often been, with a view of the meadow, the railway and the great Cathédrale de Notre-Dame, we decided to take our food and go straightaway (19.00) to Arromanches. On our way we purchased petrol – 42 litres, €1.51 per litre = €63.42 – at the Esso Station on the ring road which we often visit and we parked at the usual car park near the small supermarket in ARROMANCHES at 19.25. It was a lovely evening, although as we enjoyed our food and then sent text messages the temperature began to fall. We have no idea of how many times we have visited this historic site, where the remains of the famous Mulberry Harbour are ever more visible, but they have been very, very numerous. Again, we had to leave one of our favourite places in France and return to Bayeux for our final night in the Hexagon. Back at the Campanile at 21.15 where the temperature was now only 17°C we made a cup of coffee in our room.

(175 miles)

Day 40 – Tuesday, 5 July 2011

We are not accustomed to leaving our last étape so early in the morning but here we are able to have an early breakfast and at 8.50, with temperature 16°C, we had done so, returned our key, etc., and were ready to leave the Bayeux Campanile for Cherbourg. Not the occasion to take the interesting slow coastal road, but the direct N13 route. It was a lovely morning and at 9.50 we were doing well; at 9.55 we saw the first sign for 'Car Ferry – 7 km' and at 10.07 we arrived at the ferry port; at 10.15 we were ready to embark on the 'Condor service'. It was a very smooth and fast crossing and the vessel is comfortable and convenient, but it does not have the atmosphere of a cruise ferry. We docked at Poole at 13.03 (English time) but it took nearly 30 minutes to pass through the Border Control. It was 24°C.

As it was daylight on this occasion the journey to Trowbridge was not difficult, but we were suddenly very conscious of the far greater volume of traffic on the English roads, the impatience and lack of consideration of many drivers, the varying types and poor state of road signs often concealed by uncut verges and overgrown hedges and trees, the lack of white lines at the edge of roads and the litter on the roadsides. We were back in England!!! What a contrast! We reached

Green Lane at 15.00 exactly; the temperature was 19°C and the total distance of our journey was 1,683 miles.
(116 miles.)

What a remarkable 39 days! A holiday 'at home' midst an extensive tour of France. Day by day we appreciated the many hours spent earlier in the year – considering an outline of our journey, preparing a detailed plan of our route and, of course, making all the necessary reservations. Our plans then unfolded as we had hoped into another enjoyable, satisfying, rewarding and memorable experience, culminating in the feeling of a project successfully accomplished.

Before the end of next month, we set off on another France Journey – possibly our last!

One feature of this journey which I have not mentioned is the Tour de France. It was purely a coincidence that, it seems, on many occasions we were driving along part of the route of this year's Tour where preparations had been made and often with remarkable displays in nearby fields which were, no doubt, primarily for the attention of the helicopter cameras and thus for the benefit of the vast television audience. Fortunately, we have been able to see much of the television coverage of the race, but it was not easy to recognise roads which we had driven along and places we had visited, as the quiet roads, villages and towns we had known, were then thronged with vast hordes of excited spectators.

Margaret, feeding the ducks at our favourite and frequent refreshment stop at La Fleche.

At the Plus Beau Village of Ségur-le-Château
by the River Auvezère.

Chinon – Richelieu – Chenonceau – Sologne – Chambord – Orléans – Saint-Amand-en-Puisaye – Vézelay – Noyers-sur-Serein – Château-de-Malaisy – Abbaye-de-Fontenay – Alesia – Flavigny-sur-Ozerain – Source de la Seine – Châteauneuf-en-Auxois – Abbaye de Cîteaux – Nolay – Château de Sully – Cluny – La Chaise-Dieu – Conques – La Taillade – Cahors – Cènevières – Albussac – Beaulieu – Argentat – Moussais-la-Bataille – Fresnay-sur-Sarthe – St-Evroult-Notre-Dame-du-Bois – Cerisyla- Forêt – Arromanches – Formigny

AUGUST/OCTOBER 2011

<u>Day 1 – Tuesday, 30 August 2011</u>

Our visit to Vézelay last year was such an impressive experience that it left us with a desire to return. However, it is not only Vézelay which attracts in the region of Bourgogne, but its wealth of varied historic and interesting treasures and features not least, of course, Cluny itself. Our interest was aroused still further following the gift of a book entitled *Back Roads France* which describes a particularly interesting route from Beaune to Nolay and we decided to use this route, albeit in the reverse direction, as a basis for our visit to this fascinating area. So it was that we arranged to spend a week or so in Burgundy. Also, on this second périple of the year we planned to visit the various friends, French and English, we are fortunate to have in various parts of the Hexagon. But that is not all; there will be further interesting discoveries and experiences to come!

We left Green Lane at 8.55, rather later than we had hoped to do. This initial part of our journey was trouble free with the exception of a confrontation with a family of pheasants who threatened to bar our route. At first it was rather cloudy and somewhat maussade, but on reaching Charlton Marshall at 10.00 we saw glimpses of the sun. We reached the Port of Poole at 10.25; after the usual passport and ticket checks, with a sigh of relief, we were allowed to board the *Barfleur* without any inspection of the contents of the car or interrogation with such tiresome questions as, "Do you have any knives, weapons or guns with you"; also the weather was improving! We sailed at 11.00 and we remained outside in the warm sunshine for some while. There were not too many people or cars on board, but many caravans. As we passed through the route of the Sandbanks Ferry and out into the English Channel we found that the sea was exceptionally calm and still; so much so that we decided to have a plate of frites which were greatly enjoyed. After a wonderful crossing, almost certainly the best we have ever known in the past 30 years, we reached Cherbourg at 16.30 and it was not long before we were driving off the *Barfleur*, who knows perhaps for the last time. Although on some occasions we are met by police standing in the road who look at our passports and then our faces and even remind us to fasten our seatbelts, there were no border checks whatever and we were going into a foreign country! Is there some communication between the UK boarding control and the French landing authorities perhaps? Soon we were heading up the hill on the N13 and down the Cotentin peninsula towards Carentan. What a pity that it is always necessary to speed past the little town of Valognes with a population of less than 8,000. It is only about 12 miles south of Cherbourg and, although greatly damaged during the Battle of Normandy, it has a rich history and is known as the 'Petit Versailles Normand'. Perhaps one day! As we passed Sainte-Mère-Eglise we acknowledged, as usual, the effigy of John Steele hanging from his parachute suspended from the tower of the church. Remembering that, on 27 May, we overlooked the junction for St-Lo, we were particularly vigilant when approaching the signs for the N174.

Work is still progressing on this new road and no doubt there will be a new junction the next time we pass this way. (This was the last time!) At 18.15 we felt it appropriate to make our customary break at Torigni-sur-Vire where the temperature was still 24°C. Many times, have we spent a half hour or so at one of these very convenient parking spaces just alongside the main road which has been relieved of much traffic following the construction of the new N174. It is extremely pleasant here amidst the floral displays and with, on the one side, a view looking down into the leisure grounds and, on the other, Le Lac des Charmilles. At this stage we were still able to tune in to BBC Radio 4 and we were also able to locate the wavelength for France Musique which would stay with us for the rest of the journey. At 19.00 after adequate refreshment from our store we continued on our journey to Vire reaching the Campanile Hotel at 19.25. It is now 18°C and we have travelled a mere 130 miles by car. Fortunately, it was a pleasant evening and there was still sufficient daylight to permit a stroll along the D55B from the hotel in the general direction of Burcy. We like to observe the well cared for and productive vegetable gardens and, particularly, the remarkable long and high 'wall' of tightly knit leylandii trees which surrounds one property; it always looks as if it has just recently been meticulously trimmed. We walked as far as the newly constructed property which stands on the site of a plot which was for sale a few years ago; at that time, we actually made a note of the address and telephone number of the agent but, needless to say, we never pursued the matter! Maintenant c'est l'heure d'aller se coucher!

(130 miles so far!)

Day 2 – Wednesday, 31 August 2011

We have made the Vire Campanile our first étape in France for many years now as it is extremely convenient at a reasonable distance from Cherbourg. The facilities and services at these hotels are largely identical and uniform and always of a high standard; they also appear to always have adequate parking facilities. It was sunny and 16°C when we left the Campanile at 10.40 and after about 10 miles we reached our first village – TINCHEBRAY. The Battle of Tinchebray on 28 September 1106 lasted only one hour. The opponents were two sons of William the Conqueror – his eldest, Robert Curthose, Duke of Normandy and his fourth son, Henry 1 of England; the result was a decisive victory for Henry and, subsequently, England and Normandy remained united until 1204. Although the battle was spread out over several kilometres, most of the fighting took place in the centre of the village. Robert was captured about three kilometres north of Tinchebray and imprisoned for the rest of his life, initially in the Tower of London, then for about twenty years in Devizes Castle and he eventually died in Cardiff Castle in 1134 at the age of about 84. He was buried in the abbey church of St. Peter in Gloucester which is now Gloucester Cathedral. From Tinchebray we drove about two miles northwards on the D22 in search of the tombstones of three knights who died in the battle. We stopped first at the crossroads with the D265 where a cross stands high on a bank, but I was unable to identify it. We had noticed a couple of ladies walking along the road and we had waved to them. As we sat in the car studying the map we were surprised by a knock on the window; it was the ladies we had seen. They were English and asked if we were lost; on explaining our mission they admitted that they did not know the purpose of the memorial we were looking at, but that a little further along the road there was a memorial relating to the battle.

After an interesting conversation we thanked Rita and her friend for their help and they remarked that they would not be walking along such a road in England! Although we were parked on the corner of the junction and felt somewhat vulnerable, the only traffic was a tractor with a farm vehicle the driver of which gave us a friendly nod. We continued along the D22 in the direction advised, passing a stone marking the boundary of the departments of Orne and Calvados until, after a short distance, reaching a further memorial on the left-hand side of the road. I could not interpret the Latin inscription and, therefore, I took a photograph which, hopefully, may provide an explanation later. To satisfy ourselves that we had found the memorial we were looking for we continued a little further towards Bernières-le-Patry until we could see the railway level crossing, but we saw nothing else of interest. It was apparently near this road, D22, that Robert was captured at a place where now is situated a farm called 'prise' (taken). We returned to Tinchebray as the actual battle occurred in the centre of the village in an area which is a large open space and a place of various leisure activities. We found a convenient place to park and I walked across the 'field' to a memorial to Robert, the English inscription on which reads, "This is the reputed site of the Battle of Tinchebray 28th September 1106 where Robert Duke of Normandy fought Henry 1 of England. Both men were the sons of William the Conquerer". It was a very interesting discovery, but having spent more time here than we had anticipated we must continue our journey.

Near Domfront we spotted a number of bicycles decorated with geraniums – no doubt prepared for the

Tour de France which passed this way a few weeks earlier. Once again, we passed Mayenne and joined the D24 for Montsûrs and Vaiges; at Ballée we met 12 motor cyclists – English perhaps – it is quite likely! Midway between Sable-s-Sarthe and La Fleche, a total distance of about 15 miles, and near the autoroute junction is the Centre Hospitalier Sarthe et Loir. We have observed the construction and completion of this hospital during the course of the past few years; it is a very large building and although not an attractive structure it is in open country and easily accessible with a vast car park. It has 741 beds and rooms and, no doubt, the facilities are the best available. A principle which could be adopted to provide an adequate hospital to serve the towns of West Wiltshire perhaps? But this is England, this is Wiltshire!

We reached LA FLECHE at 14.00 and again under the plane trees by the river Loir we ate our sandwich lunch; it was 22°C, but cloudy. Although it was market day, we arrived only in time to see the last rites of the methodical cleaning up process and we could hear the ducks, but today we have little food to give them. La Flèche is twinned with Chippenham and it possesses the National Military Prytanée which was founded by Henri IV, none other, in 1604 and prepares students for the baccalaureate and entrance exams for military high schools. While we were having our lunch a 'car' arrived and parked alongside us; we were surprised to see that it had a British registration. However, it was not a recognisable or identifiable model; indeed, it was very original. As we were preparing to leave, the driver returned and entered into conversation with us. He lives for about six months of the year near La Flèche and the remainder of the year in England and he was pleased to tell us about the superior quality of his life in France and the fact that local taxes (council tax) are so much less. It was very interesting to listen to him, but we had to tear ourselves away and at 16.30 we left for Chinon, which was another 50 miles ahead of us.

After Le Lude we pass through Noyant, ensuring that we take the D141, pass the silo on our right and continue before dropping down into Breil. After travelling so many thousands of miles in France and some of them on a number of occasions, it is inevitable that certain sections of the route become memorable and enjoyable; the some 20 miles from Noyant to Bourgueil, passing through the villages of Breil, Parcay-les-Pins and Gizeux and then the thickly wooded section before breaking out into the vineyards near Bourgueil is one of them. What a contrast as we cross the A85 and the Loire and pass alongside the EDF Centre Nucléaire and other commercial establishments, but then a very different scene again on entering pleasant Avoine and then Beaumont-en-Veron. More vineyards and soon we are alongside the Vienne and heading into Chinon. I cannot say how many times we have driven from Vire to Chinon – a distance of about 170 miles – but it has always been a journey of sheer pleasure. Sadly, this was to be the last occasion!

Many times we have approached this ancient town of 8,000 inhabitants and no traffic lights, often from this westerly direction, but frequently also from the direction of L'lle-Bouchard and each route following the course of the river. CHINON is always guarded by the preserved remains of its château with, particularly, the newly restored royal apartments; this was, of course, the residence of French and English monarchs. It was 18.05 when we parked in the large square, which is dominated by a huge equestrian statue of Jeanne d'Arc, who, of course, has a special relationship with this town. We hurriedly made our way into Le Plantagenêt where we were warmly greeted by Martine who took us to the room we like on the ground floor (No. 39). Unfortunately, Barbara had already left for home, but she had left a message for us renewing her invitation to visit Keith and her for lunch tomorrow; she had also provided us with very detailed instructions to enable us to find their home. Our first task was to telephone Barbara and to formally accept her invitation. It was a very pleasant evening and after a short walk and some refreshment in the car and, before returning to our chambre, we must park the car at the far end of the square near the gendarmerie premises as tomorrow is market day here and it is a very big market.

(164 miles today)

Day 3 – Thursday, 1 September 2011

Petit déjeuner at Le Plantagenêt is always a pleasant occasion in a very friendly atmosphere and with ample choice. Again, it was a warm sunny morning (24°C) and after a brief walk amongst the very busy stalls of the market we left for Ceaux-en-Loudun at 12.15. CEAUX-EN-LOUDUN is a village of 600 inhabitants (2006) in the Department of Vienne in the Region of Poitou-Charentes of which the president is Segolene Royal, who was a candidate for the presidency of France in 2007. This small village has suffered much from plagues in the past; during the peste of the year 1632 there were 97 deaths and during the countrywide influenza epidemic of 1918 there were 33 deaths in the first 30 days; this latter figure would have followed the number of men killed in the Great War itself. Fortunately, no such disaster threatens today. It is a journey of only 12 miles from Chinon and at almost exactly 13.00, as arranged and without difficulty, we found Barbara and Keith sitting outside their home with a Welsh friend who lives nearby. We joined them until their friend left when we were invited inside to an excellent and enjoyable meal which Barbara and Keith had prepared for us.

Afterwards, sitting outside again, we also had the company of their two cats. One is named Rooney, perhaps because our hosts have some affection for a certain football team in the north of England, but the second, its name escapes me for the moment, is very young and lively. Naturally there was much conversation throughout, particularly about the comparisons of life in France and life in England. After a much appreciated and enjoyable afternoon, we left Barbara and Keith at 17.15 and returned to Chinon. It was a beautiful warm evening (25°C) and we walked through the town where many people were strolling leisurely around and many sitting out on the pavements enjoying a meal; it was a most relaxed and agreeable atmosphere. We left the town to return alongside the river, but first to inspect the complex engineering works to renew the foundations of the pillars supporting the ancient bridge – a very difficult and costly operation.

(Only 24 miles)

Day 4 – Friday, 2 September 2011

With the temperature already at 28 degrees it was to be a very hot day; nevertheless, we decided to visit Richelieu. At 11.54 we took the D8 alongside the north bank of the Vienne to L'ILE BOUCHARD with a view to visiting the Prieuré St-Léonard. However, we came first to L'Eglise St Maurice and we decided to park the car and go inside. We were interested to find a statue of Sainte Jeanne d'Arc and a record that in 1429, when on her way to Chinon, where she identified Charles VII, she had entered this church to pray; had we had used the same door? I should add that, according to a comprehensive and seemingly authentic history of this town, it was, in fact, in 1483 that Louis II commenced the construction of l'Eglise Saint Maurice. It would be interesting to know if these two records can be reconciled. Also, we found a statue of another familiar and significant saint, Saint Antoine de Padoue, who is commemorated in very many churches. Saint Antoine was born Fernando Martins de Bulhoes at Lisbon in 1195 and died on 13 June 1231 near Padoue (Italy). He was a Franciscan priest and a descendant of Charlemagne. This church also possesses a very beautiful spire of stone, which is decorated with ornamental apertures. Discovering this interesting building has delayed our journey to Richelieu, but we appreciated the time spent in the cool of the church; consequently, we must postpone our visit to Prieuré St

Léonard and indeed to historic L'Ile Bouchard to a future occasion.

At 13.00, after 40 minutes, we continued to RICHELIEU along the D757 and parked just inside the boundary of the town; it was still 28°C. Armand Jean du Plessis, CARDINAL de RICHELIEU, was born in Paris on 9 September 1585. At the age of nine he began to study philosophy and then trained for a military career, but subsequently joined the clergy. By 1606 he had been nominated by Henri IV as Bishop of Lucon; he became a cardinal in 1622. He had risen in power in the church as well as in government, having become Secretary of State in 1616. In 1624 he became the principal minister of Louis XIII and remained in office until his death in 1642. He is considered to have been the world's first 'Prime Minister' in the modern sense of the term. He is also known as the founder of the Académie Française, the learned body of 40 members, known as 'immortels', which is responsible for matters concerning the French language.

The du Plessis family had settled in Richelieu in the 15th century and Armand Jean spent his childhood there. To celebrate his wealth and status and with the permission of Louis XIII, the cardinal created from scratch a walled town on a grid arrangement and, enclosing within it the modest home of his childhood, an adjacent Château de Richelieu. Both the château and the town were built to the designs of Jacques Lemercier, the King's architect. Building work began in 1631 and was virtually finished when the Cardinal died on 4 December 1642. Many of the craftsmen employed came from Paris and almost

2,000 tradesmen worked on the site. The town is laid out in the shape of a large rectangle approximately 700m by 500m; it is surrounded by walls and is entered via three high gates, the fourth one being false. Much restoration work on the buildings in the town centre has been carried out over the years and much is in progress today. However, although the château was reputed to be one of the finest in Europe and housed some magnificent works of art, it had a relatively short life. At the time of the Revolution towards the end of the 18th century it was confiscated by the state and the works of art distributed or sold. The estate was later returned to the heirs of Cardinal Richelieu, but in 1805 it was sold, and the château was subsequently demolished and sold as building materials; only a few vestiges remain.

It was very hot as we had refreshments sitting in the car, but we must explore this remarkable, even unique, town! From the car park in the Place des Religieuses we decided to seek the Office de Tourisme. We walked along the Grande Rue which is 12 metres wide and lined by 14 'houses' on each side, which were all built to the same plan. From the Place du Marché we eventually found the Office de Tourisme, where the staff were very helpful; we purchased a plan of the town, some postcards and a book. On this very hot day the church was an appropriate place to visit. The church was built by Pierre Lemercier to the designs of his brother Jacques. It is baroque in style and on the instructions of the cardinal it was dedicated to Our Lady of the Assumption. There are elaborately designed altars and a beautiful statue of Ste Thérèse, which was inaugurated at Easter 1927; we noted the inscription, "Action de grâce pour la veneration des Relique de Ste. Thérèse de Lisieux à Richelieu – 2009". The post-classical organ dates from 1853; we would like to have heard what sounds it produces! Also, we observed the inevitable long list of the names of the 'Morts pour la France' during the Great War. While we were in the church a number of men and women were busily engaged in dusting and polishing the pews, etc., perhaps in preparation for a special occasion. A most interesting building! After leaving the church we felt that a cup of tea was appropriate, and we found further shelter from the sun in a nearby salon de thé. The covered market was completed in 1638 and is well worth a visit.

We left the town by the Chatellerault entrance, paused in the Place du Cardinal to admire the magnificent statue of the great man himself and entered the Parc. It was a long walk along an avenue of trees before we found a seat conveniently situated under a tree. Unfortunately, it was a chestnut tree and was in the process of shedding its fruit. Before we received a direct hit, we moved on to explore a little more of this vast estate. We liked, particularly, the rose garden which occupies the site of the main body of the château.

Remembering that it was a very long walk to reach this point we must begin our return journey. As we walked back along the Grande Rue, we photographed the impressive three-story houses. We know that the cardinal had specified that all the houses should be built to the same plan; each house had to have a frontage of 20 metres and be 8.50 metres deep; each had to have an arched carriage way leading into a 16-metre-deep courtyard. We saw that the doors of one property were open and tucked away in the courtyard was a beautiful little chapel, which is dedicated to the Très Sainte Trinite; we found that it was open, and we were able to go inside and we took some photographs. In the window of one of the buildings as we passed, we noticed an advertisement 'Tim Lawrence – Music Teacher'. Perhaps this is the gentleman Barbara had told us about and who lives in Ceaux en Loudun? We eventually reached the car and left Richlieu to return to Chinon via Champigny-sur-Veude; this is an interesting village and well worth a visit. In Chinon at 20.00 the temperature was still 28°C, but it had been a very good day.

(39 miles)

Day 5 – Saturday, 3 September 2011

Once again, we must say au revoir to Martine and leave Le Plantagenêt and Chinon. Indeed, we must return as there is so much of interest in this area. (Sadly, this was to be our last visit and our last farewell to Martine. However, I have been in contact with her during 2020) It was 11.30 and 26°C as we took the D8 to L'Ile Bouchard; at Noyant-de-Touraine we purchased petrol at the Total garage – 57 litres – €1.595 per litre = €90.92; then on the D760 to Manthelan, where we joined the D58 for Reignac-sur-Indre. Shortly after leaving Cigogne and before reaching the silo we took an unlikely route, the unclassified and virtually single-track road across open country for Sublaines and then Luzille. From here the D80 took us under the autoroute to Francueil; then we crossed the Cher to join the D40 leading to Chenonceau at 14.00.

CHATEAU DE CHENONCEAU, an architectural gem from the French Renaissance, is the most visited château in France other than The Royal Palace of Versailles. The château straddles the River Cher and is on the site of an old mill; the original 'manor house' was probably built in the 11th century. The château was built and rebuilt until finally it was acquired by Thomas Bohier, Chamberlain for Charles VIII of France, in 1513. He destroyed the existing château and between 1515 and 1521 built an entirely new residence; the work was sometimes overseen by his wife Katherine Briçonnet. Over the centuries the château has had a number of owners, occupants and uses.

In 1547 Henri II gifted the château to his mistress, Diane de Poitiers, who had the arched bridge constructed, joining it to the opposite bank; she also saw the creation of the flower and vegetable gardens. In 1555 Diane eventually gained possession of the property, but after Henri died in 1559 his widow and regent Catherine de Medici forced Diane to exchange it for the Château Chaumont. As Regent of France, Catherine spent a fortune on the château and on spectacular parties. In 1560 the first ever fireworks display seen in France took place during the celebrations marking the accession to the throne of Catherine's son Francis II. In 1624 Gabrielle d'Estrées, mistress of Henri IV occupied the château. A Scotsman, Daniel Wilson, who had made a fortune installing gaslights in Paris, bought the château in 1864 for his daughter. In 1891 it was purchased by a Cuban millionaire. Finally, the Menier family, famous for their chocolates, bought the château in 1913 and still own it to this day.

During the Great War the gallery was used as a hospital ward; Simone Menier, a nurse, ran the hospital with her husband Georges. During the first part of the Second World War, when only Northern France was under direct German control, the Gallery was the only passage over the Cher to the free zone in the south even in spite of a German sentry box situated at the entrance to the château. The Menier family helped refugees, Jews and resistance fighters escape from the Nazi tyranny. Unfortunately, on 7 July 1944 an American plane bombing the nearby station also destroyed the stained-glass windows of the chapel. In 1951 much work was carried out to restore the dilapidated building and gardens to its former glory.

There are many visitors today, but in the large free parking area which is sensibly laid out with trees we quickly found a space. Again, it was 28°C and under the shelter of one of the young trees we enjoyed our lunch of mainly sandwiches prepared at home on the previous Monday! We were clearly some distance from the château and we made our way to the entrance and, particularly, to the visitor shop where we purchased the essential book. After passing through the entrance gates it was a long walk of nearly one kilometre along the avenue of tall plane trees "a cathedral of greenery" until, there it was, resplendent in the bright sunlight, a magnificent sight. However, first we spent some time on the terrace admiring the remarkable château stretching across the river Cher and also the amazing garden of Diane de Poitiers. At night these gardens are illuminated to the accompaniment of music of Corelli. Inside, we visited the Guard Room, where on the mantelpiece are written the words of Thomas Bohier, "If I manage to build Chenonceau, I will be remembered", next the Chapel 'The Sacred Room', then Diane de Poitiers's Bedroom, the Green Study, used by Catherine de Médicis when she was Regent of France following the death of Henri II, the Library, used by Catherine de Médicis who was a great bibliophile and Catherine de Médicis' Bedroom. During the course of our tour there were splendid views of the river. We emerged from the château into the still hot sun and found a table and chairs where we enjoyed an ice-cream. It had been a wonderful experience – six centuries of remarkable history revealed within these walls and gardens. It is little wonder that Château de Chenonceau attracts visitors in such vast numbers; it is open for 365 days per year and brochures are available in 15 languages. Much appreciation and gratitude is owed to the Menier Family. It was a long slow walk to the car, but at 17.20 we left this unforgettable treasure to continue our still long journey to Salbris.

The D176 took us to Montrichard and the D764 to Pontlevoy. When planning our route we had considered that at this point it may be possible to visit Chaumont-sur-Loire, but because of the advancing time we had to abandon this option. Therefore, we continued on the D30 to Thenay and Contres and on the D102 to Cheverny, where we visited the Château last year, to Bracieux, the D923 to Neuvy and Neung-sur-Beuvron. We are now deep in Sologne country and the D121 leads to Marcilly-en-Gault and to SALBRIS. At 19.20 we found the Hôtel Le Dauphin on the road heading south to Vierzon without difficulty. On meeting Céline we felt very welcome; being a very warm evening at 25 degrees we had the option of having un repas in the restaurant or in the garden; we chose the former. It was an excellent meal with lots of little surprises in a very pleasant atmosphere. Afterwards we talked to a French couple who were looking forward to an early morning tour of the Loire Valley châteaux by hot air balloon; unfortunately, we did not meet them again to know if the trip was successful. Our room, overlooking the rear of the property, was very comfortable.

For administrative purposes France is divided into 22 regions, each one comprising several departments of which there are 96 in all. However, there are a number of 'regions' which are identified and recognized by their natural features and characteristics. We have visited several in recent years – the Camargue, the Plateau de Millevaches, the Brenne, the Larzac and the Alpes-Mancelles. Now we are in the SOLOGNE. The Sologne region extends over an area of some 1,900 square miles and is bounded to the north by the River Loire, to the west and south by the River Cher and to the east by the districts of Sancerre and Berry. It comprises vast expanses of forestland, moors, lakes, pools and marshes; there is little manufacturing, but some arable farming and breeding; there are charming villages with red brick houses while the main towns are Romorantin-Lanthenay, La Ferté-Saint-Aubin, Salbris, Lamotte-Beuvron and Aubigny-sur-Nère. Some 75% of the area is occupied by forests and there are about 3,000 lakes covering 12,000 hectares. Wild boar and deer roam, ducks, geese, quails and pheasants are numerous – game is abundant! The multitude of wild or maintained lakes give the region a wealth of bird life; there are 220 bird species of which 140 are nesting birds; there are also 56 species of dragonfly. Yet another remarkable region!

(114 miles)

Day 6 – Sunday, 4 September 2011

SALBRIS is a town of some 6,000 inhabitants in the Department of Loir et Cher. Its history goes back to the Celtic period and perhaps it and its name originates from a crossing, a ford or bridge, of the river Sauldre, which in the Gauloise language was 'Salera Briva'. Our choice of Salbris for three nights was not only to experience the Sologne, but also to visit Orléans by train tomorrow, Monday. Therefore, we drove to la gare to assess the option of doing so again in the morning or walking from the hotel. Unfortunately, the exercise did not help us to decide, as the route by car was different from that which we could walk and, being Sunday, the car parks were deserted! However, we did at least verify the times of trains and fares. Although we passed by and had an excellent view of the Château Chambord on 3 September 2010, there was not sufficient time to visit it and so, at about 12.15, we set off in that direction. Shortly after leaving Salbris on the D121 we pass a Camp Militaire, the boundary of which stretches alongside the road for about one mile. Through the village of Marcilly-en-Gault and passing the Forét de Bruadan leads us to Neung-sur-Beuvron. Although we felt that we should not spend time here, we had noticed that it is twinned with Williton in Somerset (since 1984). It is an interesting place as it is believed to have been the site of a battle between Vercingetorix and

Julius Caesar in 52 BC. Also, Joan of Arc passed through this village after the liberation of Orléans in 1429. We continued on the D923, densely wooded on each side sometimes with young fir trees, to Neuvy and to Bracieux; then over the Beuvron, through the Forét de Boulogne and into the Parc de Chambord. Along the D33 towards Thoury one finds a splendid view of the rear of the Château and not for the first time, and not alone, we took some photographs.

The CHATEAU de CHAMBORD was constructed by François I between 1519 and 1547, but was never completed. However, it is instantly recognizable and is the largest château in the Loire Valley; it was built as a hunting lodge and has 440 rooms. It would appear that it could be a long walk from the car park to the château and so we decided to restrict our visit to the views of the exterior; we will move on to a village we are particularly keen to visit.

We continued on the D84 through Montlivault to, at 14.10, ST-DYE-SUR-LOIRE which is on the southern bank of the Loire. At first, we observed nothing remarkable about the village and on the D951 leading out of it we found sufficient space, where we would not be obstructing any access, to spend a little time for refreshments – bananas, bun, biscuits and water; it was very warm and 26°C. But where is the river? We returned to the centre of the village and took a narrow turning to the right into a street of old buildings, which quickly revealed an unobstructed and wonderful view of this wide expanse of slowly moving calm water; there was a track for the passage of cars and here was room to park and we are also on the route of the National Footpath GR3; it was 15.30 and warm and sunny. In the distance we could see the bridge over the river at Muides-sur-Loire. We spent some time in this beautiful and peaceful location, watching various forms of passing traffic on the river as well as many passers-by on foot all of whom were pleased to exchange a friendly 'Bonjour'. This spot is particularly interesting as, in the first half of the 16th century, it saw intense activity, being the site of the port for the delivery of stone for the construction of the Château de Chambord; there are still traces of that activity.

We could see, not far away, the spire of L'EGLISE and that was to be our next destination. However, after returning to the road through the village, we could no longer see the spire until, at the second attempt, we spotted a corner of the church just visible in another narrow street. Of course, there was room to turn in and, apparently, somewhere to park, but part of the church was shrouded in scaffolding, etc., and obviously undergoing much restoration work. Disappointingly, we assumed that the building was closed until we noticed a couple of bicycles near a closed doorway – belonging to workmen perhaps? I decided to investigate and to my relief I found that the door was open. We then both went in and were greeted with an amazing sound of voices and organ filling the church. There was much to see and to learn about this church. There were statues of Saint-Déodat and Saint-Baudemire; St Antoine and Ste Thérèse were there too; we noticed also that the Bible was open at Le Livre de la Sagesse! There was the inevitable plaque, "A La Memoire des Soldats de SAINT-DYE-sur-Loire – Morts Pour La France", which records that, even from this small village, 27 men died in, or following injuries sustained in, the Great War; interestingly it also records where they died. We were exceptionally fortunate in that there was a lady present who, as well as being able to tell us verbally about the church, had some booklets for sale detailing its history. She was very pleased to draw our attention to and lead us to the 6th century tomb of Saint Déodat, which is situated below the level of the floor; it is visible, being illuminated and protected by thick glass. While in the church there was a heavy storm of rain, but "we enjoyed it all". As we left we thanked Madame for her help; she was also very interested to know that we were going to Vézelay and Cluny during the following weeks.

We have since read that the 12th century manuscript conserved by L'EGLISE of SAINT-DYE contains information regarding the life of the saint and of legends relating to him. Apparently, he was born at Bourges in the middle of the 5th century; he entered a monastery at Chabris and came to know a deacon named Baudemire or Baumaire. Together they left the convent and came to the banks of the Loire to live a hermitic life; they apparently completed the journey in one night. Baudemire isolated himself on an island near the port of Saint-Dyé, while Déodat built himself a hut on the shore. Later, the latter occupied a cave at the site of the chevet of the church. According to legend, in about 507 Clovis came to consult Déodat before a war and after the victory he endowed him with a large area of land surrounding his cave and enough gold and silver to enable him to found a small convent. Subsequently, a group of about 40 of his followers gathered here. After the death of Déodat in about 530, some miracles occurred and then the first church was built to shelter his tomb; it soon became a place of pilgrimage. Following the destructions during the passing of the Normands between 854 and 868 a second church, a basilica, was built; evidence of this building was discovered during the course of excavations in 1962. A 'town' developed around the basilica and in the Middle Ages it had become important with some fortifications; it received and kept until the Revolution the title of 'Ville'. Thanks to its river port and other resources it became a kind of 'siège social' of the 'entreprise Chambord' launched by François I. The sarcophagus of St Déodat dates from the 6th century; it is of rose sandstone and was probably transported from Anjou by boat. The vault in which it rests is hardly bigger than the stone coffin itself. The sarcophagus is partly within the vault; it was brought forward to this position to take out the reliques in 1482. There is much more fascinating information in the book of Jean Chavigny; I hope that what I have recorded here represents a faithful translation. In 1482 the reliques were placed in a silver and golden reliquary provided by Louis XI. However, this was stolen about thirty years later and has never been found.

In addition to the commercial use of its port Saint-Dyé was an important etape on the route from Tours to Orléans; the town saw the funeral processions of Louis XI, Charles VIII and Anne de Bretagne; François I visited in 1523 and there were many other illustrious visitors. The town's prosperity lasted until 1 June 1773 when the new route from Paris towards Spain on the right bank of the Loire was opened. At the end of the 18th century the cotton industry maintained the population and at 1 January 1779 it employed 2,100 workers, but the industry declined in the 19th century and closed in 1875. From 1782 to 1962 the number of inhabitants declined from 1600 to 511. Saint-Dyé would now be a very tranquil village were it not for the traffic on the departmental road, D951. However, it appears on the map as a very small and insignificant place, but what treasures it has stored! It was an amazing experience.

We left by that same D951 for Muides-sur-Loire, where we then returned to Chambord and along the D33 to Thoury. Passing through La Ferté-St-Cyr, Neung-sur-Beuvron and Marcilly-en-Gault, we reached Salbris at 18.00; it was 22°C. Although we have travelled much of that same route three times during the past two days and observed several warnings of the presence of wild animals, boar and deer in particular, we have seen none. How better now to end a splendid day than with another excellent meal at Le Dauphin? It was 18.00 and 22°C.

(88 miles today)

Day 7 – Monday, 5 September 2011

Petit déjeuner is a flexible, informal and pleasant ceremony here with ample sustenance; it is interesting and enjoyable to witness, in a detached manner, the daily comings and goings at the hotel, the movement on the road outside and the activity outside the supermarket on the other side, but we must not linger here today. Having located la gare yesterday, we decided that the car could remain at the hotel and that, provided we allowed sufficient time, we could walk to the station. We did so and we were in good time to catch the 10.43 train to Orléans Centre. We purchased tickets for a single journey so that we would be free to return on the most convenient train for us; they cost 7.80 each and the journey of about 60 kilometres took about 40 minutes. We travelled on a train of the TER Centre network. TER trains are fast and comfortable and serve towns and villages on 21 regional networks covering the whole of France; they are usually, as ours was, modern and spacious and probably built in France by Alstom! When we alighted in Orléans we were, of course, confronted with an entirely unfamiliar scene; in addition, one side of the extensive 'foyer' was concealed from floor to roof by scaffolding and polythene sheeting; clearly extensive renovations or improvements are in progress. At first we could not see an obvious exit, but we did identify a spacious cafeteria and, therefore, the first priority was a cup of coffee. After a little while, I set off to reconnoitre the area; behind the plastic 'wall' I found a shop and was able to purchase a street plan and a copy of *Le Monde*; within the station complex I came upon a taxi rank, but on emerging outside the station I still could not decide which way it would be sensible to proceed. On returning to the cafeteria we decided that, to avoid unnecessary walking, we would take a taxi to the Cathedral; this surely would give us a good starting point. Although the taxi journey was, in fact, very short and cost the minimum of €7, it was well worth it.

We are now in ORLEANS in the Department of Loiret and in the Centre Region; it is the chief town of six cantons and has a population approaching 120,000. The Carnutes, one of many Gallic tribes that invaded France in the 6th century BC, settled here at Cenabum, as Orléans was then called, and it became an important crossroads and trading centre; they took part in the uprising against Caesar in 52 BC led by Vercingetorix, but were defeated and Cenabum was destroyed. It was rebuilt by the Roman Emperor Aurelian, renaming it Aurelianum which evolved into Orléans. The name which is inseparable from Orléans is that of Jeanne d'Arc, 'la pucelle d'Orléans'. During the Hundred Years War Henry VI of England was claiming the kingdom of France and, indeed, was holding large parts of the country. In 1428 the English decided to capture Orléans in order to secure a crossing point of the Loire and to trap the army of Charles VII, then based in Touraine, in a pincer movement. They captured the Fort des Tourelles and surrounded the city and thus began the long siege. In 1429, the besieged were short of food and their morale low.

On 25 April of that year Jeanne crossed the Loire at Blois with the royal army, rode through the Sologne, via Ligny and on the 29th joined Earl Dunois south of the city. They could not cross the swollen river and Dunois and the troops returned to Blois to cross the Loire and then march along the north bank. Jeanne crossed the river at Chécy with a small band of men and entered Orléans at nightfall, by the Porte Bourgogne; she was acclaimed by the people. Four days later Dunois arrived with reinforcements and attacked the Bastille St Loup;

Jeanne joined them in the storming of the fort. On 6 May, at the head of her troops, she again drove back the English, who abandoned the Bastille de St Jean le Blanc. They went on to carry the Fort des Augustins by storm. However, on 7 May Jeanne was wounded during one of the assaults on the Fort des Tourelles, but after having the wound dressed, she went back to the fray at the head of the besieged. Troops from inside the city then sallied out on to the bridge and took the English, who were holding the fort, in the rear. The Fort des Tourelles, which protected access to the bridge from the south, then fell and Jeanne crossed the Loire by the bridge and entered the rejoicing city. On the following day, 8 May, the English raised the siege and retreated. What a significant date, as it also marked the end in Europe of the Second World War!

After the Hundred Years War, Orléans became prosperous again. The University contributed much to the city's prestige; it specialized in law, was highly regarded throughout Europe and among its students was John Calvin and Molière; Henry VIII of England offered to fund a scholarship there. Orléans was the birthplace of the poet and essayist Charles Péguy, whose writings were referred to by the President of France in his address at the Armistice Day Ceremony at the Arc de Triomphe on 11 November 2011. Péguy died in battle in Villeroy on the 4 September 1914, the day before the beginning of the Battle of the Marne.

We are at La CATHEDRALE SAINTE-CROIX; the first known reference to the Saint-Croix (Holy Cross) is on a coin dating from 670 – 'Sancta Crux Aurelianis'.

There has been a church in this place since about the year 375, which itself was on the site of a building, probably a pagan temple, of the 1st century; there are vestiges of this first church. It was destroyed by fire in 989 and was rebuilt, but too rapidly; from the beginning of the 13th century it began to subside and, eventually, to collapse. It would have to be rebuilt. The construction of the present Gothique Cathédrale took more than five centuries, from 1287 to 1829. It suffered much damage at the hands of the Protestants during 40 years of the Wars of Religion towards the end of the 16th Century. However, it was completed and officially inaugurated on 8 May 1829, the fourth centenary of the deliverance of the city by Jeanne d'Arc. The Cathédrale presents a blend of the styles of the gothic and classical periods with elegance. The façade is impressive with its identically designed twin towers and three delicately decorated arches; the entry is through a large narthex; the nave is huge – 130 metres long and 40 metres wide – but its sober appearance contrasts with the classical exuberance of the exterior. The Chapelle Jeanne d'Arc must not be missed; it contains a statue of the Sainte and also a marble statue of Cardinal Touchet. Of particular interest is the Grand Orgue; this instrument had been constructed for the Abbaye de St Benoît-sur-Loire in the 17th century and was transferred to Sainte Croix in 1830. It was reconstructed by Aristide Cavaillé-Coll in 1878; restored in 2003–08, it is again in the condition in which it was left by Aristide Cavaillé-Coll in 1880. We were interested to find a memorial to "Les Deux William Douglas Seigneurs Ecossais tombés à Verneuil en 1424 pour la défense de La France contre les Anglais" and a memorial to "John Stewart of Darnley Connétable d'Ecosse" (supreme commander of the

French armies) who died in the defence of Orléans in 1429. We are reminded that Scottish soldiers fought with the French against the English during the Hundred Years War. Another significant memorial is "to the Memory of One Million Dead of the British Empire Who Fell in the Great War 1914 – 1918 and of Whom the Greater Part Rest in France". One could spend much more time here in this fascinating cathédrale, but we wish to see more of the city.

Unfortunately, the book shop in the cathedral was not open, perhaps because it was Monday! However, just a short distance away we found and visited the Office de Tourisme where, with the helpful advice of an assistant, we were able to select a couple of very useful books. While there we enquired if there were public toilets nearby and were directed to a building across the road. The 'road', however, was the scene of complete disruption as it is the route of an extension to the city's tramline system; the work is being carried out by the company, Alstom. We negotiated the 'crossing' to the building opposite, but there was no evidence whatever of any public toilets. Facing us, happened to be the HOTEL GROSLOT; in the main courtyard is a statue of Jeanne d'Arc on a flight of steps leading to a small doorway. We ventured up the steps and through the door into a passageway; being unsure whether we should be in this building, we proceeded circumspectly along the corridor until we met two ladies; they assured us that we were welcome to use the toilets further along the passage which, incidentally, provides a lovely view of the gardens at the rear. When we returned to the 'reception' area we realised that this building is open to visitors without charge and that it has an interesting history. Hôtel Groslot was built in the Renaissance style for the bailiff, Jacques Groslot, between 1549 and 1555; it was the town hall from 1790. The kings of France, passing through Orléans, used to stay here – Charles II, Charles IX, François II, Henri III and, inevitably, Henri Quatre – in fact, François II, the son of Catherine de Médicis and Henri II, died here on 5 December 1560. Before leaving we took time to visit a number of rooms which are open to the public, including that in which the King died. What an interesting discovery, leading from our enquiry for public toilets; in fact, this was the place of kings!

From the Hôtel Groslot, we walked along the Rue Jeanne d'Arc, turning right into the arcaded Rue Royale, which was built in the 18th century and then became the main street; this leads into the Place du Martroi. This is the main square in the shopping district and in the centre stands a magnificent equestrian bronze statue of Jeanne d'Arc. On the south side of the square stands the 'ancien pavillon de la Chancellerie' built in 1754 it used to hold the Duc d'Orléans' archives, but the façade is the only part of the original building that survived the bombing in 1940. From here we made our way back towards the Gare SNCF along the Rue de la République, which is a tramway route bordered by shops; we were attracted to a particularly splendid façade which we felt compelled to photograph; it testifies to the past prosperity of the city.

Back at the Gare SNCF, we decided, foolishly as it proved to be, that we had ample time to purchase our tickets and that we could first enjoy a cup of tea. However, when we eventually entered the booking office, there was a very, very, long queue, which we joined; progress was very slow and as the minutes passed, several times we considered leaving it and to attempt to purchase our tickets at one of the automatic machines. As the time of our train continued to approach we became more anxious and we took the risk that we would be able to understand the process of producing our own tickets! It was, to us, a somewhat complicated procedure and we made several attempts, each time making a little more progress. However, there was a young man waiting to use this machine and, eventually, I asked him if he knew more about them than we did. Even he did not seem very sure, but he kindly offered to operate it for us. We gave him the information it required, destination, time of train, etc., etc., were we pensioners – yes, we entered credit card details and then suddenly we have a ticket, but only one; he had to repeat the process. Finally, we were so relieved that we had two tickets and the cost was less than for the outward journey. We were so grateful to this young man; we thanked him, and we hope he caught his train. This is by no means the first time that a young person has come to our aid and assistance when we have been in doubt or difficulty in France! It was only two or three minutes to the time of our train; we rushed out and, by chance, the contrôleuse was standing by our train and so we were able to board without further delay; we were so relieved. However, when this same contrôleuse came to examine our tickets, she looked at them very purposely and asked if we had evidence of our entitlement to that particular rate of fares. Clearly, although being pensioners, we were not entitled to the same concessions as French pensioners; perhaps the machine provided an option for our category; I don't know! I offered to pay the balance, but she immediately rejected the offer and with a smile wished us "Bonne soirée". When we left the train at Salbris she was there to assist us and again wished us "Bonne soirée".

After a leisurely walk back to Le Dauphin we were certainly looking forward to another excellent repas prepared by Jean-Pierre and served by Céline and we were not disappointed. It had been a very full, interesting, rewarding and, in spite of the considerable distances of walking required, enjoyable day.

(Mileage – 0)

Day 8 – Tuesday, 6 September 2011

We have much enjoyed and appreciated our stay, our days and nights, at Le Dauphin; it has also enabled us to visit some wonderful places and to meet a number of such friendly and helpful people. We were sorry when it was time to say, "nous devons partir" and so, we felt, was Céline; she gave us a gift of biscuits (Les Sablés de Nançay) as we said, "au revoir". It was 11.10 and the temperature was only 18°C. After driving from the hotel, but with our thoughts still lingering there, we realised we had taken a wrong turning. We had not gone far and were soon on the D724 and heading towards Souesmes; then leaving the Department of Loir et Cher and entering the Cher we now have a new road number – D924. The route of 20 miles from Salbris to

Aubigny passes through thickly wooded country and we observed the fir trees and laurel and wild purple heather and ferns on both sides of the road. Ménétréol-sur-Sauldre, a village of about 250 souls, has a history which goes back to the early part of the 11th century. It is in the heart of the Sologne and its main activity nowadays is connected to the forestry industry. We passed into the natural region of Berry, which consists of the departments of Cher, Indre and part of Vienne; it was a province until provinces were replaced by departments in 1790.

At AUBIGNY-SUR-NERE we wished that we had time to linger; first known in Roman times it became a royal town in 1189. While in the cathedral of Orléans we had observed the memorial to John Stewart of Darnley. A junior member of the House of Stuart, he arrived in France in 1419 with a large contingent of Scottish soldiers, to fight for Charles VII. Among the many titles he was awarded, was that of Duke of Aubigny; the family stayed here for 400 years. We noticed some sixteenth century houses, but we failed to see the fifteenth century castle of the Stuarts. This town of about 6,000 inhabitants displays a number of Scottish features. Indeed, there is a Museum of the Auld Alliance which emphasizes the alliance between France and Scotland which was at its zenith under the Stuarts of Aubigny during the Hundred Years War.

From Aubigny we had intended to proceed to La Chapelle d'Angillon, but after travelling a short distance along a rather uninteresting D940, we decided to return to Aubigny and to take a much shorter route, along the

D923 via Oizon, to Vailly-sur-Sauldre, a farming village of about 800 people. The D926 took us to Santranges, an even smaller village, more farming country and then to Beaulieu-sur-Loire. Shortly after leaving Santranges we re-entered the Department of Loiret at exactly 600 miles into our journey. This department takes the name of the river Loiret; a river which is only 12 kilometres long and is a tributary of the Loire; its entire course is within the department. Next, along the D951 to Belleville-sur-Loire, cross the Canal by the weight restricted bridge at the traffic lights, alongside the Centrale Nucléaire, over the Loire and negotiate Neuvy-sur-Loire. We are now in the Department of Nièvre and the Region of Bourgogne (BURGUNDY). It was then a much more straightforward and pleasant drive on the D957 to Arquian and to Saint-Amand-en-Puisaye. At this point last year we made a detour to visit the Chantier médiéval de Guédelon, but as medieval type materials, tools and building methods are being used in the construction of this château, we would not expect to see a dramatic change in its appearance after a period of 12 months.

However, SAINT-AMAND-en-PUISAYE appears to have its own particular character to offer and, at 13.30, it was an appropriate time and place for rest and refreshment – bars, bananas, etc. The display near the car park shows the wide range of enterprises here and, with its artisans, it is the centre of the Puisaye pottery craft. In the district of Saint-Amand, which has about 1,400 inhabitants, water is found everywhere, in springs, streams, ponds and the river Vrille and the subsoil possesses clay of an exceptional character, which can stand a very high firing temperature. The combination of the natural elements of water, wood, clay and fire determined the establishment of the pottery industry in this village; this craft has been practised here for more than 600 years and continues to this day. The first artisan known to have exercised his talents as a potter here was in 1316. Before exploring any town or village for the first time, it is always wise to visit the Office de Tourisme and here it is, just across the road and looking more like a lavoir for, indeed, that is what it is called. Inside, in addition to the usual considerable volume of interesting leaflets and information about the area, we observed some of the creations of the local artisans. Before leaving, we enquired if there were any public toilets nearby and, once again, we were directed across the road to a very large red brick building. We found an entrance door and, sure enough, the toilets. However, we then realised that this 'building' was, indeed, the village château which was open free to visitors. This is the most important Renaissance style château of the Niévre; it was constructed between 1530 and 1540 on the site of a feudal fortress, which stood on the route of an ancient Roman way that linked Autun to Paris and, no doubt, Orléans and which had been destroyed in 1402. The château houses Le Musée du Grès, which contains some interesting local works of art. Well, what an enquiry for toilets can lead one to! Realising what we had discovered, we paused outside to more appreciate this edifice and its environment; we walked along the road and viewed the ancient potteries with their architectural features, which bear witness to the importance of the craft of pottery in this place; we stood on the bridge over the river while some men were fishing and we were attracted to une petite maison nestling low in the garden nearby. We were interested to learn that Saint-Amand was the adopted land of Jean Carriès, Sculpteur, Ceramiste and Potier; by chance we had noticed a memorial to him when passing through Arquian last year and we had stopped to take a photograph.

Eventually, we returned to the car and resumed our journey. Continuing along the D957, at 16.30 we stopped very briefly at Le Moulin Blat, near Bouhy, but it was uncomfortably windy at this exposed spot; after Entrainlon and Billy-s-Oisy, we joined the not very busy national road, N151, to avoid the centre of Clamecy, but quickly left it to take the D951 towards Vézelay. At Dornecy, we stopped for petrol at the Esso Auto Station – 43 litres - €1.539 per litre = €66.18 – where we had an unexpected experience; after successfully completing our purchase, we were approached by a young man explaining that his credit card had been rejected and asking if we would be willing to use our card to pay for his petrol and he would, of course, give us the appropriate amount in euros. He first spoke in French, but when he realised that we were English he repeated his request in our language. He was not French and certainly not English; I suspect, perhaps, he was Dutch. I declined his request; in any case I expect, and hope, that our bank would have declined a second fairly substantial amount at the same location within minutes. Shortly after leaving Dornecy, we were troubled by the very close proximity of a very large camion behind us and by its repeatedly flashing lights; as soon as I saw a suitable area at the side of the road, I allowed it to pass, but as it did so the driver continued his expression of annoyance. Although it was a French vehicle, I wonder if the driver was one of the many thousands of foreign drivers, who apparently spend much of their lives in the lorry in order to earn as much as they possibly can. I cannot recall any other incidents of this kind while driving many thousands of miles in France. Shortly before Chamoux we entered the Department of Yonne; as we passed Vézelay we saw again the Basilique sitting majestically on the top of the hill. Again on the D957, we reached Hôtel Les Fleurs, PONTAUBERT at 18.22 and we were pleased to find that we could park at the side of the hotel. When we were here last year, we were told that extensive refurbishment work was planned, and it has now been completed. We were directed to the same room as before and we found it to be excellent. We recalled the excellent meals we had here last year and with no hesitation we decided to have a meal this evening. The waitress service was most friendly, helpful and efficient; the meal, with the 'little surprises', was very enjoyable. We are pleased to be here again.

(108 miles today)

Day 9 – Wednesday, 7 September 2011

It was a wet and rather maussade morning and only 17°C, but after breakfast we prepared to visit VEZELAY, one of *Les Plus Beau Villages de France,* as planned. After the short journey of about eight miles, we first toured parking areas near the foot of the village, but they appeared to provide for specific periods of parking; we returned to the large car park near the entrance to the village, where we were able to park for the day for three

Euros; it was 11.50. Fortunately, it was becoming drier and a little brighter. It is quite a long and not an easy walk to the entrance to the village and the hill which leads up to the Basilica is no less steep than on our last visit! Eventually, we reached the summit and there ahead of us is the impressive west front of the BASILIQUE SAINTE-MARIE-MADELEINE. Vézelay has always been associated with the Crusades; Pope Urban II had planned to announce his call for a crusade to rescue the Holy Land for the Christians in 1095 at Vézelay, although he did, in fact, preach the First Crusade at the Council of Clermont in that year. However, at Easter 1146 Bernard of Clairvaux preached the Second Crusade at Vézelay in the presence of Louis VII; Richard Coeur de Lion and Philippe Auguste met here in 1190 with their armies to prepare for the Third Crusade. The façade of the Basilica is noteworthy; for its incomplete north tower; for its 13th century decorated gothic pediment, the bays of which are separated by statues permitting limited light to the narthex; also, for its 19th century tympanum representing the Last Judgement.

One leaves the outside world of the profane and enters the dimly lit narthex, a transitory place. The nave tympanum, completed in 1130, is remarkable and so different from its counterparts across Europe; instead of depicting Last Judgement scenes, it presents a spiritual defence of the crusades. Thus, Vézelay's portal reflects the unique importance of this place in the development of the crusades. Proceeding through the doors into the bright light of the warm straw-coloured nave one realises that light is one of the principal materials used in the construction of this church. This truly is a place of inspiration; it is necessary to surrender to the mighty character of the edifice. Inspired were the architects and builders of the 12th century. They considered the position of the earth in relation to the sun and designed the nave so that, at the exact time of the winter and summer solstices, the nine clerestory windows of the southern wall allow the sun's rays to reach precise locations along the north wall and the pavement of the nave. Thus, at noon on June 21 nine spots of light appear on the pavement marking a line along the nave midway between the north wall and the south wall. Similarly, on December 21 the sunlight reaches each and every one of the upper capitals of the north wall with perfect accuracy. What remarkable skills; what an achievement! We sat in the nave for some while. Then into the Gothic choir with its whiter stones, its large windows and its even greater light. I made a second visit to the crypt and to the relics of Mary Magdalen. We paused at the memorial to Saint Bernard. In 1946, 800 years after the great gathering addressed by Saint Bernard, another great gathering assembled – the CRUSADE FOR PEACE. Europe had been torn apart and ruined and there was a call to Christians to gather in prayer to overcome the forces of hatred and to celebrate the anniversary. This pilgrimage was an event of pardon and a promise of peace; 14 wooden crosses were carried on foot from England, Luxembourg, Belgium, Switzerland, Italy and different parts of France to the Basilique. Then some German prisoners, interned in a nearby camp, asked to be allowed to join the procession and a 15th cross was hastily prepared. These crosses are displayed around the walls of the nave and have become a powerful sign of reconciliation for the world. About 30,000 people attended this crusade and Vézelay wants to continue to be a place of prayer for reconciliation and for a Europe at peace.

In more recent times and in a different way, this place, this architectural and spiritual monument, was inspirational to the Luxembourgeois conductor, Pierre Cao. One day in 1999 on entering the Basilique he was amazed by what he perceived, and it inspired him to create here in Vézelay one of the outstanding professional choirs of Europe – ARSYS BOURGOGNE. More than 500 auditions were held to select a nucleus of about 40 professional singers. Many hours of rehearsal are devoted to ensuring that each and every singer achieves exactly the same interpretation of the music and that the choir as a whole produces an incredible homogeneity and clarity of sound. Its success is largely due to the exceptional skills and inspirational leadership of Pierre Cao. When we were here last year we became aware of this choir, which is now firmly established here, and we bought a short CD of examples of their performances. A few months ago I watched and recorded the first part of a performance by the choir in the Basilique of Brahms German Requiem broadcast rather late at night on the Arte Television channel and I had hoped that we could purchase a DVD of the whole performance. I made enquiries at the shop in the church and was advised to visit the shop L'Or Des Etoiles in the village. We had spent a considerable time in this remarkable building and we had to re-enter the world of today, but before doing so we purchased a DVD 'Vézelay – la Colline Eternelle' as a reminder of our visit.

Following the 'successes' of the First Crusade in 1099, towards the middle of the 12th century some of the 'gains' had been eroded; for instance, Edesse, the first Latin state of the Orient, had been lost and Jerusalem itself was threatened and there was a decree by the Pope for a Second Crusade. However, there was little enthusiasm for another crusade, but the one preacher who could revive the flame was Bernard of Clairvaux. In the presence of Louis VII, Bernard exercised his rhetorical skills on the heights of Vézelay on 31 March 1146 before an enormous crowd and when he had finished the crowd enlisted en masse. Unfortunately, this crusade led by Louis VII (with his wife, Alienor d'Acquitaine) of France and Conrad III of Germany was a complete fiasco; an outcome which haunted Bernard for the rest of his life. We are not aware of any indication as to where more precisely the tribune from which Saint Bernard had performed may have been positioned, but we walked around the north and east side of the Basilique; we noticed the cemetery below and continued until we found a convenient seat where we could survey the hillside, the valley below and the countryside beyond; we tried to imagine the enormous crowd here some 865 years earlier and wondered how he had been able to convey his message to such a vast throng.

It was now a very warm and pleasant day, but eventually we began our way back to the west front of the Basilique and then the descent of the steep route down between the ancient and interesting buildings. We came to a pâtisserie/salon de thé; there were no customers, but it was still open and we decided to have a cup of tea. However, on the opposite side of the road was the shop we had been advised to visit – L'Or Des Etoiles. We went in; it was a fascinating shop full of books, cards, souvenirs, CDs, DVDs, etc. I asked the gentleman in charge if I could purchase a DVD of the performance which had been televised, but he had to disappoint me by saying that it was recorded for television only. As a form of compensation, we purchased a compact disc of the choir's live performance in the Basilique of Dixit Dominus by Handel.

Fortunately, our cup of tea was still available and even more welcome. We had not long been sitting when another couple entered for some refreshment. We quickly realised that they were speaking in English and we made contact with them. They were, in fact, Canadian and were extremely interested to know and made notes of what we were able to tell them about Arsys Bourgogne and we expect they too visited the shop opposite before leaving the area. We were very interested to learn that after leaving Vézelay they were going to Le Puy-en-Velay and intended to walk from there some of the pilgrimage route to Santiago de Compostela. Vézelay itself is, of course, the inspiration for one of the four starting points in France of this demanding adventure.

When we eventually reached the car, we were surprised to find on the windscreen an envelope containing a note pointing out that we had not displayed a parking ticket and that, consequently, we must purchase a ticket otherwise we would be sent a formal notice of penalty. Of course, we had already purchased a ticket, but by then it was resting on the seat. We were able to complete a satisfactory explanation and deposit it in the box provided and so that was the end of that. On our way back to Pontaubert we realised that we had again not had the time to visit the ancient village and surroundings of St-Père-sous-Vézelay other than to pass through it. Shortly before reaching Pontaubert, however, we did follow the sign for the Chapelle de Templiers hoping that we could, at least, locate this building. After some distance along a narrow road we came to a notice explaining that the Chapelle could only be visited, "par rendez-vous". It was now 19.30 and so we promptly returned to the main road and to our hotel. We had experienced a very full, rewarding and memorable day and it was appropriate that we should end it by enjoying another excellent meal in the very amicable atmosphere of the Hôtel Les Fleurs.

(15 miles only)

Day 10 – Thursday, 8 September 2011

Our first recorded experience of this day is 'A red squirrel!' Whether this apparition occurred while we were still at Hôtel Les Fleurs or after we had left I cannot now say. In any case, we certainly had a very enjoyable breakfast and after thanking Madame for the warm welcome and hospitality, the meals and comfortable room we said farewell; it was 11.25 and the temperature 17°C. Pontaubert is a small village in the Department of Yonne with a population of about 400. I cannot add any further information but, no doubt, given time one could discover some interesting facts about this village. It has certainly been an extremely convenient base for our visits to Vézelay and as a starting point of our tour of Burgundy. Avallon, with its near 8,000 inhabitants is the nearby town; it is the site of a roman settlement.

However, we left Pontaubert by a minor road to VAULT-de-LUGNY. After a very short distance we pass the Château de Vault-de-Lugny. This dates from the beginning of the 15th century; it was dismantled in 1478 and reconstructed at the end of the 16th century; it is now a moated luxury hotel. We had travelled all of one mile when we made our first stop. Vault-de-Lugny lies in the valley of the Cousin and there was a Roman presence here. We could not resist parking very conveniently outside the church in this so neat and tidy little village of little more than 300 souls. Opposite the church was the appropriately imposing Mairie, but it was the church which attracted our attention. First, we respected the inevitable, faithfully cared for, memorial, "A Ses Enfants Morts Pour La France" standing prominently in front of the church. I wonder if there was a single 'Thankful Village', however small, in the whole of France at the end of the Great War! L'EGLISE SAINT-GERMAIN was reconstructed in the 16th century – there is no trace of the original chapelle. This building is a beautiful example of a flamboyant gothic style. On the façade, perched in a buttress, is the statue of Saint Germain. There is much of interest inside the church and there are some notable features. The floor is paved with beautiful, inscribed tombstones; there are beautiful stained-glass windows; the walls present an exceptional display of wall paintings which probably date from before 1564 and which recall stories from the

Old and New Testaments; there is a remarkable chaire à preacher (pulpit) in beautiful white stone, richly sculptured with plant and character motifs in neo-gothic style dating from 1878. This is a church well worth visiting; however, we must now move on, but not before buying a postcard.

Continuing to Vermoiron, then Valloux to join the D606 towards Blannay; with the village of Sermizelles on our left we noticed a direction sign to NOTRE-DAME d'ORIENT on our right; we must investigate! The first couple of hundred metres of the narrow road was bounded by generously spaced unspectacular pavillons (bungalows); the final one having a separate dwelling in its grounds being the home of a rather fierce sounding chien who appeared to have a message for us. From there on the route was a very uneven and rough single track from which we could see nothing but trees; we were in the Bois de Boulu. As we drove slowly forward, always hoping that we would not meet another vehicle, each straight section of the track ended with a bend, and another and another, until eventually we reached a junction. We had a choice of going to the right or to the left; it was fairly obvious that to reach our goal we should go to the left. However, as there did not appear to be a way of returning to the main road in that direction, we knew that by continuing we increased the risk of meeting another vehicle and so, reluctantly, we decided to return to the D606 from that point; fortunately, we met no one. We were disappointed, but we know that Notre-Dame d'Orient is a tower which was constructed in 1858 by the young people of Sermizelles returned from the Crimean War; the chapel and the stained-glass windows were completed just a century later in 1958.

At Voutenay-sur-Cure we left the route of the Via Agrippa (Roman road), which linked Avallon to Auxerre, to join the D32, a road which passes through picturesque countryside. First it skirts Précy-le-Sec, where about 300 people live. This village has a recorded history which goes back to the early part of the 12th century; its name derives from the fact of its isolated situation on a bare plateau without water.

Next, to JOUX-la-VILLE at 13.25, where we paused for a while. Resting at the bottom of a large depression this very ancient village has a recorded history dating from 1104. The church of la Nativité de Notre-Dame seems to date from the late 15th century and is classified as an historic monument. It has a square tower and a flamboyant style; we noticed, particularly, the very old, sculptured stalls which date from the 18th century. In 1815 Napoleon 1 passed nearby on his way to Paris after escaping from the island of Elba; it was the beginning of the famous One Hundred Days which culminated in his defeat by British and Prussian armies at Waterloo on 18 June 1815. Taking the D11, over the A6 Autoroute, through the Forêt d'Hervaux we reached Dissangis, a village of about 140, situated at the bottom and on the side of a little valley well-watered by several sources which feed into the river Serein; then another delightful drive of about eight miles along the D86 through the village of Massangis took us to the entrance to Noyers.

NOYERS-sur-SEREIN has a population of about 700 and is one of *Les Plus Beaux Villages de France*; this charming little town snuggling in a meander of the Serein, sealed from the modern world in a medieval time warp, must surely be one of the most beautiful villages of even that select group of 150 or so exceptional villages. A town existed here in the Gallo-Roman period; from about the 12th century it was owned by the powerful Miles family. In 1303 Miles X became a Maréchal de France and commanded the French cavalry at the Battle of Crécy in 1346. After the extinction of the illustrious Miles dynasty the seigniory was sold to the Duchesse de Bourgogne in 1419. At the end of the 12th century Hugues de Noyers, Bishop of Auxerre and guardian of Miles VII, had transformed the primitive château into 'un des plus fiers castels de France'; he also constructed the ramparts, gates and towers around the town. In 1217 the château resisted the siege of the troops of Blanche de Castille. During the Wars of Religion in the 16th century, Noyers became a Huguenot stronghold; later it flourished under the Dukes of Luynes. However, following a period of looting of the surrounding area by the then occupant, Henri IV decided to demolish the château in 1599. There are vestiges of the château to the north of the town.

We entered NOYERS through La Porte Peinte at about 15.10, into Place de l'Hôtel de Ville and were able to park nearby in the ancient Place du Marche au Blé (wheat), which is a reminder of the town's agricultural significance. After surveying the scene, we walked into and along a paved pedestrian street where we were able to enjoy a welcome cup of tea. We had already noticed a gentleman in a 'uniform' and it became evident that a wedding had just taken place nearby; soon appeared a photographer leading the bride and groom to specific locations to be photographed, at one of which they lay prostrate on the ground. We walked further along the 'street' and out into the Place de la Petite Etape aux Vins, which indicates that this is a viticole area. We strolled back to the Place de l'Hôtel de Ville, everywhere observing and admiring the splendid medieval buildings – the medieval arcades, the half-timbered houses, the carved pilasters and, not least, the climbing wisteria. There are, in fact, some 78 buildings which are registered Monuments historiques, many dating from the 15th century and which have been altered little since that time. It is only a very short walk from Place du Marche au Blé to l'Eglise Notre-Dame. In the 15th century the inhabitants found the existing parish church too distant and decided on 25 June 1489 to build a church in the centre of the town. The first stone was laid on 3 May 1491 and 24 years later in 1515 the church was completed. It has a square belltower; on entering, one is struck by its regularity and its flamboyant gothic style; the choir stalls are 17th century and the pulpit probably 18th century; there is no crypt; the organ apparently dates from 1740! Before leaving Noyers we felt we would like to purchase an appropriate souvenir. We spotted a likely shop and the helpful lady introduced us to the perfect reminder of our visit – an excellent little book *Promenade Dans le Vieux Noyers*, written in 1935 by l'Abbé Marcel Terre, who was born at Noyers in 1907. This village is a real gem and one could spend much more time here, but it is now 17.05 and we have a reservation at the Château de Malaisy for tonight.

However, before proceeding out of the town and along the Rue de la Republique we can note that about 15 miles north-west of Noyers is the town of Chablis. The grape vines around Chablis are almost all Chardonnay which produce the dry white wine renowned for the purity of its aroma and taste. The best vineyards in the area all lie in one small southwest facing slope located just north of the town.

We left Noyers on the D956 for Sanvigne and Aisy-sur-Armançon where we left the Yonne and entered the department of Côte-d'Or and, at the same time, joined the D905 for Montbard; this road follows the route of the river Brenne. Montbard is a small industrial town on the Brenne with a population of about 5,500; the Burgundy canal also passes through the town; it also has the distinction of having a cricket team! Just three or four miles beyond Montbard we found FAIN-lès-MONTBARD, but it was when passing through in the opposite direction that we spotted a very clear direction sign for le CHATEAU de MALAISY. From there on every turning was well signed and led us into the grounds of the Château and to the entrance – at 18.05. We were greeted in a very courteous and friendly manner and invited to have a meal, which we accepted. First we were introduced to our room – chambre 22, which was located in a large building detached from the main château; it was on the ground floor and entered directly from the exterior; it was quite acceptable and comfortable and, from the doorway, we had a splendid view of the château. For our meal we were taken into a large and grand dining room where all the tables appeared to be fully laid. However, so far as we recall, there was just one other couple and a single gentleman dining, and it was not very long before we were entirely alone. Nevertheless, we were served in a most helpful and friendly manner and we enjoyed the meal. It was a balmy late summer evening and, on our way back to our room, we lingered to appreciate the remarkable silence and the atmosphere of the place. We had had a splendid day, experiencing so much to absorb and remember and, yet, we had travelled no more than 57 miles!

(57 miles)

Day 11 – Friday, 9 September 2011

We awoke to a beautiful morning – 20°C – and after a very satisfactory conventional continental breakfast in the dining room, together with a surprising number of other guests, we encountered two 'permanent' residents while on our way back to our room – a peacock and its friend, a white Silkie hen of the bearded variety. We also had the pleasure of meeting and talking to the gentleman of the couple with whom we had shared the dining room during the previous evening. He was trying to form a friendship with the peacock, but the bird did not appear to share his emotions. We were interested to learn that they (the couple) were on their way to the Pyrenees; in fact, their home is in Berlin and, although they are very fond of France, they also like to explore countries to the east of Germany, such as Poland, Ukraine and Belarus. It was an interesting conversation during which he referred to Berlin as being a very spacious city compared to some other capitals; I wonder if that fact could have anything to do with the Second World War.

Here, at CHATEAU de MALAISY we are in the north of the natural region of Auxois and at the heart of the valley of Fontenay. In 1623 these lands were acquired by Pierre de Damas, whose family constructed the château. During the 18th century a tower and some additional buildings were added. In the 19th century it was in the ownership of the wife of the Count of Maleyssie and, presumably, this is how it acquired its name. Since 1986 it has been owned by the Gilinsky family. One of the attractions of the château is, undoubtedly, the 15-hectare park which surrounds it; this is adorned by ancient trees and a variety of animals; here we meet deer, sheep, donkeys, Vietnam pigs, goats, horses and cows in their specific enclosures and, almost anywhere, and certainly not least, "nos petits compagnons les chats".

We chose to spend a couple of nights at the Château de Malaisy to enable us to visit, in particular, l'ABBAYE de FONTENAY; in fact, it was no more than about a five mile journey. Fontenay arose near a spring, close to a lake and a small hermitage, tucked away in the hollow of a wooded valley and watered by a flowing stream. The Abbey of Fontenay is a vast monastic complex founded by Saint Bernard of Clairvaux in 1118 and built on land received from his uncle. The church was constructed from 1139 and consecrated in 1147; it is in the Romanesque style; simplicity is a principal of its design; in accordance with the intention of Saint Bernard, that nothing should distract the eye from the primary purpose of the place as a house of prayer, the capitals, etc., are barely sculptured; accordingly, the builders were masons and not sculptors. Architecturally,

Fontenay is a faithful expression of what Saint Bernard, founder of the order, believed should constitute a Cistercian foundation; its layout reflects the daily life of the monks; the Cistercians wished to reform monastic life and to strictly apply the Rule of Saint Benedict dating from the 6th century. Everard of Calne (Wiltshire), an Archdeacon in the diocese of Salisbury, who became Bishop of Norwich, resigned his see in 1145 to be a monk at Fontenay; he used his wealth to finance the building of the Abbey; he died here, probably in 1146, and is buried here. Sadly, Fontenay was plundered during the Hundred Years War and during the Wars of Religion. It was closed at the time of the French Revolution and became a paper mill until 1902; it was owned by the Montgolfier family (of hot air balloon fame) for most of the period of this operation. In 1905 the Abbey was bought by Edouard Aynard, a banker from Lyon, from his father-in-law, Raymond de Montgolfier. He undertook an immense task to restore the Abbey to its original state – to what we are able to enjoy today; it is still in the ownership of the same family. L'Abbaye de Fontenay is one of the oldest and most complete Cistercian abbeys in Europe; it has been a UNESCO World Heritage Site since 1981.

At noon we approached the Abbey along the valley of the D32 from Marmagne to find a very spacious parking area – even extending to the adjacent meadow; it was noon. First we visited l'eglise; the nave is 66 metres long and 16.7 metres high; in the north transept we saw a remarkable example of late 13th century Burgundian statuary – Mary, crowned, carrying the child Jesus – this is especially remarkable as it was sold at the time of the Revolution and was exposed to the elements in a village cemetery for more than a century before being returned to the Abbey in 1929; in the sanctuary is the tomb of the Bishop of Norwich. The dormitory is accessed by a staircase directly from the church; it is vast, 56 metres long and is where all the monks slept together on the floor; it is covered by an oak frame, resembling an upturned ship's hull, which dates from the second half of the 15th century. During the course of our tour of the church we met and talked to a German lady, who, like us, was exploring the area by car. Later, as we descended the lower and open section of the wide stone staircase from the dormitory we met her again and, observing our caution on the steps, kindly offered a hand of support. Incidents like this we have experienced often, and they are all the more remarkable when one recalls that tens of thousands of innocent civilians were annihilated by the Royal Air Force in cities such as Cologne, Hamburg and Dresden during the 1940's. The significance of the 'European Union' is often questioned; perhaps we should think of it more as a union of Europeans! Fontenay is a very extensive complex and, in addition to the imposing abbey church, we circulated in and around the various buildings, etc., the most impressive of which is the cloister. We then spent some time walking around, sitting in and admiring the elegant modern gardens where flowing water is a prominent characteristic. Here one can be transported back to the early days of the Abbey in the first part of the 12th century. However, before departing from this haven of peace and tranquillity, we were soon reminded of the present-day world; we visited the bookshop to purchase a book; we bought a cup of coffee from a 'machine' and we discovered that Fontenay had been the rendezvous for a large gathering of veteran cars. I wonder what Saint Bernard might think of Fontenay today – probably he would be amazed that it has survived so much and for so long and, no doubt, gratified that, structurally, it is now preserved for the benefit of many future generations to experience, much in the form of his vision. We left at 16.30.

From Fontenay we decided to go back in history a few centuries from the Middle Ages to the Roman Period. We returned to the D905 and to Fain-lès-Montbard, continuing alongside the railway and the Brenne to Venarey-les-Laumes and then Alise-Ste-Reine. From here we followed the signs for Mont Auxois and the site of ALESIA; after a short distance we found a convenient parking area and decided to complete the ascent on foot. It was 17.00. Although it was a rather steep climb, the surface was good and it was not very far to the top. Prior to the first millennium the approximate area covered by present day France, together with Luxembourg and Belgium, most of Switzerland, parts of Italy and the Netherlands and Germany formed the region of Gaul. It fell under Roman control during the 2nd and 1st centuries BC, but it was during the campaigns of 58 to 51 BC that Julius Caesar finally subdued the whole of Gaul. Roman rule lasted for some five centuries until AD 486. The oppidum of Alésia was a particular obstacle to Caesar; it was occupied and strongly defended by Gallic tribes led by Vercingétorix. It was placed under siege by Caesar for two months in 52 BC and, following the ensuing battle, the town surrendered. Vercingétorix was imprisoned and later taken to Rome and executed. There had been uncertainty regarding the location of Alésia, when in the 1860s, Napoleon III, whose view was that Alise-Ste-Reine was the site of the ancient town, funded research and excavations which revealed evidence of a Roman camp in the area; he also dedicated a memorial statue to Vercingétorix.

Recent excavations have confirmed previous findings; there is also evidence of 2,000 years of settlement prior to the time of Caesar. The consequences of the siege and battle which occurred here at Alésia 2,000 years ago were of such significance that the events have been referred to as the beginning of the History of France. As we reached the top of Mont Auxois we were immediately struck by the sight of the massive statue of Vercingétorix which is seven metres tall and bears the inscription, "Gaul united, Forming a single nation, Animated by a common spirit, Can defy the Universe". We sat to admire it and then walked around the statue. Nearby is an information area containing a plan of the 'Siege d'Alésia d'Apres Les Fouilles Ordonnees Par l'Empereur Napoleon III'. We returned to the point where we had reached the top, but continued across a field and found some cellars dating from the 1st century AD. Now they are almost filled in, but they were the basements of urban houses, dating from the Gallo-Roman period in Alésia, which served to store foodstuffs. A little further in the distance we could see a collection of buildings; visitors we met told us that they were part of a museum, etc., but they thought that it was by then closed. However, we returned to our car and drove to the entrance of the site. Through the railings we could see that it was a very extensive and interesting area, no doubt full of archaeological discoveries. We could see the very modern and impressive Centre d'Interprétation and we learn that the Centre and Musée will be open to the public from the 26 March 2012. It would certainly warrant a visit of a whole day!

It is now 19.00 and we must return to the Château de Malaisy, but as we left Alise-Ste-Reine we stopped to photograph an equestrian statue of Jeanne d'Arc. It was 22°C when we reached the hotel at 19.30 and being such a very pleasant evening, we spent some time walking around the animal park meeting the various 'residents' in their respective allotted habitats. We took one or two photographs which remind us that at that time we had entered into a period of twilight or, perhaps we should say, 'entre chien et loup' As we strolled back to our room we were very aware of a particularly remarkable feature of this place – the silence, silence which is rarely pierced day or night other than by the sound of a TGV speeding between, presumably, Paris and Dijon. We have had a most interesting and varied day and all within a distance of 24 miles.

(24 miles)

Day 12 – Saturday, 10 September 2011

It was a wise choice to spend a couple of nights here at Château de Malaisy, not only because of its proximity to so many interesting sites, but also for its special setting and its atmosphere; perhaps one could even use the word 'unique'. After petit déjeuner we were in no hurry to leave and we still had the company of peacock and Silkie – the latter, with its calm and friendly temperament is very appropriate here. Eventually, we returned our key and said farewell and as we drove away at 'midi' – it was 27°C – we realized that peacock did not wish to be left behind for it was trotting alongside us. We were considering whether to use our superior speed when a call from a member of the staff diverted its attention and we were allowed to continue independently into Fain-lès-Montbard. This is a village with a population of about 300; in the gallo-romaine period, a villa was built near an older temple and some traces still exist. Returning to the D905 as far as Venary-les-Laumes where we could have taken the road for Alise-Ste-Reine and made a further visit to Alésia.

However, we would prefer to spend some time in a nearby village which was closely linked to the Roman campaign of 52 BC, FLAVIGNY-SUR-OZERAIN is situated on a rocky spur and one is conscious of this fact when approaching the village and when entering and exploring its ancient streets. During the siege of Alésia, Caesar set up a military camp on the hillside of Flavigny and after the withdrawal of his army he offered one of his generals, Flavinius, some land on which would be built the city of Flavianiacum; this is now Flavigny, one of *Les Plus Beau Villages de France* with a population of about 300. We approached the village by the D9 and on the hillside just below we found a designated, indeed, 'obligatoire', parking area and, although informal, it was very convenient; it was 12.30 and just a few steps to mount and a short incline to climb took us to one of the gates of the city – Porte du Bourg. However, we walked along the esplanade to the left to the Porte Sainte-Barbe to find the remains of the ancient Abbaye Saint-Pierre, particularly La Crypte Sainte-Reine. The first abbey was founded in the 5th or 6th century; soon destroyed, it was rebuilt by Wideradus in 719 and, with him as Abbot, it became a Benedictine monastic community. It was restored in the 15th century and reconstructed in the 17th century. In 1632 an Ursuline convent was founded here. The Benedictines returned in 1644, but at the time of the Revolution there were very few monks and the abbey was probably little more than a ruin. In 1791 the abbey was sold and much of the remainder destroyed at the beginning of the 19th century. The remains of the carolingienne crypt are remarkable; built in the 9th century to receive the relics of Sainte Reine, it has been classed as an historic monument since 1906 and is one of the oldest religious buildings in France; it is surely the oldest 'building' we have ever entered.

Part of the old abbey, reconstructed in the 18th century, is occupied by the sole producers of the anise-flavoured candy, Les Anis de Flavigny. Manufactured here by the monks since 873, these small aniseed flavoured pastilles are known world-wide and the current recipe has been used since 1591. It is said that aniseeds were used by the men of Caesar's army. We visited the shop and purchased a sample of this famous bonbon. From this ancient site we followed the Rue de l'Abbaye and Rue de l'Eglise to the parish church of Saint-Genès. This church was built in the 13th century on vestiges dating from the 11th century and enlarged in the 15th century; the façade was damaged by lightning in 1663 and was reconstructed in the 18th century. An exceptional feature of this church is the choir and its most remarkably decorated wooden stalls of the 15th century – we had to photograph them! Outside the church, in the Place de l'Eglise, visitors were enjoying a drink, etc., but we walked along the Rue de l'Ancien Couvent at the side of the church and noticed a courtyard with some tables with parasols; was it a café; there were no customers, but was it open? We found an open door and asked Madame if we could possibly have a croque-monsieur and a drink; indeed, we could. We enjoyed our refreshment in the very warm sunshine and, as is the case in most such establishments however small, toilet facilities were available. Eventually, we made our way back down the old, narrow and sometimes quite steep streets of Flavigny to our car which we reached at 16.05 after a very absorbing three and a half hours. The temperature was now 32°C.

We left the village to join the D9 for Jailly-les-Moulins; here taking the D117 for Boux-sous-Salmaise, then the D103c for Présilly and Blessey towards St-Germain-Source-Seine until following signs for the Sources de la Seine. These two parishes of Blessey and Saint-Germain were fused as from 1 January 2009 to form the single commune of Source-Seine with a total population of about 50. Much of the route of some 8–10 miles from Jailly is picturesque with hillsides covered with pastureland, but it is narrow, very undulating and circuitous.

In September 2009, after two aborted planned attempts in previous years, we reached the SOURCE of the RIVER VIENNE; it involved a long walk along a rough track through thickly wooded, wild and deserted country deep on the Plateau de Millevaches in the Limousin Region; when, after negotiating some particularly unfriendly terrain, we eventually reached one of the sources it simply rained and rained.

What a contrast here today at 17.00 with the temperature a comfortable 25°C at the SOURCES of the SEINE; although there is no formal car park, we were able to leave the car at the side of the very quiet road. As we crossed towards the entrance to the site, we were surprised to see the sign stating that this is part of the Ville de Paris; we descended a flight of steps into the pleasant 'visitor area' of the sources. We quickly came upon a little rivulet, then, nearer its source, a small stone bridge crossing it and finally, at the site of the spring, a man-made cave containing a reclining nymph. This site has a very interesting history. Archaeological studies have revealed vestiges of a Gallo-Romain shrine dedicated to the goddess Sequana from which the name of the river derives. From the considerable number of discoveries, particularly of an *ex voto* nature, it is evident that this has been a place of pilgrimage for centuries and since the 1st century BC. Towards the end of the 4th century AD pagan temples were replaced by Christian establishments; in the 17th century Parisians became interested in the reputed healing powers of the Seine and in 1864 the area was acquired by the Ville de Paris and in 1868 the citizens of the capital financed the construction of the grotto dedicated to the Seine Nymph. Significantly, these latter events occurred during the reign of Emperor Napoleon III. Here at an altitude of 445 metres is the modest beginning of one of the most famous of rivers, which then flows 482 miles, under a total of 37 bridges of Paris, through the city and port of Rouen and into the English Channel at Le Havre. There are many families here appreciating this natural and historical site.

However, it is nearly 18.00 and we must leave as our destination this evening is Pouilly-en-Auxois. We left on the D103 to join the D971 for St-Seine-l'Abbaye; here taking the D16 to Sombernon. From there on, it was the D16 towards Aubigny-les-Sombernon; although we had intended to approach Pouilly from the Civry-en-Montagne direction, our route became closely entwined with that of the A38 Autoroute and we reached the Hôtel de la Poste at POUILLY-en-AUXOIS from Beaume; it was 19.10 and still 27°C. What an interesting day!

(Our mileage for the day – 58)

Day 13 – Sunday, 11 September 2011

Hôtel de la Poste is situated in the Place de la Libération in the centre of POUILLY-en-AUXOIS and from our very comfortable room on the second floor we had an excellent view of the activity in this town of about 1,600 inhabitants on a Sunday morning; the little supermarket opposite had opened its doors and the first customers were making their purchases for the day, as well as at a nearby boulangerie. After a while the bells of the church began to ring. However, the weather was maussade but dry, and we wondered if such ideal conditions might prevail at Bristol for the occasion of the half-marathon race later in the morning in which

AUGUST/OCTOBER 2011

Paul will be running. An interesting fact about Pouilly is that the Burgundy Canal apparently passes through a tunnel underneath the town. We chose Pouilly as an étape on our particular tour of Burgundy as it represents a very convenient stage on our route. Having had a satisfactory breakfast, we left the hotel at 11.20 – it was then 20°C.

As we arrived at Pouilly on the previous evening we had passed a very convenient petrol station and being conscious of the fact that many such stations are closed on a Sunday we hoped to buy petrol before we left the town – unfortunately, it was closed! We had decided to visit Châteauneuf-en-Auxois today and shortly after taking the D18 we were relieved to find a supermarket petrol station still open. We bought petrol at Pouilly Carrefour – 38.02 litres - €1.539 per litre = €58.51. We continued through the village of Vandenesse to Châteauneuf, which is only six miles from Pouilly and about 25 miles from Dijon.

Sitting proudly on the top of the hill, CHATEAUNEUF-EN-AUXOIS is one of *Les Plus Beaux Villages de France*. As we entered the village we noticed a direction sign for the church and we parked near a restaurant where there appeared to be no restrictions – it was 11.50 and 22°C; we could see that it was close to the entrance to the château and, in view of the approaching inevitable closing period, we made that our first destination. Fortunately, there was still time to purchase a guide book and to make a worthwhile if somewhat cursory tour of much of the interior. This Château, built on a rocky outcrop, is a massive and impressive stone structure dominating the valley below; it is one of the few medieval castles of Bourgogne which have been largely preserved. It was built in 1132 by Jean de Chaudenay for his son who became Jean I de Châteauneuf; the reign of the Châteauneufs came to an end nine generations later in 1456 when the last heiress, Catherine, was burnt alive for poisoning her second husband. In 1457 the Duke of Burgundy gave the fortress to Philippe Pot, his godson. At the time of the Hundred Years' War the defences of the château were strengthened, but during the ownership of Philippe Pot it was made more comfortable and, in particular, the chapel was built. Philippe Pot died in 1493 without leaving an heir and after various ownerships the building was donated to the state in 1936. We were interested to see a most unusual monument in the Chapelle; on the floor in front of the altar is the cast of the recumbent figure of Philippe Pot with four mourning figures on each side; this was created in 1993. However, the original memorial is preserved in the Louvre in Paris; this depicts the mourners carrying the slab, on which rests the reclining figure, on their shoulders. We also visited the large room which contains seven panels of tapestries dating from the early 17th century which portray the life of Moses. Perhaps the time for closing came a little too soon for us, nevertheless, our visit had been worthwhile.

After leaving the château we walked up the steep main street observing, particularly, the ancient houses some of which still display coats of arms and also an impressive 1914–18 war memorial; we took some photographs. Near the top we reached the sign for a Belvedere and, although it was not a comfortable surface to walk on, we could not fail to continue to that point. What a magnificent view it offers – a large area of the Auxois, the Burgundy Canal and, in the distance to the west, the MORVAN hills. This is probably as close as we shall come to this natural area in the centre of Burgundy. Morvan in Celtic means 'Black Mountain' and the region saw resistance to the Roman occupation and against another occupier in more recent times. The Parc Naturel Régional du Morvan was created in 1970 and features wooded hills, close and rounded rather than mountainous, rising to up to 900 metres; it is home to a wide variety of foliage, flora and wild animals and is an ideal area for exercising outdoor pursuits. However, the Morvan can attribute much of its present-day recognition to the influence of a former local politician and mayor of Château-Chinon, after he became president of the Republic, François Mitterrand. Walking back down to our car by the same route gave us a second opportunity to appreciate and admire the impressive buildings.

Before leaving the village we must locate the church of Sainte-Philippe et Saint-Jacques the sign for which we noticed on our way up to the centre. It was just a short walk but, unfortunately, it was closed as it is undergoing extensive restoration work; we had to be content with taking a photograph of the exterior. We have learned that three stages of the work have been completed; the bell tower and the facades have been restored giving the building an 'aspect nouveau'; also, close examination of the framework of the roof of the nave has enabled it to be dated from 1491. There is now an appeal for funds to assist in the completion of this work!

Although it involves branching off from the main route of our journey through Burgundy, we decided that it would be an opportunity to visit the Abbaye de Cîteaux about 30 miles from here. Before leaving Châteauneuf at 14.05, we had crisps and a drink and Margaret recorded that her ankle ulcer was very painful and that she had taken two paracetamol tablets. We proceeded on the D18a to join the D18 which took us alongside the Canal de Bourgogne as far as Pont-d'Ouche; through Bécoup to Bruant, where we joined the D25; much of this route is wooded and picturesque. Near Arcenant we observed extensive vineyards reminding us that this is a very important wine producing region. This small village was the scene of a battle on 15 June 1944 when a contingent of German troops together with men of the French militia attacked a hundred Maquis guerrillas holed up in a place called The Cave. The outcome was that 39 of the attackers and only six of the guerrillas were killed and this feat continues to be commemorated at the site each year. There are other interesting features here, but we continued through Meuilley to Nuits-St-Georges. Unfortunately, we had some difficulty in finding our way through this town of about 5,500 inhabitants and, particularly, in traversing the main D974, the railway and the autoroute. Eventually, we were relieved to reach Agencourt and from there on it was a straightforward D8 road through more wooded lands and the village of St-Nicolas-lès-Cîteaux to the junction with the D996.

After turning left here we quickly came to the entrance to the ABBAYE de CITEAUX. As we parked at 15.30, a heavy storm broke and prevented us from leaving the car for a little while. Our impression was that the various buildings are spread out over a large area. There were a lot of visitors and many coming to and from a particular entrance; we took the same route – it was a very well stocked boutique where we were able to purchase a useful book. Following signs, we then walked some distance to the entry to another building; outside was a statue of Saint Bernard. We went in and discovered that all visits to the site are guided; after some deliberation we reluctantly concluded that in view of the remaining time available, the cost, etc., would not be justified. However, on our way back to the car we came upon an open door which allowed us into a very modern church. We would have liked to have experienced and learned more of this historic establishment but, of course, these buildings are occupied by a living working community and there is no uncontrolled public access. We know that towards the end of the 11th century Robert, Abbot of Molesme and 21 companions came here to a wild uninhabited place; they found a small stream and a marsh covered with rushes and course grass which was called, in the language of the day, *cistels*, from whence came the name, Cistell or Citeaux. Their aim was to establish a community where the Rule of St. Benedict would be strictly observed. A new monastery was built, and it was inaugurated on the feast of St Benedict, 21 March 1098. St Robert was elected Abbot of Cîteaux, but a year later he returned to Molesme and was succeeded by St Alberic. The third Abbot was St Stephen Harding, who had been a monk at Sherborne; he held the office from 1108 to 1133 and during this period he was joined by St. Bernard and 30 of his companions. The Cistercian

Order had been founded and Cîteaux became its mother house. St Bernard left Cîteaux to found Clairvaux Abbey in 1115. The construction of the great church of Cîteaux was commenced in about 1140 and was completed in 1193. In 1244 the abbey was visited by Louis IX (Saint Louis) and his mother, Blanche de Castile. During the Hundred Years War the monastery was pillaged, and it suffered again during the Wars of Religion. At the time of the Revolution it was seized and sold by the government. However, in 1898, the remains of the abbey were repurchased and populated by monks of other abbeys. Today, about 35 monks live in the Abbey. The Order has spread and Cistercians are now found on every continent; in all there are about 180 men's monasteries and a similar number of women's monasteries; since 2010 there has been a branch of Anglican Cistercians in England. Before leaving the car park we had some refreshments from our still plentiful supplies.

It is now 17.00 and as it is quite a long way to our destination for tonight, Couches, we decided not to attempt the option of negotiating the minor roads as planned, but chose a much more straightforward route. We returned to Nuits-St-Georges, where we joined the D974 which took us through the town of Beaune which, as it was a Sunday, was relatively quiet. Beaune is a very ancient and historic town and is the wine capital of Burgundy; it has a population of about 22,000. Continuing southwards to St-Léger-s-Dheune we reached the junction with the D978 from Chalon-sur-Saône; about four miles along this road towards Autun is COUCHES, a village of about 1,500 inhabitants in the Saône-et-Loire department of Burgundy. The village is spread out along each side of the road and towards the far end we eventually noticed the Hôtel Des Trois Maures. It was now raining heavily and the daylight was fading but, fortunately, we were able to park in a public area immediately in front of the hotel; it was 18.35. We were taken to one of several rooms, each with its own external entrance, in an attractive annex, accessed by a flight of wooden steps, at the rear of the main building. In fact, we somehow quickly acquired a special liking for this room (18); it felt particularly comfortable especially, perhaps, in view of the less clement weather. We had not planned to have a meal, but we were warmly welcomed in the restaurant, where we enjoyed a cup of coffee. A rather longer journey today – 76 miles.

Day 14 – Monday, 12 September 2011

Petit déjeuner in Les Logis de France is usually a much less formal occasion than any other meal; it is often in a room other than, or in a designated part of, the main restaurant; usually served by different staff and often by the husband/chef of les propriétaries. The service and ambiance at HOTEL des TROIS MAURES this morning was typically personal and friendly. As we left the hotel we expressed our thanks for the warm welcome we had received. In the clear light of the morning we were more easily able to view and appreciate the exterior appearance of the building, which incorporates a round tower; it would be interesting to know more about the history of this hotel.

Before driving away at 11.20, we walked a short distance along the road through the village and we bought a copy of *Le Monde*. It was 18°C. However, the château is some distance away at the eastern end of the village and so we drove to a convenient parking place opposite the entrance. Construction of the CHATEAU de COUCHES, which is also known as the Château de Marguerite de Bourgogne, began in the 11th century and was finally completed in the 19th century. It was built as a fortress to protect the route from Paris to Chalon via Autun, but is now in private occupation. In 2009 it was acquired by the Poelaert family, who initiated a programme of renovation; it is now open to the public and is the venue for concerts, conferences, etc.; also, apparently, it offers chambre d'hôte accommodation! Unfortunately, we did not have the time to go in, let alone to stay overnight!

As we did not approach Couches by our planned route through Nolay we decided to first drive in that direction instead of going direct to Cluny. Leaving Couches by the D1, first for St-Maurice-lès-Couches and then finally on the D33, it was about eight miles of tiny villages and hamlets in lovely undulating rural countryside; truly the back roads of France. We reached NOLAY, which is just inside the Côte d'Or, at noon. This beautiful medieval market town, with its 1,500 inhabitants, is in the heart of the Cozanne Valley and lies between the forests and plains to the north and west and the vineyards to the south; the D973 from Beaune to Autun passes through the town. Nolay was constructed on a gallo-romain site and the first recorded date of the town is 885. It originally had a château situated in the present Place Carnot, but any remains are concealed in the existing properties. According to legend the name of Nolay came from the noyers (walnut trees) which were very plentiful here in past times. When visiting such towns and villages throughout our many years of journeying in France we have rarely had difficulty in finding somewhere convenient to park and without charge; here was no exception. Shortly after entering the town we came upon an 'open area' at a junction on our left where, obviously, we could leave the car; however, the surface was exceptionally uneven and rough, but we accepted the opportunity. Just around the corner is Place Carnot. Lazare Carnot was a mathematician, physician, general and politician; he was born here in 1753; we photographed his impressive statue which stands in front of his birthplace.

It was just a short walk to the heart of the ancient city with its wonderful alleyways and half-timbered houses. It seems that there was much commercial activity and many skilled carpenters here in the Middle Ages. We visited l'Eglise Saint-Martin which stands on the foundations of a roman church. It was constructed in the 15th century; collapsed in 1641; was reconstructed in about 1643 and only a chapel remains of the original church. The bell tower is 38 metres high and supports two Jacquemarts, Jacquot and Jacquotte; the spire was rebuilt in 1763–65. Inside we photographed the memorial to those who Morts pour la France – 1914–1918; even for this small village the list contains some 59 names! We also admired the lovely figure of St Jacques de Compostelle. Near the church is the most remarkable structure in Nolay – Les Halles, the covered market – a superb building of the 14th century. It has a robust framework of oak and chestnut with the pillars standing on blocks of stone; it all supports a magnificent roof in limestone weighing 800kg per square metre. However, some additional supporting timbers have been introduced more recently and which has enabled, no doubt, two markets to be held here each week as well as four fairs every year. Although we did not see it, the 16th century Chapelle Saint-Pierre is noteworthy in that its bell tower with an onion-shaped dome is evidence of its use as a leper hospital. It is surprising that Nolay does not appear to be a member of that prestigious association, *Les Plus Beaux Villages de France,* but perhaps the town does not meet all the 30 criteria required.

Having, in recent years, visited the Château de Sully-sur-Loire, the home of Henri IV's well-known minister, Maximillien de Béthune, we were attracted to another CHATEAU de SULLY. Along the D973 towards Autun we turned right at La Forge on to the D26 which took us directly to the village of Sully and on to the château; it was no more than 11 miles from Nolay. Not surprisingly – it was 13.35 – the entrance to the château appeared to be closed; however, there were signs of activity and we discovered that it would be open for the afternoon. It was a suitable opportunity to take some sustenance while sitting in the car in front of the wrought iron gates through which we had an excellent view of the gardens inside and of the impressive building. Here on Sully Plain one of the last great Gaul battles against Caesar took place some 2,000 years ago. Gauthier de Sully fought in the Crusades and while a prisoner of pirates at Rhodes he swore an oath to the Virgin Mary that he would build a church in her honour if he escaped and returned home to Sully safely. He did so and he kept his word, building the Priory of St Benoît in the Forest of Sully. The Château was originally an impressive, moated fortress of the Middle Ages; it was owned by the Montaigu family by the 14th century and until the death of Claude, killed in battle in 1470. His daughter, Jehanne, took Sully as a dowry into the Rabutin family. Modifications in the 16th and 18th centuries made Sully a masterpiece of French Renaissance architecture and one of the country's most romantic stately homes.

The Morey family bought Sully in 1714. In the 18th century the MacMahon brothers arrived from Ireland and the wife of Jean-Baptiste inherited Sully. Maurice de MacMahon, the 16th of 17 children and grandson of Jean-Baptiste, was born in Sully in 1808; he was created Field-Marshal and Duke of Magenta in 1859 by Napoleon III; the present Duke is his great-great grandson. In 1873 the Field-Marshal was elected President of France; a national hero who would lead France into happier times. He was the first President to occupy the Elysee Palace in Paris. In 1876 he made an official visit to Sully and for three weeks it became the Presidential Palace from which France was governed. Today the château is lived in by the Scottish Duchess of Magenta, the 4th Duke's widow, and their children; they are the descendants of the medieval Dukes of Burgundy. We joined a guided tour of the château at 14.40; we had a very lively and charming young lady guide, who did not hesitate to interrupt her description in French to speak to us in English to ensure that we fully understood what she was describing; it was a very interesting and enjoyable tour and we expressed our appreciation of her individual attention. It is an interesting fact that at dawn on the spring and autumn equinoxes the sun's rays pass straight through the centre of the house and across the 'sleeping' bridge. At the conclusion of the tour we returned to the boutique area and, particularly, to the café where we enjoyed a very welcome cup of tea in a very friendly setting. We left Château de Sully at 16.25 feeling that our detour had been well worthwhile; it was then 25°C.

Back on the D973 we were only about 10 miles from AUTUN; it would have been very interesting to visit this town, of about 16,000 inhabitants. Founded in the late 1st century BC at the time of the 1st Roman Emperor, Augustus, after whom it was named; its main attractions include the remains of the Roman amphitheatre which could seat 20,000 people, two monumental Roman gateways and the Cathédrale St-Lazare with its tympanum of the Last Judgment. We are so near, but it has not been possible to allocate sufficient time to include this further step into antiquity in the itinerary of this journey.

We returned to Nolay and Couches; then to St-Léger-s-Dheune and continuing on the D978 towards Chalon-sur-Saône until the junction with the D981 for Mellecey; we were soon in GIVRY. We have 'met' Henri IV, the "best King France ever had" in so many connections in the past, but never before in that of advertising; in Givry, we were somewhat surprised to be confronted with a very prominent display proclaiming "Givry le vin preferé par Henri IV"! Continuing southwards we passed through BUXY, a Village Touristique. What an interesting area; it was probably known to Neanderthal man (150,000 to 35,000 years ago) and his successors; it experienced Roman occupation; Christianity came here in about the 5th century; there was an important Jewish colony here in the 14th century until removed from the kingdom by Philippe le Bel; there were many victims among the 'poilus' (French soldiers) of the Great War; on 17 June 1940 German troops entered the village which aroused strong resistance; in July 1940 the demarcation line cut the Canton de Buxy in two. As we drove slowly through the village we noticed a memorial at the side of the road; we were unable to stop immediately, but at the first opportunity we turned around and returned to the site to take a photograph. It records that, at this place, the Germans assassinated three members of the Resistance on 20 July 1944 – "Francais Souviens-toi".

We continued on the D981 through St-Boil to Cormatin shortly after which we noticed the entrance sign for Taizé. In 1940 Brother Roger Schutz founded the TAIZE COMMUNITY here; an ecumenical monastic order of about a hundred brothers from both Protestant and Catholic traditions and from many countries of the world. Taizé is one of the world's most important Christian pilgrimage sites with more than 100,000 young people from around the world making a pilgrimage to the centre each year. The project began following the fall of France in 1940 when Roger, a Swiss, purchased a small house in this desolate village near Cluny, the birthplace of western monasticism. His work was interrupted on 11 November 1942 when the Gestapo occupied the house while he was in Switzerland; Roger was not able to return to Taizé until late 1944, after the liberation of France. Brother Roger continued to be Prior of the Taizé Community until, when in his 91st year, he was sadly stabbed to death during the evening service in Taizé on 16 August 2005. The assailant was Luminita Solcan, a Romanian woman of 36 and a diagnosed schizophrenic. Passing the sign for Taizé was a distinct reminder of an interest in the 1960s in the method of singing the Psalms developed by Joseph Gelineau of Taizé, which respected the original Hebrew rhythms. This was another place we would have liked to have been able to devote some time to.

It is now only a short distance to CLUNY, where we have a room at the Hôtel de l'Abbaye reserved for two nights. As we entered the town we realised that it was rather larger than we had anticipated, but we imagined that if we found the Abbey our hotel would be nearby. This was not so and after extricating ourselves from the congested area of the Abbey we returned to the entrance to the town and began to search nearer the main D980. Eventually, in the Avenue Charles de Gaulle, we spotted the hotel sign; it was 19.00. We quickly reported our arrival and discovered that the restaurant was closed for that evening, but le propriétaire had been waiting for us; he gave us instructions for accessing the hotel by a rear door and assured us that breakfast would be available in the morning. Although we did not see anyone, we felt that there may have been some other 'guests' in the building for the night. We could not see the Abbey from the hotel and it appeared to be quite a distance to the centre of the town and so we resorted to our own supplies for a 'meal'. We did, however, walk some distance along the road of the hotel towards the Place des Martyrs de la Déportation, as far as the junction with the D980; it was quiet, but not an inspiring environment – Cluny must wait until tomorrow!

(82 miles)

Day 15 – Tuesday, 13 September 2011

Petit déjeuner was available as promised and what a different atmosphere it was compared to that of the previous evening, with several guests, or perhaps external customers, for breakfast and, of course, the staff. CLUNY, in the Saône-et-Loire Department of Bourgogne and in a valley drained by the River Grosne, has a population of about 5,000; the village grew following the economic activity created by the Abbey. Before setting off in search of our objectives we were given instructions for reaching the town centre. However, after a short distance, we made further enquires in a little shop and, what is more, we were able to purchase an invaluable street plan. It was then not long before we found ourselves amongst old buildings in narrow streets and we felt we were actually in Cluny. We walked along the Rue des Trois Carreaux to the Place de l'Hopital where we photographed the Hôtel Dieu and the nearby Monument aux Morts 14–18. Hôtel Dieu, a town hospital, was founded in 1646 following a bequest by a priest of l'église Notre-Dame, Julien Griffon, and was constructed at the beginning of the 18th century at the initiative of the Abbot of Cluny.

Continuing through the Place de la Liberté and along the Rue de la Liberté took us to the main street of the town and the Rue Mercière; here we found a very convenient seat near the Tour des Fromages and opposite the Monument 11 Août 1944 situated in front of l'Eglise Notre-Dame. The Tour des Fromages was formerly called the Tour des Fèves (Bean Tower) and is the oldest building still standing in the entire abbey; its lower part dates from the early 11th century; it once formed part of the surrounding wall of the Abbey.

We did not feel inclined to climb the necessary number of steps, but we read that the top affords splendid views of the Abbey, the town and the surrounding countryside; in addition, a screen version provides a view of the recreated image of the great Abbey Church of Cluny III in its entirety, in the context of the surrounding town of today. Instead we visited l'église Notre-Dame, the parish church. Construction of this church was spread over the period from 1159 to the 14th century. It has some interesting features; the present belltower was constructed in the 18th century with salvaged materials; unfortunately, the 18th century stained-glass windows were lost in the course of the German bombardment on the 11 August 1944. After leaving the church we walked along the rue 11 Août 1944 into the Place du 11/08. It was the midday period when the Abbey is closed, and it was very convenient that we were able to have a cup of coffee sitting in the square in the warm sunshine close to the entrance.

The first recorded human activity here was in the 9th century and in the early 10th century William, Duke of

Aquitaine and Count of Mâcon and Bourges offered some of his land here to the Abbot of Baume-les-Messieurs and suggested that he establish a house of prayer. The formal agreement was signed on 11 September 910 and an abbey was founded; it was accountable directly to the Pope. Twelve monks took up residence on the site; they followed the rule of Saint Benedict written in about 540. Thus began the long and, for the first two centuries, the illustrious history of the ABBEY of CLUNY. The monks of Cluny were able to choose their own abbot and under the leadership of men of such outstanding merit as Odon, Mayeul and, particularly, Abbot Odilon de Mercoeur (994–1049), the abbey grew considerably until the 12th century. Following a right granted by Pope John XI in 932 the Abbot could direct any other monastery wishing to follow his precepts, and the abbey's spiritual influence grew and Cluny became the mother house of more than 1,000 monasteries in Europe from as far afield as England and Poland; it was the headquarters of the largest monastic order in the west, the Cluniac Order, representing a major constituent of Christendom. Devotion to the dead was a major feature of intercession and in 1030 Odilon inaugurated All Souls' Day on 2 November, which is still celebrated today. Following the end of Odilon's long abbacy in 1049, came the appointment of a very young abbot, Hugues de Semur, perhaps the greatest of them all, who served for 60 years.

There were several successive churches during the first 200 years of the abbey's existence. The abbey church consecrated in 927 is known as Cluny I; Cluny II refers to the one built from 981 onwards, while Cluny III was built from 1088 to 1130 and this project was reaching completion when Hugues died in 1109. It is the remains of this church which can be seen today. Regarded as a masterpiece of classical Romanesque art it represented the work of several generations of builders. It was a monumental building and the largest church in the whole of Christendom until Saint Peter's, Rome was rebuilt in the 16th century. It was constructed at about the same time as Saint-Sernin in Toulouse and Santiage de Compostela. During the 12th century the Cluniac influence began to decline; it never truly recovered. During the Wars of Religion the Abbey was looted by the Huguenots in 1563 and 1573 when many valuable manuscripts were destroyed or removed. During the period from 1510 to 1790 Cluny had only sixteen abbots; one of which was Cardinal Richelieu, from 1629 to 1642, who reformed the abbey to bring it back to a stricter monastic life. During the 18th century a reconstruction programme restored the abbey to something of its former glory.

However, before the end of that century, came the French Revolution; the decree of the Constituent Assembly on 13 February 1790 signalled the suppression of religious communities; finally, in 1791, the last forty monks were expelled and their property confiscated. In 1798 the sale of the buildings as building materials marked the beginning of the dismantling of the church. Preservation of the abbey ruins began in 1821; it was listed as a historic monument in 1862. The future of the monastic complex thus became very uncertain and steps were taken to integrate the site into the town, which provoked further major demolition work resulting in the almost complete destruction of the abbey church. For example, the market moved into the classical cloister, transforming it into the town square. Not only the dismantling of the abbey, but also, and especially so, the urbanization work carried out over the remnants of the monastic buildings have made the interpretation of archaeological remains particularly difficult. Apparently by the early 20th century the destruction and alternative use of the area had been so extensive that some local residents did not know that such an abbey had existed on the site.

The first major excavation work began in 1928; it was financed by the Medieval Academy of America and was led by the archaeologist, Kenneth John Conant. The principal aim was to establish the layout of the gigantic building by uncovering the foundations of walls and pillars which had been concealed by the rubble. Work of excavation and preservation continued throughout much of the 20th century and, indeed, some work was continuing while we were there, but much remains to be done in order to, eventually, have it recognised as a world heritage site. However, there is now much for the visitor to see, absorb and digest, but one visit is not sufficient to comprehend and appreciate every aspect of the magnitude of the structures, powers, influence and authority which existed here in past centuries.

We were able to visit various parts of the abbey site but found it difficult to relate what we saw to the original whole. We saw and photographed the magnificent Richelieu Door which was removed from the palace's façade during 19th century restoration work and is now displayed on the floor of the abbey cellarage. We also saw a facsimile of La Charte de Fondation; the Office de Tourisme has confirmed – in 2020 – that, "the Charte de Foundation is in the cloister of Cluny, in its right place!" After perusing the various books, etc., in the boutique we left this very impressive modern entrance to such a memorable historic site and returned to the present day. Although we had spent some time in the enclosed area of the 'Eglise Abbatiale', there is much of interest in the wider area of the 'Enceinte Abbaye', but time did not permit further exploration.

However, we thought that an appropriate 'memento' of our visit to Cluny would be a bottle of local wine and in this area of ancient streets and buildings, at 13 Rue Municipale, in the Cellier Abbaye, we bought three bottles of wine – it was as much as we could carry! Nearby, at No.16 in the same street, at the restaurant Le Cloitre, we were able to enjoy a crêpe and some fruit juice before returning to our hotel. It was a very worthwhile visit to Cluny, but we were left with the feeling of a task unfinished. In particular, I would like to learn more about the circumstances of the German bombardment on 11 August 1944 – and now – in 2020 – the Office de Tourisme has kindly informed me of the circumstances. As the German Army left Cluny, they bombarded the city. The top of the medieval tower – the Tour des Fromages – and the adjoining square was severely damaged. After the war the top of the tower was rebuilt. The memorial represents three superimposed figures – woman with a lion skin symbolizes the victory, a child symbolizes hope and a man breaking his chains is a symbol of freedom.

Day 16 – Wednesday, 14 September 2011

It was virtually the end of our tour of Burgundy as we left Hôtel de l'Abbaye at 10.45 to head south-westwards into the regions of Rhone-Alpes and Auvergne; it was 18°C. We left Cluny to join the D980 for about three miles towards Macon, to the complex junction with the N79, which we took in the direction of Moulins. At 11.00 we purchased petrol – 29 litres – €1.58 per litre = €45.82 – at the Total Garage at the Relais de Ste Cecile and then continued on this fairly busy main road as far as Clermain. It was only about five miles on the national road, but we were pleased to return to a much more relaxed form of motoring on the D987 towards Trambly. Although there were plenty of clouds it was mainly sunny with much blue sky and the countryside was just beautiful. Matour, nestling in an attractive valley, is a popular holiday destination for a wide variety of pursuits; it is followed by the climb to the summit of the Col de la Croix d'Auterre where we entered, for a brief while, the Puy-de-Dôme Department of the Region of Rhone-Alpes and then on to the village of Aigueperse (population 2,500). What a joy it is to be able to drive at one's chosen pace without being hurried or harassed at all by other motorists and thus be able to enjoy and appreciate such glorious countryside, even if is it no more than the many cream cows grazing in areas between forests. After about five miles, at Le Sordet, we are back in Burgundy country and in the Brionnais area of the Saône-et-Loire Department. At approximately this point, and at about 11.50, we had completed the first 1,000 miles of our journey and also encountered some busy roadworks. In the commune of Saint-Racho we passed, at the bottom of a valley, the Château de Chevannes, which was built in the 16th century and is a private property. Taking the D989 at La Clayette leads us to Semur-en-Brionnais; this village, with a population of about 700, is another of *Les Plus Beau Villages de France*. It possesses the oldest château in Burgundy, Château St Hugues, which dates from the 9th century and it is the birthplace of Saint Hugues, the Abbot and 'builder' of the great abbey church of Cluny III.

In view of the length of today's journey, we must not linger here. Next we pass through Marcigny, where Adela, daughter of William the Conqueror, sister of Henry I and Robert, Duke of Normandy, who fought each other in the Battle of Tinchebray (Day 2) and is also the mother of King Stephen, died in about 1137. Shortly afterwards, at Chambilly, we crossed La Loire and about seven miles beyond and on the D990 we finally leave the Region of Burgundy. We have travelled through all four departments of this region – Nievre, Yonne, Côte d'Or and Saône et Loire – which owes its name to the Burgundians, ancient Germanic tribes who settled here in the 5th century. At Urbise we are briefly in the Department of la Loire and the Region of Rhône-Alpes before entering the Department of Allier and the Region of Auvergne and, more particularly, very picturesque countryside.

MONTAIGUET-en-FOREZ is a very attractive little village with a population of about 300; a fortified village with beautiful houses and the 12th century château. Being now 13.15, we decided it was an appropriate place to stop for a break, some refreshments and a little exploring. We drove onto a large, tarmacked area somewhat above the level of the road; it was very quiet apart from a workman apparently doing some repair work on farm machinery in a workshop at one end; there was a bus stop sign and it appeared that we would be inconveniencing no one and so it proved to be. It was 19°C. A little further ahead we could see a most interesting archway over the road. On closer investigation we found that it was a fortified gate constructed by Pierre de La Fin, Abbé de La Bénisson-Dieu, in 1496; the arch linked le Bourbonnais to the Forez. In a niche is a small statue of Pierre de La Fin; the statue and gate are classed as monuments historiques. An upper room above the arch was probably the chapter house of the church which was constructed at the same period. A short distance beyond the gate is an interesting and less traditional Great War Memorial. This village is another little gem! We continued on the D990 until joining the D994, then the D990A to Lapalisse; here we took the D907 in the direction of Vichy. We did not wish to head for the centre of this town and, therefore, made our way very carefully and successfully around the D67, D6 and D2209, until unintentionally following the D426 to Abrest, where we were able to join our planned route, D906, to St-Yorre.

Continuing in a southerly direction, we stopped at PUY-GUILLAUME for a cup of tea; it was 15.20 and 21°C. We parked in a public car park in the centre of the town (population 2,600) close to the busy road and on the other side was a convenient salon de thé; it was a generous cup of tea; in fact, it was a pot each, sufficient for 1½ cups of tea – in glasses and cost €3.80! While sitting inside the café we observed the considerable volume of traffic slowly piercing its way through this bottleneck. We noticed, particularly, that amongst it there was a good proportion of new looking heavy goods vehicles. After more than an hour we decided that we must re-join it and at 16.35 we continued our journey; immediately after leaving the town there was, in fact, no congestion. Soon there was more beautiful countryside; in fact, much of the next 40 miles is designated a 'scenic route'. Passing to the west of Thiers, then on to and beyond Courpière the road is mainly straight. When our D906 converges with the D225 and the River Dore it follows the meandering of the river along its eastern bank virtually all the way to Ambert; the tourist railway lies close to the western side of the river. Much of this route is outstandingly beautiful; some excellent photographs of the area around Olliergues can be found on the internet. We are, in fact, in the Parc Naturel Regional de Livradois-Forez, which is a protected area of woodlands and traditional farmland of the Auvergne and Rhône-Alpes Regions; it covers an area of 730,000 acres.

We recalled that we bought petrol at AMBERT when on a journey in the opposite direction in June 2010. This is a fairly large town of 7,000 inhabitants in the Puy de Dôme Department of the Auvergne Region. It is the birthplace, in 1841, of the composer Emmanuel Chabrier. Also, the Agrivap Chemin de Fer Touristique operates from here, providing local steam train journeys and, in order to more appreciate the wonderful campagne, the Panoramique Autorail. This association provides tourist trains on the 85 kilometres of single track from Courpière to Sembadel, passing through La Chaise-Dieu, in the midst of the Livradois-Forez Natural Parc; the line was constructed between 1883 and 1902 and for much of its route it lies in the valley of the Dore. In contrast to the road to the north of Ambert the road to the south is remarkably straight at least as far as Arlanc and even then, it was a straightforward drive to La Chaise-Dieu. We noted that we were a mere 25 miles from Le Puy-en-Velay, reminding us of that memorable day in 2010.

We had little difficulty in finding our accommodation for tonight at Hôtel de la Casadei, in LA CHAISE-DIEU, which we reached at 18.30 and it was 16°C; the restaurant was not open, but breakfast would be provided. We were given the keys of our room and were a little surprised to find that it was at the top of the building involving a climb of 50 steps. However, it was a very comfortable room with a view of the abbey, immediately opposite, which we had come specifically to visit; we could also see our car parked in the street below. We took to our room only that which was absolutely necessary to avoid unnecessary climbs to the 'summit'. Although we were advised where we could find an open restaurant, we found that a patisserie nearby was still open and we purchased a quiche for our 'meal'. This is a small village with less than 1,000 inhabitants and we took a short walk amongst the ancient buildings before returning to our room.

Our mileage for today is – 159
(I had calculated that it would be 158)

Day 17 – Thursday, 15 September 2011

Petit déjeuner was a generous meal and we were kindly invited to take with us any food we were not able to eat at the time; we were provided with bags to enable us to do so. We visited La Chaise-Dieu (from the Latin 'casa dei' meaning 'House of God') on 23 June 2010 after leaving Le Puy-en-Velay. Unfortunately, much of our time there coincided with the midday period when the abbey was closed; we decided that we would like to return. La Chaise Dieu is in the Department of Haute-Loire in the Auvergne Region. When Robert de Turlande and some of his disciples arrived here in 1043 they found, 1,000 metres high, a harsh plateau of woods and some pasture land, a desolate area almost surrounded by the river Senouire; there were some ruins of a chapel built in the 5th century. Robert had been an apprentice at Cluny under Abbot Odilo and became a canon at Brioude. However, after returning from a pilgrimage to Mont Cassin (Montecassino – founded by Benoît de Nursie in about 530) he decided to leave the hustle and bustle of life in the town and install himself in this wild place and establish a monastic community adopting the rule of Saint-Benoît. By the time he died in about 1067 the abbey had more than 300 monks and many outlying priories depending on it. Robert was canonized in 1095 and La Chaise-Dieu continued to grow throughout the Middle Ages; it was described by 12th century contemporaries as "le miroir de la perfection monastique". Among its abbots were Richelieu, Mazarin and Rohan, but the most illustrious name associated with this place is one Pierre Roger who was a novice here and who became Pope Clément VI. He was responsible for the expansion of the abbey and in 1344 he ordered and financed the demolition of the existing church and the construction of a new building; it would be the site of his own tomb. When he died in 1352 the work, although very advanced, was not entirely finished. The abbey was finally completed by his nephew when he became Pope Grégoire XI in 1370. Although the monks were expelled and the abbey became the parish church at the time of the Revolution, Clément's vast abbey church, his tomb and the abbey cloister remain – an austere and majestic architectural masterpiece. Today, the Brothers of Saint John maintain a religious presence in this place.

In 1965, when searching for a place large enough and with good acoustics, to perform a concert, the Hungarian pianist, Georges Cziffra, was directed by his friends to La Chaise-Dieu. An incident involving the discovery of a coin near the organ reminded him of a Hungarian proverb, 'Là où tu trouves un sou jaillira la fortune'. Perhaps inspired by this omen, but especially seduced by the atmosphere of the place, the pianist offered to play at La Chaise-Dieu in the following year and decided to devote his fee to the restoration of the organ. Thus was born the prestigious international annual festival of music which has been held here for the past 45 years; this year some 1,500 artists participated. In addition, L'Académie de Musique de La Chaise-Dieu maintains much musical activity throughout the year.

We came here especially to view the interior of the Abbey and after descending the 50 steps from our room for the last time we then found that there were 40 steps up to the west door. This church, although quite plain, is impressive; it is rectangular like a basilica and broader than it is high; it is in the depressed Gothic style typical of the Gothic style of the Languedoc in southern France. In fact, we entered the church by the side entrance and almost immediately we are witnessing the main features of the interior of the church – the sanctuary and, on the left, the monks' choir. The sanctuary is illuminated through very high double lancet windows; the choir is adorned with tapestries and stalls and is closed by a rood screen and side walls. This partitioning of the liturgical area is typically medieval. There are 144 stalls made of sculpted oak wood and each is adorned with a cul-de-lampe representing vices, virtues, faces, etc. It is the tapestries that are the jewels of this abbey church; they were ordered from a Flemish workshop at the beginning of the 16th century and are woven with threads of wool, silk, gold and silver. In the middle of the choir is the tomb and effigy of Clément VI. The Dance of the Dead fresco can be seen in the north aisle. To enter the nave, we had to leave the church, proceed under the cloister and enter the church again through a gate and up a staircase. Here we found Saint Robert's tomb and the organ. This instrument was built in 1683 and the main organ added in 1727; it has four manuals and pedalboard and forty stops; it was restored in 1995 in its original design. Planning our route to include an etape at La Chaise-Dieu, this place of such historical and current significance, was fully justified. At breakfast we collected a very informative and descriptive information sheet which included a detailed plan of the village and a suggested walking tour; unfortunately, at least a whole day would be required to fully explore this ancient village.

However, we have another long journey ahead of us today and at 11.30 we left on the D499 in the direction of Brioude; although it was a bright day the temperature was only 14°C and it was feeling *très fraiche*. This area is one of the most densely wooded of the Massif Centrale and almost immediately we were seemingly surrounded by many thousands of trees. After a short distance we left the D488 and continued on the D19 passing through Cistrières, a small village of about 140 residents and apparently 10 cows! We are in the Forêt de Lamandie and, although there are occasional signs of habitation and small pockets of verdant pastureland, the forest is omnipresent. We crossed the little river Doulon and the only signs of life we saw were a few sheep; it was still trees and more trees. Although this was a wonderful part of the journey it was a strange feeling of relief when we reached the village of Javaugues, with a population of less than 200, and shortly afterwards leaving the Parc Naturel Regional de Livradois Forez to see open countryside, fields of sweet corn and a bus stop! From La Chaise-Dieu it was a distance of about 16 miles and we had seen about a dozen other vehicles, but thousands upon thousands of trees. We continued via Fontannes, crossing the Allier and into Brioude, an interesting town of about 6600 inhabitants.

We made a half hour refreshment stop on the D588 before joining the autoroute A75 – the Méridienne – at junction 22 in the direction of St-Flour. We normally avoid resorting to the use of motorways, but sometimes it is a very helpful means of travelling longer distances. On this occasion we are heading somewhat further south and other routes would extend the travelling time considerably. In any case this motorway is particularly interesting and, indeed, often quite spectacular. The building of this route across the Massif Centrale was a formidable achievement and was only completed in June 2010 after construction work extending over 35 years; it involved surmounting many challenges before creating a link between Clermont-Ferrand and Beziers, a distance of 334 km, thus facilitating travel between Paris and the south and also providing access to many small towns and villages. Shortly after the junction we entered the Department of Cantal in the Auvergne Region and passed the village of Massiac. The road reaches a height of 990 metres between junctions 24 and 25 and between junctions 26 and 27 it overcomes the Col de la Fageole at 1107 metres. Midway between junctions 30 and 31 is the Viaduc de la Truyère which is 308 metres long. In this area there are excellent views of the nearby Viaduc de Garabit, which was constructed in 1884 by Gustave Eiffel to carry the railway line. At junction 32 we left the autoroute temporarily to have a break in the Aire de Lozére; here we purchased petrol – 35 litres – €1.63 per litre = €57.05 – and, after parking amidst rearranged natural features of the landscape, we enjoyed a cup of coffee. Returning to the autoroute and approaching junction 37 the route rises to 1121 metres at the Col des Issartets. This is, in fact, the highest point of this and any motorway in France; it is situated in the Department of la Lozère and on the volcanic and granitic plateau of L'Aubrac. Between junctions 38 and

39 there are the Viaduc du Piou, Viaduc du Ricoulong and Viaduc de la Planchette. After junction 39.1 we passed through the Tunnel de Montjezieu which is 616 metres long at an altitude of 650 metres. Finally, for us, between junctions 40 and 41 is the Col de la Fayette at a height of 882 metres.

We left the A75 at junction 42 in the direction of Rodez; we had travelled about 80 miles on this amazing route. Far more than simply being a fast route one is witnessing a masterpiece of highway engineering and yet the outstanding achievements of the A75 lie further south – namely the Viaduc de Millau and the Pas de l'Escalette. After junction 42 there is a short section of motorway as we pass Sévérac-le-Château at 16.00, a town in the Aveyron Department and Region of Midi-Pyrénées dominated by its château; nearby is the Source de l'Aveyron. Soon we are heading west on the N88 in the direction of Rodez. At Laissac (about 1500 inhabitants) we saw, from a distance, and Margaret sketched, the church with its tower and spire; I have found and recognized a view of this church on the internet. After another two to three miles we reached Bertholène, where traces have been found of the presence of man going back to the Paléolithique Age and in subsequent periods; the 13th century château, restored in later centuries, was abandoned in the 19th century; coal was extracted here in the second half of the 20th century, but the three mines are now closed. We continued on the N88, which generally follows the course of the Aveyron, taking us around the north of Rodez; we intended joining the D840 which passes the airport and leads to Decazeville, but we unintentionally followed the signs for Conques, the road D901. In fact, this was a more direct and surely more picturesque route to our destination – St-Cyprien-sur-Dourdou. We passed through Marcillac-Vallon, a very ancient village which was given its name by a Roman officer – Marcellus; the monks of Conques planted the first vines here in about the 9th century. After about a further seven miles and at 17.30, we reached l'Auberge 'Aux Portes de Conques', at SAINT-CYPRIEN-sur-DOURDOU. We reported our arrival and were given the key to our room. We were able to park in a public area at the rear of the hotel and adjacent to its terrace. We found our room very satisfactory and we soon felt very comfortable here. In fact, we had the privilege of being introduced to the two-week-old daughter of les propriétaries. When we arrived at 17.30 and it was still a warm and pleasant evening – 30°C – as we absorbed the atmosphere of the place and walked to the bridge over the little river Dourdou. Yes, it is at the gate of Conques and that is to be our agenda for tomorrow.

(Our journey today – 160 miles)

Day 18 – Friday, 16 September 2011

We had hoped to spend two nights in Conques itself and to experience the atmosphere of this ancient village in the morning before the visitors of the day arrived and, in the evening after they had left. However, we found that our chosen establishment was fully booked, but we were able to make a reservation 'Aux Portes de Conques', just six miles distant; we are pleased we did so. Saint-Cyprien-sur-Dourdou, in the Department of Aveyron, is 'un village authentique' as it is described in its excellent booklet of welcome and information regarding shops, services, facilities (including a swimming pool and tennis courts), and events, together with a list of fairs which are held throughout the year. In the words of Monsieur Le Maire, *Nestling in its setting of greenery at the entrance to the Gorges du Dourdou, Saint-Cyprien offers a festival of beauty, calm, peace and history. The dynamism which exists can be attributed to the diversity of the retailers and artisans who are very much involved in the life of the community.* This is a quite remarkable village, largely self-sufficient, and yet it has a population of no more than about 800. Immediately opposite our room there is one of those fascinating shops une Quincaillerie – an ironmonger's store. Each morning many of its wares are displayed on the pavement outside, a task which is frequently interrupted as the assistant exchanges a greeting and, no doubt, some local news with passers-by. There is always time for a chat! We could spend more time in this village, but the purpose of being here is to visit Conques. However, before doing so we were pleased to be able to purchase a copy of *Midi Libre*, which obviously has a wide circulation area. Every day, *Midi Libre* features a particular Saint and today it is Sainte Edith of Wilton, the daughter of King Edgar of England (10th century). We were also interested to notice in this edition a news item relating to the Collège Voltaire at Florensac which was the scene of the tragic event in June when 13 years old Carla was killed by the 14 years old brother of a rival. This article records that on the previous day the teachers had been on strike following conflict with the Principal regarding the lack of adequate administration; there was no direct link with the death of Carla.

However, mindful no doubt of the deep and widespread concern which that tragedy aroused, l'inspecteur d'académie de l'Hérault (department) was anxious for a prompt resolution of the dispute and has proposed the provision of an assistant principal with effect from la semaine prochaine!

Eventually, at 11.00 and 23°C, we set off on the D901 towards CONQUES; suddenly the scenery changed as we entered the Gorges du Dourdou with the river on our left flowing towards the Lot and we were reminded that we were approaching one of the 'Grand Sites de France'. The Pont Romain (pilgrim's bridge) which crosses the river is, in fact, of medieval origin and reconstructed in the 15th and 16th centuries; it carries the GR 65 footpath which forms part of the Chemin de Saint-Jacques from Puy-en-Velay. We continued and turned right on to the D42, which winds its way up to the ancient village. Shortly afterwards we were 'intercepted' by a lady who invited us to purchase a ticket for €3 which would entitle us to park in Conques, which was a further couple of kilometres ahead. However, at 11.20, we quickly found a very convenient parking place at the top of the hill leading into the village and with an attractive view overlooking the valley below. Conques, in the Department of Aveyron and Region of Midi-Pyrénées, is one of *Les Plus Beaux Villages de France*. Its population in 2008 was 281, but it is interesting to note that throughout most of the 19th century it had a population in excess of 1,000 and in the Middle Ages there were in the region of 3,000 inhabitants. Conques is situated in a deep hollow in the plateau, and owes its name to its shell-like setting – 'shell' in latin being 'concha'. The village rests on the sunny slope, sheltered from northerly winds, but above the humidity and mists of the valley of L'Ouche, which soon feeds Le Dourdou. Christianity had been spreading into the countryside and a religious building may have been constructed on the site during the Merovingian Period from the mid-5th century to be destroyed by the Saracens in the 7th century.

However, Conques appears to owe its origin to a hermit, Dadon, or Datus, who established his hermitage here, in a wild and spectacular terrain, "Once the sanctuary of wild beasts and song birds", in about 795; the site of which was, no doubt, the Plô fountain which still flows near the entrance to the abbey-church. Dadon soon had many followers and the first Benedictine Monastery was established. However, its future was to be greatly influenced by an event which occurred many miles away in Aquitaine. During the persecutions of the reign of the Roman Emperor Diocletian, a 12-year-old Christian girl in Agen, named Foy, who refused to worship the pagan gods, was put to death in 303 and was martyred. The relics of Sainte Foy of Agen were highly venerated throughout Aquitaine. However, by means of a 'secret transfer' the relics were brought to Conques in the year 866. This acquisition attracted much attention. Towards the middle of the 10th century a three-nave basilica was built to house the reliquary statue of Sainte Foy. In the 11th century Conques became an important staging post on the route of pilgrims from Puy-en-Velay to Saint Jaques de Compostela. After crossing the difficult and inhospitable Aubrac they would have reached the Lot at Espalion and continuing through Estaing, Saint-Marcel to Conques, a walk of some thirty kilometres. With the increasing numbers of pilgrims, the abbey became wealthy and powerful; a monastic empire independent of Cluny. From the middle of the 11th century into the 12th century the present-day Romanesque abbey church, the façade and the tympanum depicting the Last Judgement was completed. Subsequently, the monastery's fortunes began to decline and particularly so with the advent of the Black Death and the Hundred Years War. During the Wars of Religion, towards the end of the 16th century, Conques was seized by the Calvinists. It suffered again at the time of the Revolution in 1789, but fortunately its priceless treasures were saved by the inhabitants of the village. The Abbey, close to collapse, was rescued by the actions of the Historical Monuments Inspector, Prosper Mérimée, from 1837. Restoration and improvement of this prestigious heritage site has continued since that time.

From the car we began the descent into the village, our first stop being the Office de Tourisme. This is accommodated in a very interesting 18th century house; we collected an invaluable 'Guide of the Town'. However, at 'Au Tympan', a gift/bookshop, we purchased two excellent guidebooks in English. We made our way to the church square, the buildings of which surround, as if to protect, the church; in the centre is the Fontaine du Plô. One's attention is soon attracted to the façade of the abbey church itself and, particularly, to the remarkably preserved tympanum of the Last Judgement; its 124 figures represent one of the major works of art of the 12th century. Inside, one is struck by the height of the Romanesque building, accentuated by the alternating half round and rectangular pillars; the nave reaches a height of 72 feet. There are numerous interesting capitals, some 250 of them, displaying amazing and delicate craftsmanship. The wrought-iron gates of the choir have to be admired; they allowed the relics in the choir to be seen whilst providing necessary protection. They date from the XII century and represent one of the finest examples of Romanesque ironwork still preserved in France. The 20th century is represented here in the form of the stained-glass windows of Pierre Soulage which have been added since 1995. We were interested to find a memorial to Saint Thomas Becket who was of Norman ancestry; it recalls that, following his conflict with Henry II, he spent nearly two years of exile at Pontigny, in the Yonne Department in Burgundy; the now disappeared parish church of Conques was dedicated to the English Saint. Nearby we observed a grand piano! We did not discover any information about the organ, but it appears to be an 1898 Puget instrument.

We had spent much time inside the building, but there is much more to see in the surrounding buildings, etc. The cloister almost completely disappeared at about the end of the 18th century, probably due to the lack of maintenance and only traces now remain. Prosper Mérimée arrived too late to save it. However, the discovery of an inscribed lintel has enabled the cloister to be dated to the year 1100; it was, therefore, constructed during the abbotship of Bégon III (1087–1107). Also, it was thus a contemporary to the cloister at Moissac which remains standing and which we have visited. In the centre the large Romanesque ornamental serpentine basin is overlooked by the transept façade and the stairway tower. From the edge of the 'cloister' we could look down upon the cemetery, which is obviously still in use and it also offers splendid views of the spectacular valley. In the former refectory of the Benedictine monks we saw various exhibits, including capitals from the original cloister. Finally, there is Le Trésor de Conques, the most remarkable feature of a remarkable abbey church.

Many adjectives have been used to describe the priceless treasures of Conques, but unique may be the most appropriate – in quantity and quality it is exceptional. From the beginning of the 11th century until the 13th century Conques received successive gifts and donations of gold, silver and gems from powerful figures, emperors and kings, as well as from the many pilgrims of Sainte Foy and those en route to Santiago de Compostela. Some items were made in the Abbey's own workshop. However, the treasure is remarkable in that it survived at all. At the time of the Revolution, at the end of the 18th century, the National Convention ordered the confiscation of all precious metal objects so as to be melted down. Being somewhat isolated and some distance from administrative centres, the community of Conques chose to ignore the order and hid their treasures in all manner of unlikely places. At the end of the Revolution all the treasures were returned to their places in the abbey church. Thus, survived the richest collection of medieval and Renaissance gold treasure in France and probably in Western Europe. Until 1875 the treasure was kept in the church, but in

1911 it was installed in the specifically constructed south wing of the cloister. By the law of 1905, on the Separation of the Churches and the State, the treasure became the property of the state and commune, but some objects are still used regularly in the catholic liturgy. Of the numerous exhibits the most celebrated is the gold reliquary statue of Sainte Foy, which is studded with gems and other jewels presented by the pilgrims. Historians agree that the making of this statue, in its initial condition, can be dated to immediately after the arrival of the saint's relics at Conques in 866; the top of Sainte Foy's skull is still enclosed. A significant item is the 'Croix processionnelle'; made by a goldsmith from Villefranche-de-Rouergue, who was known from 1493 until his death in 1512, it has a cavity which contains remains of the True Cross. The reliquary known as Charlemagne's 'A' was made in the period of Abbot Bégon III (1087–1107).

There is much more to see and admire in this Trésor and indeed in the village of Conques, but we have spent many hours here and it is time to begin the climb back to the car. It was now very warm and, near the top of the hill, what a welcome sight to find a small drinks kiosk; we were able to sit and enjoy a cooling 'minute maid'. Although the main centre of attraction in Conques is its ancient buildings, we noticed something much more contemporary, the 'Auditorium du Centre Européen d'art et de civilisation medieval'. On reaching the car at 16.15 we found that the temperature was 32°C! We must now leave Conques; it is indeed one of the 'Grand Sites de France'; it was a memorable visit and a rare experience.

After returning to 'Aux Portes de Conques' at 16.38, it was a lovely warm evening (28°C) and we were able to enjoy an excellent meal sitting on the terrace of L'Auberge'. When describing our interesting day to Madame we were informed that the pronunciation of Conques is 'konka'.

(An excellent day – 12 miles!)

Day 19 – Saturday, 17 September 2011

It is Saturday morning and there is much more pedestrian activity in the street below; once again a selection of items for sale are being set out on the pavement in front of the shop opposite. It is fascinating to watch, but we must not dawdle as today we move into another phase of this particular journey. We will find ourselves in much more familiar regions of the country and often amongst longstanding friends and, perhaps, even establishing new friends. After petit déjeuner we hurried to ensure that all our luggage was returned to the car. However, before leaving L'Auberge we expressed our thanks and appreciation to les propriétaires for the warm welcome, the hospitality and the comfortable accommodation which had made our visit to Conques so memorable. As we were finally securing the car, a gentleman at the adjacent car made some comment to me. At first, I was not sure what he had said and thought that perhaps we had been occupying his parking place. It was nothing of the kind; for when he realised we were English the couple were so pleased to enter into a most friendly conversation.

We left Saint-Cyprien, therefore, on a very happy note. It was 11.05 and a much cooler day at 21°C.

About five miles on the picturesque D22 took us to the junction with the D840, the route from Rodez to Decazeville. We have passed through Decazeville in the past, but from the direction of Maurs and Aurillfac. DECAZEVILLE is a town built on coal and was a centre of coalmining from the 16th century. However, the last mine closed in 2001 but, as in the Somerset (Angleterre) we know, there is still ample evidence of this past industry. In fact, I have read that a British company was considering the reopening of some mines here, but the idea did not appear to be particularly welcomed locally and I have seen no more about the proposal. In the early part of the 20th century steel production was a major industry and in the 1930's the population reached 15,000. Although it is now in the region of 6,000 there are still a number of seemingly thriving industries in the town. After climbing out of Decazeville we continued on the D5 and D1 southwards, skirting the town of Villefranche-de-Rouergue, until it reaches the junction with the familiar D911.

We have driven through VILLEFRANCHE-de-ROUERGUE on a number of occasions, but because there has not been a suitable parking opportunity and sufficient time we have not been able to make a worthwhile visit. (There are lovely views from near the top of the hill as it descends into Villefranche from the Rieupeyroux direction) Deep in the valley of the Aveyron this ancient town, situated on the place of an earlier village, was founded by Alphonse de Poitiers in 1252; Alphonse was the son of Blanche de Castile and thus a brother of King (Saint) Louis IX. There were mines of copper, lead and iron here. Now it is classed as a Ville d'Art et d'Histoire. Villefranche is also remembered as the site of a certain event during the Second World War when it was under the occupation of a battalion of the 13th Waffen SS Division composed mainly of Bosnian and Croat soldiers, including muslims and catholics, enrolled in the German Army. On 17 September 1943 the battalion rebelled against their German Commander and killed the German officers. The insurgents took control of the town and for a very short time it was liberated. However, reinforcements were quickly brought from other garrisons and the rebellion was quelled. The survivors were condemned to death and buried at 'Le Champ des Martyrs Croats'. However, two of the leaders of the uprising escaped and subsequently joined the maquis. The Avenue des Croats stands in honour of the uprising.

We continued on the D911 in the direction of Cahors. At MARTIEL – at 12.30 – we resisted the temptation to stop at the pâtisserie but, no doubt, the life-like figures of the couple in the very realistic domestic setting of bygone years are still comfortably installed. Not far from Martiel is L'Abbaye de Loc-Dieu, a Cistercian abbey founded in 1123. It was bought by the Cibiel family in 1812 and it is still occupied by their descendants. From 1940, precious paintings from the Louvre were kept in hiding here. It is open to the public, but we have not made a visit. Shortly after Marroule, at 12.35 and after 1,355 miles we crossed into the Lot Department, but we are still in the Region of Midi-Pyrénées; we were reminded of the '540 Monuments du Lot Department'.

AUGUST/OCTOBER 2011

At LIMOGNE-en-QUERCY we stopped for a break – it was 12.45. There is a very convenient small car park here just along the D24 towards Cénevières with a couple of public seats and an adequate toilet; it serves various premises including a doctor's surgery, but it is not for their exclusive use and we have always found room to park for an hour or so. Our 'lunch' consisted of all the rolls, etc., which we were not able to eat at petit déjeuner at Hôtel de la Casadei on Thursday last; it was quite adequate. As we were eating, a lady carrying a black case, perhaps she was a médecin or infirmière, left her car and headed towards the surgery; she wished us "bon appétit"! Yes, this is France! At 13.30 we left Limonge and soon we left the D911 also, to join the D19 which will be our route to our destination for today – Castelnau-Montratier. Once again we pass through familiar villages of Varaire, Bach, Vaylats and Lalbenque; the road layout as it approaches and transverses the Autoroute A20 until it eventually links with the D820 is untidy and a little difficult to follow; however, after a short distance towards Montauban we take up again the D19 for the final 7–8 miles to Castelnau-Montratier.

This is the 10th successive year that we have spent a sojourn at the gite at La TAILLADE. We found the door unlocked, the gite fully prepared and, once again, a number of gifts of welcome – a selection of drinks, a melon and a vase of flowers; it was not long before we were warmly greeted by Alain and Bernadette. Far from any road, the spacious grounds and the tall proud resolute trees standing guard help to make this a haven of peace and tranquillity. After our journey of discovery of the past weeks, and as we have explored this village and the surrounding area quite extensively during previous years, we do not plan to travel very far during the coming week. Having arrived at 14.30 we had ample time to visit the excellent Spar supermarket, on the road leading into the village a short distance away, to buy supplies for the coming days and then to prepare our first meal, a modest one, since leaving home.

(78 miles)

Day 20 – Sunday, 18 September 2011

Ten years ago, although we had visited many areas of France during the previous 25 years, we felt that there was a France which we had not yet fully discovered and appreciated, a kind of inner France – its past – its present – its soul. In the hope of doing so, we decided to endeavour to seek accommodation in gites and in chambres d'hôte in more rural areas where practicable. This policy has brought us many rewards, much interest, satisfaction and pleasure, and we have been pleased to return to several of those locations on many occasions. Also, it has led to the establishment of some very valued friendships. La Taillade was one such place.

Today was intended to be un jour de repos and so it was. However, we realised a day or two later that it should not have been entirely so. The weekend of 17 and 18 September was, in fact, Les Journées Européennes du Patrimoine which are the days on which many well-known and historic buildings, etc., some normally not open to the public, are available to visit free of charge. These include museums, historical monuments and even the Palais de l'Elysée and the Senat. Some 12 million people took advantage of this opportunity. We were disappointed that we missed an opportunity to visit the nearby Moulin a Boisse!

Day 21 – Monday, 19 September 2011

CASTELNAU-MONTRATIER, a bastide town of the 13th century, is a charming village in the Lot Department with a population of approaching 2,000. Particular features are its large central square surrounded on three sides by covered arcades, its belfry, its windmills and l'eglise Saint-Martin. In recent years we have completed a very interesting written guided tour.

Castelnau-Montratier is situated in an area known as the QUERCY, a former province and which comprises the Department of Lot and the northern half of Tarn et Garonne; its traditional capital is Cahors. More precisely, Castelnau is in that part known as the QUERCY BLANC, an area which lies between Cahors and the southern boundary of the Lot Department; it is identified by its chalky soil and white limestone buildings. In the regions official guide, the Quercy Blanc is described as a land detached from the frenzy of modern times, preserved in the beauty of its countryside and in the richness of its architectural heritage.

Castelnau-Montratier and the Quercy suffered much during the HUNDRED YEARS' WAR (1337–1453) and from an early stage. The background of this conflict between England and France is complex and extends over several centuries, but one person, Eleanor of

Aquitaine, had a considerable influence. The region of Acquitaine in south-west France has a long history during which its boundaries have fluctuated. At the age of perhaps only 13 Eleanor succeeded to the Duchy of Acquitaine in 1137. When she married Louis VII in that year the region passed to France. This marriage was annulled in 1152 and, shortly afterwards, Eleanor married Henry, Duke of Normandy. When the latter became Henry II in 1154 the area came under the control of the English crown. It remained so until the end of the War, almost exactly 300 years later. From the 13th century until the French Revolution the region was normally known as Guyenne. Castelnau Montratier was in Guyenne. Hostilities arose as Philippe VI of France attempted to take Guyenne, while Edward III (his cousin) claimed the throne of France. Soon the people of Castelnau had to bear the burden of a levy to enable the baron, Ratier IV, to raise a company to join the army of the King of France. Castelnau and the surrounding villages also became the targets of attacks and looting of their supplies, by the English. In his very interesting book, *Mémoire sur le Passé de Castelnau de Montratier,* Monsieur Jean Colomina-Grangier writes that the Quercynois were so weakened that they were unable to resist and the English Sénéchal, Thomas de Walkafara, suppressed their revolt with great savagery; churches, châteaux, farms, and the centre of villages were burnt. He retook Castelnau, which was in ruins, but was captured in Réalville and hung in Toulouse. Having begun in Guyenne the Hundred Years War ended in that region with the French victory at the Battle of Castillon on 17 July 1453.

Another mainly lazy day until, towards the end of the afternoon, we decided to explore more of the surrounding villages. We drove along the D19 towards Cahors before taking the D214 for FLAUGNAC; we have visited this small commune of about 400 in the past and on each occasion, it has been very quiet and peaceful. This is a picturesque site situated on a typical rocky spur with a valley to the east and to the west formed by a stream (the Sabatier); as such it was, in ancient times, a castrum or Roman fort or fortress. The fort, on the tip of the promontory, consisted of a château and some houses of nobility, but by the middle of the 17th century the houses were in ruins. After a rather obscure entrance, the road continues and then dips down into the valley to the east and the Combe de Flaugnac; at the junction with the D26 we turned left towards St-Paul-de-Loubressac, but then turned right in the direction of la Lécune and St-Etienne. The church of St-ETIENNE is a beautiful old building, Romanesque and simple, in a lovely setting; from the road we drove up an incline to the church and into a very convenient and spacious car park. The cemetery and graves are well cared for and just below the level of the church and overlooking the surrounding countryside is a wonderfully conceived and attractive shrine; it is illuminated so that its beauty is not lost after dark.

Nearby there is a vineyard and a small lake which enhances the setting of the church. The dedication of this church is interesting. According to the information board at the church the oldest parish register relates to about 1315; it shows that St-Etienne was independent from other churches. It also explains that the name of

(Saint) King Etienne I (997–1038) is associated with the founding of the State of Hungary at the beginning of the 11th century. Records show his actions relating to the successful setting up of the Church and of the State as well as the suppression of rebel tribes. In founding the Christian Kingdom, he united the entire country, and from that time, royal domination extended over the whole of the Carpathian Basin. After leaving St-Etienne we continued our random meandering tour, turning right for la Perade and les Bordes, turning right to join the D4 at la Croix des Moines, but leaving this road to visit Lamolayrette. The church here is in a rather agricultural setting; we were not able to go inside, but we took a photograph. We returned to the D4 which led us back to Castelnau, approaching the village from beneath the prominent rocky promontory which bears the impressive L'Eglise St. Martin. We arrived home at 18.40 after a most interesting exploration. It was 17°C.

(Only 20 miles)

Day 22 – Tuesday, 20 September 2011

Today we will make our annual visit to CAHORS, the capital of the Lot Department with a population of about 23,000. From La Taillade at 12.36, we take the D19 to its junction with the D820; this was formerly the N20, but since the construction of the A20 autoroute it is now a fairly quiet route; it takes us directly into Cahors. Crossing the river Lot by the Pont Louis-Philippe, we then drove up the Boulevard Gambetta, through the centre of the city, to park once again in the Place du General de Gaulle – it was 13.20 and 22°C.

We have visited Cahors many times during the past ten years and we love this ancient city, a treasure securely enclosed in a remarkable loop of its river – the Lot; it is a favourite. The very best way to explore Cahors is, without doubt, on foot and because of its compact nature this is not particularly difficult. There are other ways to explore the city, however. By taking a river cruise, as we have done on a couple of occasions, there are splendid views of the old city, including of la cathédrale, la Tour du Pape and la Tour des Pendus (where hangings took place). Also, on two occasions, we have completed the journey of the little road train. This is a most interesting, entertaining and exciting experience, as it miraculously weaves its way through the traffic and the maze of narrow medieval streets. There is yet another way of touring the old city, but that is for a little later.

First, we left the car to walk past the impressive war memorial and into the Avenue Charles de Freycinet, passing the Arc de Diane, a relic of ancient roman baths, and continuing down the hill until reaching la Gare. We like to spend a little time here watching the trains arrive from, and leave for, distant places, although, so far as I am aware Cahors is not yet served by TGVs. Nearby is the former booking office of the now closed autorail touristique route along the valley of the Lot to Cajarc. When we first came to Cahors this service was still operating and we very much hoped to make the journey. Sadly, it closed before we were able to do so and, now, the closure appears to be permanent. We have driven along its route as far as Cénevières several times and although the track and crossing barriers are still in place, the route and the entrances to tunnels are very overgrown; it is a sad sight. We walk on, passing the hotel where we spent a night some years ago, then through the subway underneath the railway to emerge near the famous Pont Valentré. This bridge, built in the 14th century, is the most beautiful and best-preserved fortified bridge of the Middle Ages; of course, it is said that the devil had a hand in its completion. Nearby, we had the opportunity of a tour of a different kind. Two donkeys were waiting to transport us around the ancient city in their 'coach'; they did, of course, have a guide. We couldn't resist and with just a few other passengers we set off. We were taken around the medieval streets, but it was as well that we had seen them before because, at times, we were mainly concentrating on staying securely in our seats and avoiding pointing out of the side, as we were often very close to the walls. Eventually, we returned to our starting point, but not before our 'drivers' had shown that they wished to give us a bonus by diverting on to the pavement. Soon, all was under control and we were able to alight. It was exhilarating, but in the subsequent calm we had the pleasure of meeting Suzie, who is 14 years old, and Kastor as well as their owner. Of course, we took, and had taken, some photographs.

By this time the refreshment bar on the quay was closing and we began our climb (it is not very steep, but it had become a warm day) along the Rue Wilson back to the Boulevard Gambetta near the Hôtel de Ville. There is a bookshop near here – Librairie Lagarde – which we have patronized a number of times, but not today; it is fascinating, very small and so full of books that there is little room for the customers. We have always been treated very helpfully and courteously here; it has an excellent atmosphere. More compelling, after all the exertions and excitement, was the need for a drink and one does not need to look very far for refreshment in this city. Near the fountain and the statue of Léon Gambetta, who was born in this town in 1838 and became Prime Minister of France, there is the Bistro Gambetta where we were quickly served with a very welcome cup of tea at a table in the warm September sun. During past years the area to the west of the Place Gambetta, behind the fountain, has given us much interest. Coinciding with the excavations of the Southgate area of Bath and the search for evidence of the Roman occupation, similar extensive excavations were continuing in this area of Cahors during the decade 2000. The discoveries here have been remarkable; the excavation of an area of 5,000 square metres has revealed the organization of Roman Cahors, including its basilica and amphitheatre, as well as medieval and modern artefacts. A short video can be found on the internet entitled 'Two thousand years of an urban quarter in Cahors'; it incorporates a commentary by the archaeologist on the work being done as well as pictures of various finds. Now that the work at these respective sites has been completed, the contrasts could not be greater. Yes, each has an underground car park, but while Cahors has a spacious open area for walking and outdoor events, Bath has a concentration of commercial, etc., buildings!

It was now time to begin our walk back towards the Place du General de Gaulle, but on our way we felt that we must make a short diversion into the old medieval city and to the cathedral once again, which lie on the eastern side of Boulevard Gambetta. The Cathédrale Sainte-Etienne is a national monument; it was constructed in the 11th century by Bishop Géraud de Cardaillac on the site of the 7th century church of Saint Didier and was completed in about 1135. It has the appearance of a fortified building and it has two domes. Inside there are frescos on a dome and many paintings on the walls; the cloister is in a flamboyant Gothic style. Although it was now late afternoon the church was still open and there was the usual activity. We have visited this cathedral a number of times and on every occasion we have always felt welcome in a warm friendly atmosphere; one gains the impression that it is much loved and valued by Cadurcians; this church is not a museum and a visit is a moving experience.

It is certainly now time that we should return to the car. However, as we do so we must remember one other special feature of this city, its Secret Gardens. Created in 2002, these 29 little gardens are situated in unexpected places in various parts of the city and have different themes; there is a way-marked path linking the gardens. What more could one wish for in this wonderful and delightful city; but there is more, much more, to its long and interesting history? Also, we do not recall seeing any litter – what a joy! Is it any wonder that we have returned to Cahors over and over again?

We have found in past years that, although this is a paying car park, the cash is collected from the ticket machine and the barriers raised at about 19.00; as it was now 19.10 we had had the benefit of free parking for the day! It was 24°C. Leaving the city by the Boulevard Gambetta and over the Pont Louis-Philippe we continued in the direction of Montauban, passing the many industrial and commercial establishments of the environs of Cahors. However, we must make our regular stop at the premises of L'Atrium, the company of Georges Vigouroux (Wine Distributors) which was founded in the Lot in 1887. In fact, we were only just in time as they were about to close at 19.30, but we were still welcome. Last year (2010) we bought some Chateau Lafleur 2008 red wine which was praised and appreciated. We had so little time to make any selection and so we felt we could do no better than purchase more of the same appellation, but it was of 2009 vintage. Will it be as good – we wait for the verdict! It was 19.32 when we were served by Gisele and, without doubt, we were her last customers of the day, but she willingly carried the box to our car. We reached La Taillade at 20.05. Margaret's verdict was that it had been a "Good day, but hard work for feet and legs, because of the heat." We were ready for a meal!

(36 miles)

I have described our first visit to Cahors and its Cathedral on 19 September 2002 – sadly today was our last visit!

<u>Day 23 – Wednesday, 21 September 2011</u>

From time to time we have read articles in magazines, etc., describing certain places or recalling particular events; we have visited a number of such places. Some years ago, we read with much interest about a potentially devastating incident which occurred in 1944, during the German occupation of France, in a peaceful village in the valley of the Lot – in CÉNEVIERES. We decided that we would visit this village so that we could better understand and appreciate the record of the event. From the description, we did not find it difficult to locate the properties concerned; we spoke to a local resident who promptly took us to meet two of the personalities who featured in this article, Maurice and Ginette Flaujac. It was such a great pleasure and privilege to meet and talk to them – introduced to them by their daughter, in fact – and they greatly appreciated our interest and our visit. As we left on that occasion, albeit as an afterthought, we left with their address.

Since that introduction we have visited Ginette and Maurice many times and corresponded in the meantime. In March 1943 Maurice was deported by the Germans to serve in forced labour camps in Hungary and Austria. When he was eventually freed and was able to return home in June 1945 his weight was no more than 35 kilograms. Despite his experiences he had an indomitable spirit and we have had such lively conversations about his family, country, politics, and football, usually with the assistance of a dictionary, either in their living room or, more often, sitting on their vine shaded patio. It was, we understand, the house in which he was born. We have been privileged to meet their daughter, Marie-Hèlène, and other family members as well as various friends, one of whom, Denise, has become another special friend. Maurice was proud of his garden and often, as we left, he would present us with products he had grown, radishes, tomatoes, etc. Unfortunately, Maurice had a leg amputated at the beginning of 2009, but he had a prothesis (artificial limb) fitted; his spirit prevailed and with the help of a mobility vehicle he was able to stay in touch with his friends and return to his favourite boules. Sadly, however, Maurice died on 4 December 2010, at the age of 88. It was a privilege and a great pleasure to have known Maurice; we always looked forward to our visits as we know he did.

We have remained in touch with Ginette, having visited her on 31 May last and we have arranged another visit for today. Our favourite route to Cénevières is via Cahors, and then continuing along the very picturesque route on the north bank of the Lot, but today we will go more directly on the D19 through Lalbenque to Limogne-en-Quercy and then take the D24 as it winds its way gently down to the village and indeed to the door of Ginette's home. We were able to park nearby again, close to the village store, at 15.30. We found Ginette in good spirits and pleased to see us again; with her was Denise which was an added pleasure. As usual we had some interesting conversation, not least about where we had been in France this year. Denise is very helpful in assisting us with our French, for which we are very grateful, and we find her explanations of various aspects of French life very interesting. A year or two ago she told us about the new system of the immatriculation (registration) of road vehicles which no longer incorporates the number of the department in which it is registered. After an hour or so Denise left and we said a fond au revoir to her; we then spent further time with Ginette talking about her family and her life since the death of Maurice.

Sadly, after a couple of hours, it was time to say an emotional farewell, but I am sure that Ginette was pleased to know that before leaving Cénevières we would visit the cimetière and the tombe of Maurice. This is a very short distance from their home and must be no more than a few metres from the end of his garden; what an appropriate final resting place for Maurice. It is such a peaceful setting; nearby and overlooking is l'Eglise Saint-Clair and a few metres in the other direction, is the now 'sleeping' track of the former Cahors – Capdenac train-touristique. We noted the beautiful remembrances and we took some photographs. Our visit to Cénevières is now complete. We are very pleased that we have been able to visit our friends once again; it has been a most enjoyable and memorable afternoon in lovely weather; the temperature reaching 30°C.

Cénevières is a very small village, with a population of less than 200, lying in a 'loop' of the Lot and surrounded by wooded hills. It is a very calm and peaceful place and it is difficult to imagine that any unpleasant event could happen here, as it did in 1944. Surely this is a place near to the heart of France which we sought. Also, it did apparently attract the attention of non-other than Henri Quatre in past times; he had looked favourably upon and visited the château!

We returned to the D24 and began the very gradual climb of about five miles to the Causse de Limogne. As we left Limogne we bought petrol – 47 litres – €76.14 – at the Total Service Station; it was then 18.00. We had enjoyed beautiful weather throughout the day and the sun was still shining brightly, but now it was not so welcome; we found ourselves facing that sun for most of the 33 miles to Castelnau-Montratier and it made driving difficult. However, we reached La Taillade safely at 19.35. It was still 25°C.

(71 miles)

Our first visit to Cènevières was on 16 September 2002. Today was our last visit but we have remained in contact with Ginette.

<u>Day 24 – Thursday, 22 September 2011</u>

La Taillade is, to us, unique. Never have we been able to spend so many weeks in such a place and now for the 10th year in succession. The peace, the tranquillity, the serenity and the silence, yes, the silence is remarkable. Apart from the occasional sounds of domestic or 'garden' activity of Alain and Bernadette it is virtually impossible to identify any human made sounds. At the time of crépuscule and après la tombée de la nuit it is even more memorable. It is a very rare experience and to be able to 'reside' in such an environment is a rare privilege. It had been a lovely day and perfect for relaxation and rest and, apart from a brief visit to the Spar to purchase bread and croissants (€1.85), we had no desire to abandon this atmosphere.

(2 miles)

Day 25 – Friday, 23 September 2011

Attached to the gite is a maisonette which is occupied on a permanent basis. In our early years here (2002) our neighbours were Beatrice and Marc and their lovely little son Tristan. They too made us feel very welcome and a firm friendship developed. We have since visited them in their new home at Beaumat near Labastide-Murat, some 20 miles north of Cahors, on several occasions. Marc's profession related to the natural environmental affairs of the Lot Department. He had a particular interest in birds and we recall how, in the near silence of a late evening, he imitated and called nearby owls to which they responded; it was an amazing experience. Nowadays the property is the home of a single gentleman who we rarely see during the first four days of the week when he travels to his work in Figeac. However, on a Friday he is pleased to have a conversation, to know of places we have visited, etc.; he kindly gave us a melon – "it is a tradition" he said. It was another gorgeous day and we were content to spend a few hours of our last day, relaxing and resting and making use of the table and chairs on the sheltered (from the sun) area outside our entrance.

However, at 16.20, we set off on another foray into the Quercy. A short distance along the D19 we took the D659 and then the D64 to the junction with the D55 where stands the preserved Moulin à Vent de BOISSE, situated on a mound a little above the level of the surrounding moors. It is an impressive monument with an interesting history, at a lovely spot, which we have visited a number of times as it is only four miles from

La Taillade. It previously stood at Cézac, a short distance away, but it was dismantled and re-erected at Boisse in 1813 because it was considered that here it would be less vulnerable to lightning! It was recorded as a monument historique in 1979 by reason of its state of conservation; its original mechanisms date from the 17th century. Also, it is one of only three moulins à vent in the Lot which still turn. We were disappointed to realise that it had been open to the public on Sunday, 18 September. However, it was good to make another visit on such a lovely day and we took some photographs – the temperature was 26°C. There is a private dwelling very close, but just below the level of the moulin – the owners, perhaps?

As we continued across the Causse, the limestone plateau, towards Lhospitalet we noticed a gariotte (shepherds' shelter) close to the roadside and we stopped to take a photograph. These shelters are usually circular in shape with a conical roof and are built with the limestone which has been brought to the surface by the severe winter frosts. The area generally is arid with little vegetation and the main economic activity has, for generations, been the production of ewe's milk.

LHOSPITALET has gallo-romain origins and the village is spread along an ancient roman way, the Via Podensis. Following the discovery of the tomb of Saint Jacques early in the 9th century and the increase in the number of pilgrims journeying to Compostelle in the 11th century it became part of the route from Le Puy-en-Velay. As such it was the site of a hospice founded in 1095 by Dame Hélène, wife of Pons I of Gourdon, baron of Castelnau; however, this was destroyed during the Hundred Years War. L'église Notre-Dame de la Nativité dates, in part, from the 13th and 14th centuries; it has a very short nave with the choir occupying almost half the total length of the church.

From Lhospitalet we continued to the D7, passing Pechpeyroux, along the valley of the Lendou and through the main street of Lascabanes, which the inhabitants (180) make so attractive with their floral displays. A meandering drive took us back to Castelnau and to La Taillade after a most interesting and varied tour of two to three hours.

(A total of only 32 miles!)

Day 26 – Saturday, 24 September 2011

Alain and Bernadette have always been most kind and helpful to us since the day we first arrived on 14 September 2002. On that occasion we approached Castelnau-Montratier from a southerly direction and through the village of St-Paul-de-Loubressac, rather than in accordance with the directions we had been sent! Consequently, we were unable to find the vital sign of commercial premises which marked the entrance to the lane leading to their 'estate' and which has since become so familiar. We had to telephone Alain who identified where we were and simply said, "I will come to meet you". On occasions we have been invited to join them for dinner when we have met their friends Anthony and Janine and Nigel and his wife. Only this week, when Margaret was complaining about the wear and tear on her feet after a day in Cahors, Alain offered to arrange a rendezvous with his médecin – he would come to see you here, he said. That would have been a rare experience and, on reflection, perhaps we should have accepted his offer! Very often, when coming to the end of our stay, Alain has said that we can leave when we are ready or even stay until the following day. We are very glad that we chose to spend that week here in 2002; it has given us the repeated pleasure of experiencing this special environment and atmosphere and, of course, it has enabled us to get to know much of this area of the Lot Department. It has also introduced us to Lauzerte, Montaigu-de-Quercy, Luzech, Ste-Alauzie, Molieres, Montpezat-de-Quercy, Bruniquel, St-Antonin-Noble-Val, Cordes-s-Ciel and Gaillac. Alain and Bernadette came to wish us goodbye and we were very pleased to see Jérôme also and to know that he has fully recovered from his serious illness of a few years ago. It was 14.15 when we eventually left La Taillade.

This was indeed our tenth and final visit. In fact, Alain and Bernadette have since left La Taillade.

It was a lovely day again with the temperature at 23°C and our destination for tonight is Albussac in the Department of Corrèze. Once again it was the D19 and D820 to Cahors, but immediately after crossing the Pont Louis-Philippe we turned right on to the D653 towards Figeac. This road has the old city on our left and the river to the right, then passes Laroque-des-Arcs and underneath the A20 until at Vers it leaves the valley of the Lot and then follows the course of the river (or creek) Vers. At Moulin de Guillot we took the D32 which branches off to the left of the D653 and dips down to the river valley. This road is not familiar to us, but how lovely it is, passing only very small villages such as St-Martin-de-Vers – with perhaps less than 100 inhabitants but with prehistoric and roman remains in the area and also St-Sauveur-la-Vallée, until rising to take us into Labastide-Murat. It was 15.50 and 22°C. This journey from Cahors of about 23 miles is very interesting and attractive; it is, in fact, designated by Michelin as picturesque.

We know LABASTIDE-MURAT and we like this little town with a population of about 700. We have been here a number of times when on visits to Beatrice and Marc at nearby Beaumat – on market day and meeting Tristan from his école primaire, for instance. We have seen the birthplace, in 1767, of Joachim Murat, who became the brother-in-law of Napoleon Bonaparte and also Marshall of France and then King of Naples until his death in 1815. We were pleased to have the opportunity of enjoying another lovely cup of tea sitting outside the Hotel la Garissade and surveying the leisurely activity in this smart and tidy centre of the town on this pleasant Saturday afternoon; how nice also to revive memories of previous visits. At 16.30 we must continue our journey on the D807 across the Causse de Gramat, which is within the Parc Naturel Regional des Causses du Quercy, to the capital of the Causse, Gramat.

GRAMAT, in the Lot Department, is a charming town of about 3,700 inhabitants and a church (Eglise Saint-Pierre) built in 1923. But it has a history which goes back to prehistoric and gallo-romaine periods when it was at the crossroads of important routes; as such it became subject to invasions by Arabs in the 7th century and then by the Normans in the 9th and 10th centuries. It suffered during the Hundred Years War, but the chateau survived a siege by the English led by the Prince of Wales. However, at the end of the 14th century the population had diminished to seven persons. Towards the end of the 16th century, during the Wars of Religion, Gramat was the target of both the Catholics and the Protestants. The Great War had its effects also; many young men did not return from the battlefields and the town itself became a centre for the rearing of horses. For the first part of the Second World War, Gramat was in the Free Zone, but afterwards it did not escape the attentions of its German occupiers. Although we have not visited the site, we cannot pass this way without recalling the 'Tragédie de Gabaudet'.

It was on the 8 June 1944, just two days after the Allied Landings in Normandy, that Gabaudet Farm, in an isolated situation about five miles south of Gramat, was chosen as a meeting point for nearly 300 people volunteering to join the Resistance. That same morning the notorious armoured SS Division 'Das Reich' had left the Montauban area, initially to suppress the resistance in the Brive – Clermont-Ferrand – Limoges region; a few days later it headed north to the Normandy Front. It must surely have been a collaborator that led a column of tanks and armoured vehicles to Gabaudet at the end of the afternoon, where they encircled the farm and attacked it with extreme ferocity. According to the memorial, "Almost 40 people were killed or listed as missing, 71 were arrested, including two women. Most of them were deported to the Dachau concentration camp. Very few of them would return. On the same day the same SS division set ablaze the hamlet of Donnadieu, (located at about 600 metres away from Gabaudet), went on committing atrocities and massacres in Bretenoux".

On the following day, 9 June, reprisals were carried out at Tulle, in Corrèze; all men between the ages of sixteen and sixty were arrested, 99 were hanged from lamp-posts and balconies in the town and many were sent to Dachau. However, even this act of barbarism was surpassed on 10 June at ORADOUR-sur-GLANE, near St-Junien in Haute-Vienne. Here death and destruction was meted out in fullest measure as 642 men, women and children, virtually the entire population of the village were indiscriminately slaughtered and the buildings left in ruins. Oradour-sur-Glane has been 'preserved' in the state in which it was left by the savages for subsequent generations to witness. Our visit, a few years ago, was a frightening, most moving and unforgettable experience. It is difficult now to acknowledge that these terrible acts were being committed against innocent French people when the forces of liberation were already on the soil of France.

We continued from Gramat in the direction of Tulle, almost certainly on the same route as that taken by those barbarians in the course of their appalling acts of butchery; how could such peaceful roads through such lovely countryside have been a channel for such evil? Still on the D807 we pass through the little village of Lavergne, with many roads leading off in various directions, and continue until we begin to descend from the Causse de Gramat. At this point a splendid panoramic view is revealed; we pass the Grotte de Presque on our right and nearby there is a convenient viewpoint. In the distance, to the right, is the village of SAINT-CERE and, dominating the wide valley of the Dordogne, are the remains of the Château de Saint-Laurent-les-Tours. The earliest of its two towers dates from the 13th century. Some part of the ruins was rebuilt in the 19th century and this was later acquired by the artist Jean Lurçat who lived and worked there; during the occupation in the 1940s he operated a secret radio station for the Resistance. Since 1889 the château has been classified as a monument historique; it is open to the public for certain periods of the year. Near St-Céré we joined the D940 for Bretenoux.

When we have been making a similar journey from Cahors in the past, we have sometimes taken an alternative route. At the junction with the D32 for Labastide Murat we have continued on the D653 across the virtually uninhabited Causses du Quercy with its wooded hillsides, then through the small villages of Livernon and Assier to the slightly larger and interesting village of Lacapelle-Marival; this is a most pleasant drive of about 43 km. After Lacapelle the route is very picturesque and eventually descends into the centre of St-Céré; here it is possible to park under the trees and, just a short walk away, to enjoy a welcome cup of tea! The distance from Lacapelle, on the D48 through Leyme, is 21 km.

BRETENOUX is just inside the Department of Lot and lies on the left bank of the Cère; it has a population of about 1,300. It is known that Bretenoux existed in the year 866 and in 1277 a bastide was founded by the Lord of Castelnau. On the day of 9 June 1944 members of the Resistance opposed elements of the Das Reich division here; during the course of the 'battle' 19 maquisards were killed as well as 13 civilians. We have visited Bretenoux on several occasions, to purchase films, to call at la poste and, notably, to spend time in a salon de thé in the arcaded square which is typical of so many bastide towns. Also, we have passed through on our way to the nearby Château de Castelnau. On leaving Bretenoux on the D940 we cross the River Cère shortly before it flows into the Dordogne to complete its 75 miles journey. We then bear right in the Tulle direction as the D803 heads towards Brive-la-Gaillarde. Almost immediately we are in BIARS-sur-CERE; although seemingly modern, this little town has its roots in the 9th century. Once again driving over the level crossing, we are intrigued; it is just an ordinary passage à niveau, but to where does this track lead in each direction? In fact, the line was constructed in 1891 and still provides regular services between Souillac in the Lot and Aurillac in Auvergne country; the journey takes some three hours and passes through the Gorges de la Cère; no doubt, it would be an interesting and enjoyable experience! The railway certainly brought economic benefits to the commune. Firstly, it became the only centre for the production of wooden railway sleepers; the raw material having been floated down the Cère. Industrial activity continued to increase and today there is a large zone d'activitiés (business park) which accommodates a variety of enterprises employing many hundreds of workers. One trade which has been established here for many years is that of fruit processing and preserving; the company Andros, known for its Bonne Maman brand, is based here and has earned Biars the distinction of being described as the "Capitale Européenne de la Confiture".

We are now about to leave the Department of Lot; perhaps for the last time? However, we take with us so many fond and happy memories; of many weeks spent in the area, of excursions, sometimes tentative, along often very minor roads linking village to village, of so many interesting places and history discovered, of so many days spent in the wonderful and unforgettable capital of the department – Cahors, but, above all, of those personal friendships formed and renewed year after year and long to be cherished. Now we are in the Corréze and in the Limousin.

The Region of LIMOUSIN is situated mainly in the Massif Central and comprises the Departments of Corrèze, Creuse and Haute-Vienne and is the least populated region after Corsica. It is a mainly upland rural area, famed for some of the best beef farming in the world – the distinctive chestnut-red of its cattle is a common sight. It is also a major timber producing area and its capital, Limoges, is world-renowned for its porcelain. Because of its predominantly rural nature, the Limousin has a strong tradition of traditional music in which the bagpipe and hurdy-gurdy feature. We have traversed the Limousin many times in many directions and so many of its place names are familiar:- Le Dorat, Magnac-Laval, Bellac, Mortemart, St-Junien, Limoges, St-Leonard-de-Noblat,

Rochechouart, Oradour-sur-Vayres, Châlus, Nexon, Pierre-Buffière, St-Yreix-la-Perche, Lubersac, Arnac-Pompadour, Vigeois, Brive-la-Gaillarde, Collonge-la-Rouge, La Souterraine, Châteauponsac, Le-Grand-Bourg, Gueret, Bénevent-l'Abbaye, Bourganeuf, Pontarion, Aubusson, Felletin, Eymoutiers, Peyrelevade, Millevaches, Bugeat, Meymac, Egletons, Bort-les-Orgues, Tulle, Albussac, Argentat, Beaulieu-sur-Dordogne and the martyr village of Oradour-sur-Glane. Le Limousin contains within its borders the entire old province of that name, which was one of the traditional provinces prior to the Revolution; its name derives from the name of a Celtic tribe. As of 2015, metropolitan France is divided into 22 administrative regions, but there is legislation passing through the parliament to reduce this number to 13. The sad consequence of this process is that le Limousin will disappear; it will lose its identity by merging with Aquitaine and Poitou-Charentes to form a much larger region, with a capital, probably, in Bordeaux. Although, in future, there may be no formal roadside reminders of the area of this ancient province and region, it will continue to be recognizable by the colour of its cattle! (As from 1 January 2016 Le Limousin is part of the new region of Nouvelle-Aquitaine.)

The Department of CORREZE is one of the original 83 departments created on 4 March 1790 during the Revolution; its capital is TULLE. The musical instrument which is emblematic of France is the accordion and in Tulle is the last industrial manufacturer of accordions in France. The company, Maugein, was founded in 1919 and still produces some 600 instruments each year; every year, in September, a festival dedicated to the accordion is held. But can one think of Tulle without recalling the ghastly atrocities which were perpetrated here on 9 June 1944 (referred to in Day 26)? Notable personalities who were born or who have lived significantly in the Corrèze include – Jacques Delors, former President of the European Commission; Jacques Chirac, 22nd President of the Republic and François Hollande, 24th President of the Republic. Incidentally, the basis for choosing the chief place of departments in 1790 was that it had to be no more than one day's journey by horse from all parts of the department.

Immediately after entering the Department of Corréze the D940 follows the left bank of the River Dordogne until it reaches Beaulieu-sur-Dordogne where it crosses the river. Beaulieu is only about five miles from Bretenoux and we shall not pause here today as, without doubt, we shall return. After a short distance alongside the river, the road begins to rise onto the rolling hills of Corréze, the foothills of the Massif Central! About five miles after leaving Beaulieu, there is a junction with the D38 which leads to Collonges-la-Rouge. It was the Mayor of Collonges, Charles Ceyrac, who conceived the idea of a formal association of *Les Plus Beaux Villages de France*. The suggestion quickly gained support and there are now some 150 member villages. Apart from Collonges itself there are Turenne (situated on top of a cliff), Curemonte (along a ridge) and Carennac (in the valley of the Dordogne) nearby and we have been able to visit them all in past years. We continue on the picturesque route until reaching Quatre

Routes – "the sun is still shining" – where we turn right on to the D921. There is a very acceptable hotel here and, just after the junction, up on the right, a station service; Jim has often spoken of his satisfaction with the service he has received from the propiétaire, Michel; incidentally he has also assisted us when in need of some liquide de refroidissement. About three to four miles along this winding and undulating road we turn right for Neuville then, almost immediately, we turn left. We are now in un-signposted territory and must rely on memory, instinct and guesswork as the narrow road twists and turns as it climbs quite gently through, most certainly, agricultural territory; one is not surprised to meet a herd of cows seemingly making their own way to the milking sheds or to their grazing fields; we can see that they are dissuaded from straying from their rightful route and entering private properties, by lengths of coloured twine which has been re-attached in advance, to the 'hedge' on each side of the entrance. Here, landmarks cannot be relied upon. A few years ago we found a helpful 'signpost' in the form of a long row of logs piled high alongside the boundary of a property adjacent to the road, on our right, which we should take. Helpful it was until, on a later occasion, we realised that the logs had disappeared; we were completely confused – perhaps it had been a severe winter and the supply had been exhausted! However, today at 18.10, even after one year, we reached the foot of the short sharp climb of Anne and Jim's drive at Les Bedaines without taking any wrong turnings and it was not long before they were there to greet us once again in that lovely warm welcoming manner that we have experienced many times.

AUGUST/OCTOBER 2011

We had known that we would like to spend time in the area of the River Dordogne and, early in the previous decade, we were attracted to an entry in a guide to 'Special Places to Stay', which read that Anne and Jim, "were born to do B & B; interested in others, they genuinely love having visitors, their enthusiasm for their adopted area is infectious, Anne's cooking is superb". We could not resist this introduction. Now, after visits, first to their restored farmhouse home, then many more to Les Bedaines, their newly constructed home of great character standing proudly on the hillside, we can fully endorse these observations. Our visits to Anne and Jim have been experiences we shall never forget. The guests' bedrooms, at the top of the building, are comfortable and well equipped, each with its individual balcony providing a splendid view of the peaceful rural scene below and beyond; the near total silence is occasionally broken by the distinctive sound of a bell which has been presented to a particular member of a nearby herd of dairy cows and one is then aware of her whereabouts. The large dining table is conveniently situated with an excellent view to the east; the furthest visible point is of the top of Puy Mary of the Monts du Cantal, which reaches a height of 1,787 metres and is situated some 40 miles away in that direction. The period of the evening meal is an occasion to savour – beginning at about seven o'clock with nibbles and drinks, followed by a splendid four-course meal with a choice of wine, then, retiring to the lounge area for coffee and much conversation. Yes, stimulating conversation with a seemingly endless range of topics. As the years have passed mutual interests in our respective families have developed; also, Anne and Jim always show a readiness to sympathetically understand the varying personal concerns, cares and worries of others; how welcome and helpful such opportunities can be! Of course, the problems of the wider world are not neglected, and the necessary solutions are wisely devised. Breakfasts are very informal and served by Anne, who invariably remembers the individual preferences and needs, regarding medication, etc., of guests; yet, despite her many other tasks and responsibilities she will often find the time to sit and talk about some further matter of interest. In addition, Anne and Jim have exercised great skill in integrating guests and thus creating new and interesting friendships. This truly is a 'Special Place'.

On this occasion we are the only guests and the evening followed the familiar pattern; however, the main course of the meal notably included Anne's own veal calf. Afterwards, there was much news of the past year to exchange and discuss; it was a natural continuation of our previous visit.

(91 miles today)

Day 27 – Sunday, 25 September 2011

The weather is always good at Les Bedaines – well, it seems to be. It was a bright clear morning and it was good to be able to step out on to the balcony from our room and breathe the fresh clean unpolluted corrézien air and experience the quietude, the calm and the peace while looking down upon that enviable rural scene. At the breakfast table the sun was rising and casting its rays across the room – it was going to be a lovely day.

Bedaine is a hamlet of the Commune of ALBUSSAC, which lies about 500 metres above sea level and has a population of about 700; it is well watered by several streams. The village centre is dominated by its 11th century Romanesque church of Saint Martin and the grey roofs of the dwellings are a feature.

During past years we have visited many interesting and historic places in this area. However, there are two where we always like to spend a few hours; both on the banks of the Dordogne, they are Beaulieu-sur-Dordogne and Argentat. Today, at 11.15, we will return to Beaulieu. Our route, a familiar one, is via the D921 to Quatre Routes and there joining the D940. Shortly after doing so we see the direction sign to the Roche de Vic, which reminds us of visits to that well-known landmark. ROCHE de VIC is a former Gallic oppidum that dominated the region and, although standing at no more than a modest 636 metres, it provides a magnificent panorama stretching over a remarkable six departments; we have 'conquered' it two or three times. Since 1880 it has been crowned with a small chapel and a statue of Sainte Marie.

Continuing across this so pleasurable Limousin countryside, then gently descending to the valley of the Dordogne we enter the city of BEAULIEU. On doing so we turn right into the Place du Champs du Mars where we have always found space to park and, of course, it is free. It was midi, near the Hôtel Le Manoir, with its red-shuttered windows and climbing plants; the temperature was a very acceptable 19°C. Often we have enjoyed a cup of tea at this hotel, sometimes sitting at a pavement table in warm sunshine, or even in the rustic restaurant with exposed beams and quarry-tile floors before a welcome fire in the inglenook fireplace. However, even after travelling for more than three weeks we still have refreshments in the car, which we made use of before setting off on foot. Back on the D940 – here, it is the Rue General de Gaulle, the main road and although the volume of traffic is not normally great, it is important to make use of the pavement – just a short walk to the right takes us into the Place Marbot. This square was named in honour of Colonel Marcellin Marbot, a hero of Napoleon's campaigns; his statue stands in front of the Maison du Bessol and there is further car parking here. Also, the Office de Tourisme is situated in this square and that is our particular interest today. While browsing over the books on display I was attracted to a new (2011) publication by Editions Ouest-France, an extremely interesting book, with many photographs, entitled 'Le Limousin'. Unfortunately, the office was in the process of closing and I felt I must then leave the book on the shelf.

Whenever we visit Beaulieu we always spend time in the ancient ABBEY of SAINT-PIERRE. Again, we turn to legend regarding the origins of this once great Benedictine Abbey. Legend has it that in the middle of the 9th century, Rudolph of Turenne, Archbishop of Bourges, captivated by the beauty of the place, decided to found an abbey for men here. Twelve Benedictine monks under the direction of Gairulph, the first abbot, came from the Abbey of Solignac, near Limoges, from 855 to 860. The first monks undertook the building of an abbey that quickly became rich and prosperous, thanks to the many donations it received as well as to the relics that attracted many pilgrims. Following the influence of the Bishop of Limoges, the abbey was put into the hands of the monks of Cluny. With the benefit of reinforcements, in about 1095, it was decided to build, under the direction of Abbot Geraud II, a new and much larger church. This replaced the former church and is the one we see today. Construction took place in two phases. The first period ended in about 1103 and included the building of the choir, the north and south transepts, the chancel transept, with its domed vault, and the last bay of the nave. The second phase lasted until about 1125 to 1130 when three other bays of the nave were built along with the tympanum of the south door. The building was completed in about 1140. There were additions in the 13th and 14th centuries. However, after two centuries of prosperity, the Hundred Years' War signalled the decline of Beaulieu Abbey, although no major destruction was inflicted on the abbey or the monastery. It was commandeered by the Huguenots in 1569 during the Wars of Religion. Abandoned by the surviving monks, the monastery was not re-established. However, in 1663, with the arrival of the Saint-Maur Benedictines, the abbey was restored, and the church repaired. This continued until the Revolution in 1789 when the monastery was once and for all abandoned and the abbey church finally became the parish church.

Crossing the Rue General de Gaulle it is then just a short distance to the abbey church. As we reach the Place de la Bridolle we are immediately attracted to the south portal and its tympanum – a wonderful creation of the 12th century. It represents the Parousia (the Second Coming of Christ on earth). Inside, what remains of the magnificent treasure of Beaulieu Abbey is on display in a glass cabinet that can be illuminated, and which is close to the Chapter House. It contains the most exceptional item – the Virgin with the Child Jesus, a 12th century work in silver-plated wood. This Abbey Church is a great pilgrimage church, modelled on the likes of Saint-Cernin in Toulouse or Sainte-Foy in Conques, both of which we have visited. Listed as an historic monument since 1843, Beaulieu Abbey measures 71m long, 30m wide and 23m high under the dome. The nave is vast – 17m high and 60m long.

From the Abbey we walked again along the narrow streets between the ancient buildings to the Quai Docteur René Fougère and the banks of the silent and seemingly still Dordogne. As on 20 September last year it was a charming spectacle, the so calm and peaceful river, La Chapelle des Penitents, and Les Flots Bleus for a welcome cup of tea; it was all so quiet, yet quite a number of visitors were enjoying the experience. It seemed that the river set the tone of the occasion. Sitting on the grass bank we attempted to persuade a family of ducks to welcome some surplus croissants. They were not particularly interested; perhaps they had already been well fed or perhaps the croissants contained too much butter!

Eventually, we walked back to the Place du Champs du Mars. As we approached our car, we were surprised to see two gentlemen examining it rather purposely. We then noticed, parked alongside was a Saab Sports car with a Dutch registration. We realised that they were, in fact, admiring our car and a conversation quickly developed.

They exclaimed, "No more Saabs!", "Keep it!",

"It's all over; it is finished!"

Nine years later I still own it! We were told that their Saab was bought in Germany in 1998.

Finally, we were on our way back to Les Bedaines, which we reached at 18.00. The temperature was then 20°C.

(34 miles)

Day 28 – Monday, 26 September 2011

Another lovely morning! We would like to make a further visit to Argentat, but as we left the Office de Tourisme in Beaulieu rather hurriedly yesterday, we decided to first drive again to Beaulieu for a brief and last visit. It was 11.00 and 22°C. Having parked in the Place du Champs du Mars at 11.35 and walked into the Place Marbot we bought a copy of *Le Monde* and two cartes anniversaire. At the Office de Tourisme we didn't hesitate to purchase the book, *Le Limousin*, for €15.90 – it is excellent.

We lingered in Beaulieu for a while before driving along the beautiful 25km of the D12 which closely follows the north bank of the Dordogne, to ARGENTAT. At 14.10 we parked again near le Collège to walk the few yards down to the Quai Lestourgie; it was 24°C. Established on one of the stone seats, one is mesmerized observing the mighty Dordogne as it saunters by majestically, silently and serenely. The DORDOGNE rises on the flanks of the Puy de Sancy in the mountains of Auvergne and from the confluence of two small torrents, the Dore and the Dogne, above the town of Le Mont-Dore. Its westward course takes it through five departments and the ancient regions of the Limousin and Perigord, before flowing into the Gironde north of Bordeaux at the end of its 310-mile journey. In its upper regions the river passes through deep gorges, the fast-flowing water funnelling between cliffs and steep banks. In places dams have been formed to create long deep lakes. It is at Argentat that the nature of the river changes, where the valley widens into fertile farmland. The Dordogne is one of the great rivers of France.

It was little more than one year ago that we sat in this place, enjoying almost identical conditions. I have written about that visit on 19 September 2010 and referring to the role of Argentat as a commercial port in past centuries. Today, we sat outside the flower decorated L'Auberge des Cabariers and enjoyed cups of the (tea) menthe for €6. We walked along by the still, silent water and watched a wagtail splashing; butterflies under the willow trees; we fed two small ducks and a larger one; it was an idyllic setting! At 17.15 and with the temperature now 30°C we left this delightful spot. It was indeed our final visit to Le Quai at Argentat, one of our favourite sites of France. Margaret's record for the day simply ends, "5.50pm 'Home' to dinner".

(43 miles)

Day 29 – Tuesday, 27 September 2011

Sadly, today we must leave Les Bedaines, for the last time. We are immensely grateful to Anne and Jim for allowing us to share their home and their environment and for their welcome and their hospitality during the past nine years. It has been a unique experience for us and also our gateway to just some of the many gems of the Department of Corrèze, the southernmost department of the (former) Region of Le Limousin and nearby in the Lot Department, including Aubazine, Collonges-la-Rouge, Turenne, Cressensac, Curemonte, Carennac, Bretenoux, Castelnau as well as Beaulieu and Argentat. In fact, Anne and Jim have since retired from Les Bedaines, but we have been pleased to remain in contact with them.

It was a lovely morning again – 20°C – when, at 10.50, we left this 'Special Place' knowing that 'we will never see this place again'. After joining the D1120 for Argentat we stopped at 11.05 to buy petrol at the Elan Garage in St-Chamant – 45 litres – €1.66 per litre = €74.70.

Our destination for tonight is St Savin and this is a repeat of our journey on 21 September 2010. Climbing out of Argentat on the D18 we noticed large numbers of brown ferns and "Observation des cerfs' signs. At Marcillac la-Croisille it was market day. Although not on our route, about 10km west of Egletons is the village of SARRAN. With a population of less than 300, it saw the end of stage 12 of the 2020 Tour de France. Nearby is the Château de Bity which has an interesting history.

Construction began in the 12th century and was completed in the 18th century. During the period of ownership by William Noel Lucas-Shadwell, a former colonel of the British army and a member of the British secret services, it is believed that Léon Trotsky was a resident from 1933 to 1935. During the Second World War it sheltered resistants and then became a hospital. In 1969 it was acquired by Jacques and Bernadette Chirac and is still in the ownership of the Famille Chirac.

At 13.15 we left La Corrèze and entered the Department of Creuse. Felleton, then, at 13.50, we stopped for an hour at Aubusson, where we enjoyed refreshments sitting in the sun by the River Creuse – it was 30°C. Bénévent l'Abbaye was our next stop, at 16.15. Here for the third year in succession, we had our usual cups of tea – in glasses again – for €4. It was now 26°C. At 17.00 we began the final stage of today's journey and at 19.05 we arrived at Hôtel de France, St Savin to be greeted again by Bruno and given the key to – Chambre 20! A very good journey.

(187 miles)

Day 30 – Wednesday, 28 September 2011

As the year 1066 is imprinted on the minds of English children, the year 732 is established firmly on the minds of French children. It was the year of the BATTLE of TOURS or, as it is often called, the BATTLE of POITIERS. It was fought on 10 October 732 between forces under the Frankish leader Charles Martel and the massive invading Islamic army of Emir Abd-Er-Rahman Ibn-Abdallah El-Ghafiqui Ghafiqi. The Franks defeated the

Islamic army and Emir Abdul Rahman was killed. The success of Charles Martel in halting the northward advance of Islam from the Iberian Peninsula is considered by historians to be of great significance in that it halted the Islamic conquests, and preserved Christianity in Europe when Islam was overrunning the remains of the old Roman and Persian Empires. The Arab army retreated south over the Pyrénées. Undoubtedly the victory at Poitiers preserved Christianity as we know it. It would be another 700 years before the Ottomans managed to invade Europe via the Balkans.

CHARLES MARTEL was born in 689 and died in the year 741. Like his father, Pepin of Herstal, he was a Frankish statesman. He asserted his claims to power as successor to his father and he built on his father's work. He was a military leader and he began a series of military campaigns that re-established the Franks as the undisputed masters of all Gaul. His son Pepin le Bref became the first king of the Carolingian dynasty and his grandson, Charlemagne, became the first emperor in the West since the fall of Rome.

L'EMIR ABD-ER-RAHMAN was born in about 665. He ruled over Muslim Spain and was a very fair and devout warrior, a close relative of the Caliph of the Omayyad dynasty in Damascus. He landed in Spain for the first time in 721, when the Arab Conquest is in full expansion.

Despite the great importance of this battle, its exact location remains unknown. Most historians assume that the two armies met where the rivers Clain and

Vienne join between Poitiers and Tours. We would like to visit that site!

It was a lovely morning again and the temperature already 27°C when we left Hôtel de France at 11.48. We drove along the D951 in the direction of Poitiers until, at Chauvigny, taking the D749 along the right bank of the Vienne to Bellefonds. At Bonneuil-Matours we crossed the Vienne and on the D1 into Vouneuil-Vienne. We found the D15 and then followed the signs for MOUSSAIS-la-BATAILLE. Suddenly, after passing through the hamlet of Moussais, at 12.40 we reached the entrance sign – '732 – La Bataille de Poitiers – Musée de plein air'. Yes, no buildings, but a wonderful exposition illustrating the known history of the Battle, laid on the surface of the site and on raised display panels. Adjoining was a grassed area for picnics and where we had some refreshments. It was a lovely warm day – 29°C. A delightful spot with extensive views over the Châtelleraudais countryside – in the distance we noticed a goods train travelling along the other side of the Clain on its way to Châtellerault – and we had it all to ourselves! After nearly three hours we left, and Margaret noted, "Just the most amazing place with more history to learn".

We drove back to Vouneuil-Vienne and to the Office de Tourisme where we were greeted with, "Would you like a cup of tea?" In fact, we had a cup of tea and a cup of coffee. We had a very friendly conversation about our travels, family, etc. We bought a couple of books, a video and Madame added three postcards and some leaflets, etc., which she thought might interest us and gave us a souvenir bag in which to carry it all. She suggested that, before we left, we should visit l'Eglise Saint-Etienne close by. We then spent some while in the church before leaving Vouneuil at 16.55 to return to St Savin comfortably in time for le diner.

"A very interesting and pleasant afternoon".

(54 miles)

Day 31 – Thursday, 29 September 2011

Some years ago now, when we were planning a journey, to avoid an excessive distance in one day we felt that it would be wise to spend a night in the region of Poitiers and we found accommodation in the town of Saint-Savin-sur-Gartempe, in the Department of Vienne with a population of less than 1,000 and which we had never visited.

We have since been so happy to return to this hotel many times. In fact, this is our thirteenth and final sojourn at the Hôtel de France, in St Savin. Bruno and his whole team – kitchen staff, waitresses and domestic staff have always been so welcoming, helpful and friendly towards us. It has been a particular pleasure to have the friendship of Cécile and their two lovely little daughters, Bérénice and Honorine; we did not meet Valentin, who was born on 6 February 2013, "pour la plus grande joie de ses parents". On every visit we have had the use of the same spacious and comfortable room – Chambre 20 and we have particularly appreciated the view of the floodlit spire of the great Abbey Church.

We have now visited many towns and villages in this area of Vienne and beyond, including: Chauvigny, Bêthines, Villesalem, Villemort, Moussac, Antigny, Angles-sur-l'Anglin, Fontgombault, Montmorillon, Lussac-les-Château, Le Dorat, La Trimouille and La Brenne Natural Parc. Naturally, we did not wish to stray far from this place today. However, we spent a quiet time in the great Romanesque Abbey Church, which dates from the 11th century and contains remarkable wall paintings; we had to leave via the bookshop! We also had a nostalgic stroll along the banks of the Gartempe. We shall always associate the little village of Bêthines with our sojourns here and at 16.27 with the temperature 30°C we set off to make a final visit to that interesting little church. We had "Another read of all the interesting items re André-Hubert Fournet and Jeanne-Elizabeth Bichier". It was a short but interesting visit and at 18.00 we returned to the hotel to enjoy a last meal at our corner table in the restaurant.

(13 miles)

Day 32 – Friday, 30 September 2011

Bruno has always said that petit déjeuner is "when you want it" and so we enjoyed a leisurely breakfast this morning, before taking our various pieces of luggage to the car, while the staff were preparing for another new day and to welcome new guests. Before leaving Hôtel de France for the last time we were able to say "farewell and thank you" to Bruno and as we joined the car at the rear of the hotel some domestic staff were enjoying a drink in the sunshine and we were able to say "goodbye" to them also.

We are making another visit to Les Alpes Mancelles region and returning to the Hotel Ronsin for a couple of nights as we had hoped. Our route today will be the same as that on 22 September 2010. We left Hôtel de France at 11.10 in lovely weather with the temperature 23°C. At 11.20 we stopped at the Elan Garage for petrol – 39 litres - €1.59 per litre = €62. Another 'for the last time'! Angles-sur-l'Anglin was a 'Ville Fleurie' and then, soon into La Brenne country. At Liguel on the D59 we found a new road and new roundabout.

We reached Chinon at 13.55 where we stopped for a "drink and a bite" – 28°C. At 14.55 we left for Fresnay-sur-Sarthe, but could not resist a final visit to our favourite picnic spot under the trees at La Fleche – there were many ducks but we had no food for them – it was 33°C here. After 30 minutes, at 17.15, we left for the final stage of today's journey. We eventually arrived at Hôtel Ronsin, FRESNAY-sur-SARTHE at 19.30. It was now 23°C.

(182 miles, last year 187 miles)

Day 33 – Saturday, 1 October 2011

A quiet day, with no driving. It was a great pleasure to have the opportunity of further conversation with Didier at the Hôtel Ronsin. His reminiscences and impressions of living and working in England and then of his return to France were very interesting. A common site in France has always been of customers leaving their local boulangerie armed with a supply of baguettes for the day, sometimes doing so precariously while at the control of a bicycle. Didier told us that he had now seen instances in France of bread being supplied, not from a local boulangerie, but from a mobile van – he was horrified at this apparent erosion of a tradition.

It was on 24 September 2010 that we first visited this 'Little Town of Character' and I have written about that visit. However, we were very happy to have a second opportunity to enjoy its features, not least the lovely gardens midst the remains of the medieval castle. A memorable feature of last year's visit was descending the steep route from the castle's edge to the footbridge crossing of the River Sarthe. While on the bridge we exchanged a casual greeting with a passing couple and shortly afterwards we were joined by the gentleman, François, who invited us on a little journey through his garden down to the water's edge. We took photographs at that point. In addition, he invited us to help ourselves to some of his grapes and he indicated the position of their home. We were touched by his friendship and kindness and we resolved to visit Fresnay-sur-Sarthe again and to call at their home to give them copies of the photographs we had taken.

Today we had the photos with us, and it was our intention to visit their house. Unfortunately, however, it was a very warm day and we both felt that we did not have the energy to contemplate the steep return ascent to the gardens. We were very disappointed to have to abandon our plan. We were, however, able to identify our friends' property and we took photographs. We then reconciled ourselves to the intention of sending the photographs to François by post – we could ascertain the postal code; we knew the name of the road and we could describe the recognisable property. That was our plan and our disappointment subsided. Sadly, I have to admit now that we did not fulfil our intentions. However, we otherwise had a very enjoyable day ending with a meal in the restaurant.

(0 miles)

Day 34 – Sunday, 2 October 2011

It was 11.40 and time to leave Fresnay-sur-Sarthe and the region of Les Alpes Mancelles and to say a fond au revoir to Didier. We left Fresnay on the D310 for Mamers, where, instead of taking the bypass, we decided to drive into the centre of the town. We stopped when we became uncertain of the direction we should take. At this point an elderly gentleman approached us carrying une brosse – I think he had been brushing up the leaves – and gave us helpful directions on the D3, through Aillières-Beauvoir, on the edge of the Foret de Perseigne and to Le Mele-sur-Sarthe in the department of Orne, which is twinned with Faringdon. The D6 took us to Ste-Scolasse-sur-Sarthe and to Moulins-le-Marche; the D932 to Ste-Gauburge-Ste-Colombe and then the D31 through a very extensive forest where much timber had been cut, for a return visit to St-EVROULT-NOTRE-DAME-du-BOIS. It was now 13.40 and time for a break. We parked near the lake, as we did last year, to enjoy some refreshment. It was a very pleasant 23C. We walked around the garden and the ruins of the Ancienne Abbaye. Unfortunately, there was no access to any of the buildings; perhaps some were open to the public earlier in the year. I have written about our visit on Sunday, 27 June 2010 and particularly regarding the remarkable life of one, Orderic Vital.

At 15.25 we began the last stage of today's journey, to Vienne-en-Bessin. Our route now is the D13 to Gacé and the historic village of Chambois, which witnessed the closure of the Falaise Pocket, following some of the most bitter fighting, and the end of the Battle of Normandy in 1944. With a population of about 400, on 1 January 2017 Chambois was merged to form a new commune of Gouffern-en-Auge. Its name may not now appear on the map, but the historic site, the crossroads, will remain! Continuing on the D13 through Trun and then the D63 to Falaise, the route of the escaping German armies as they were mercilessly bombed. At Falaise at 16.45, it was certainly time for a cup of tea. Along Rue Georges Clemenceau to park near l'Eglise Saint-Gervais, we soon found a salon de thé or a bar where we enjoyed some "Good cups of tea". It was 30°C here!

FALAISE, with a population of around 8,000, suffered greatly during 1944, two-thirds of the town being destroyed by bombing before being taken by Canadian and Polish troops. During the Great War it lost 274 men. Since 1974 it has been twinned with Henley-on-Thames. On 11 November 2012 we were pleased to watch a celebration of la messe from Falaise – I think, in the church of Sainte Trinite.

The year is 2011, and what a significant year in which to be visiting Normandy – 1,100 years after it was founded. Normandy grew from the Treaty of

Saint-Clair-sur-Epte of 911, between King Charles III of West Francia and Rollo, leader of the Vikings.

We left Falaise at 17.40, after nearly an hour, and first took the D6 and then followed a familiar route – Thury-Harcourt – Villers-Bocage – Tilly-s-Seulles – Bayeux to Les Châtaigniers, Vienne-en-Bessin at 19.25. We were very pleased to meet Fabienne again and to establish ourselves in our usual room for the next four nights.

(142 miles)

Day 35 – Monday, 3 October 2011

I am sure we have visited Arromanches more than any other village or town in France and at 12.22, with the temperature 25°C, we set off again on the five-mile journey, via Ryes, to park, as we have always been able to do, in the free car park near the little supermarket and the école maternelle at 12.40. We walked the short distance down the Boulevard Gilbert Longues and into the pedestrianised rue Marechal Joffre where we did some shopping in the inviting magasin de journaux. Rather than carry the items around for the next few hours we decided to return them to the car. However, Margaret was anxious to avoid unnecessary walking and I left her on a vacant seat at the entrance to rue Marechal Joffre and opposite le 6 juin restaurant and with *Le Monde* to read. When I returned, I was surprised to find her in conversation with a couple. She introduced me by saying, "It's alright, you can say Good Morning". Our newfound friends were John and Joan and they came from St Ives in Cornwall. Apparently, they had been very cautious to join Margaret as, seeing her reading *Le Monde*, they assumed that she was French. We had a very long and interesting conversation and were soon joined by daughter Suzanne who was their chauffeur. They were, in fact, spending a couple of nights in Arromanches. Eventually we said goodbye but anticipating that we would meet again, as indeed we did.

Today ARROMANCHES has about 500 inhabitants and is very much a tourist town with endless streams of visitors. Their main interest is the seafront with the Musée du Débarquement and the remains of the famous Mulberry Harbour, which local people have been proud to describe to us as 'Port Winston'. Indeed, it was a remarkable accomplishment – an artificial port which by 12 June 1944 had enabled 300,000 men, 54,000 vehicles and 104,000 tons of supplies to be landed. It was remarkable too that, as we have been told, there were no Germans in Arromanches on D-Day. In fact, Arromanches was not attacked from the sea. The town was liberated on the afternoon of D-Day by the 1st Battalion Royal Hampshire Regiment who landed on Gold Beach and descended upon the town from the heights of St Come to the east. There were six civilian deaths. However, Arromanches has other interesting features and we walked around the town. The 19th century Parish Church of Saint Peter is particularly interesting with many items that are registered as historical objects, such as its stained-glass windows.

As the evening approached it was feeling rather cooler, but people were still in the sea at 19.00. Time for another meal at le 6 juin, including jus de fruits – orange and pineapple – and glace chocolat et menthe. At 20.15 we left Arromanches – still 22°C – and reached Les Châtaigniers at 20.35 where it was only 15°C!

(10 miles)

Day 36 – Tuesday, 4 October 2011

As we had already arranged, at 14.40 we left the farm to visit Paulette and Herve in Bayeux; it was only about six miles. We had a most enjoyable afternoon and we felt hat we acquitted ourselves well in solely French speaking company. We have so much in common and there is much to talk about. As we left at 17.35, we were presented, "avec beaucoup de pommes de l'arbre a La Riviere!" La Riviere is the previous home of Paulette and Herve, which is now occupied by their son and where we have had the privilege of sojourning.

While in Bayeaux we drove to our Esso Station Service to fill the tank – 56 litres – €1.54 per litre = €86.24. We were back at Fabienne's at 18.00 – 19°C, but straightaway continued to Arromanches for le diner at 18.30. Afterwards we bade farewell to Suzanne and her Mum and Dad, who pleaded with us to visit them in St Ives and they gave us their telephone number and e-mail address. Our meeting has added to our many fond memories of Arromanches.

(In fact, we never made that journey to St Ives and, in the meantime, Margaret and also John have died. However, I am pleased to say that we established contact with Joan and John, and, in 2020, I remain in contact with Joan.)

We left at 21.10 for the five-mile journey, through Ryes to Vienne-en-Bessin. We have driven along this route at this time of the evening many times and have met very little traffic. Tonight, we recorded that we passed three rabbits and we saw a vehicle travelling along the D12 between Bayeux and Creully, before we reached the junction. It was 21.30 and 17°C when we reached 'home'!

(23 miles)

Day 37 – Wednesday, 5 October 2011

Poets of the Great War are well remembered – Wilfred Owen, Seigfried Sassoon, Rupert Brooke, Laurence Binyon, Edmund Blunden, John McCrae, etc. Poets of the Second World War are less so. However, one lies near where he died, in the fields of Normandy. KEITH DOUGLAS was born in 1920 and was an Exhibitioner of Merton College, Oxford where he was a student of Edmund Blunden. He served in the North African campaign and on the 6 June 1944, he took part in the D-Day invasion of Normandy. On 9 June as his unit was pinned down on high ground overlooking Tilly-sur-Seulles and, while making a personal reconnaissance, he was killed by a German mortar. His chaplain buried him by a hedge close to where he had died. After the war his remains were reburied in the Tilly-sur-Seulles War Cemetery.

It is the penultimate day of our journey and at 12.36 we left Les Châtaigniers to drive the 18 miles to Tilly-sur-Seulles War Cemetery, which is situated on high ground above the village, to visit the grave of Keith Douglas. We parked at the roadside opposite the entrance to le Cimetière at 13.25 – it was a pleasant day with the temperature 19°C in this peaceful spot. We made directly for the register of burials and found that his grave was in plot 1, row E, grave number 2; it was easy to find.

On his tombstone is inscribed –

"CAPTAIN K.C. DOUGLAS
2nd DERBYSHIRE YEOMANRY – ATTD.
THE NOTTINGHAMSHIRE YEO.
ROYAL ARMOURED CORPS – 9th JUNE
1944 – AGE 24 – POET. ARTIST.
PHIL. IV. 8 'THESE THINGS' HE LOVED –
HE DIED IN THEIR DEFENCE".

We had been joined by another couple who were already in the Cemetery. They were from Halifax, but the lady's home was St Ives! They like France too, but they were much more widely travelled than us – Thailand, for example!

After more than two hours in the Cemetery, which contains 1,222 graves of which 986 are British, we returned to the car to contemplate the scene. At 15.40 Margaret recorded that we, "Had (late) tablet and bars and a drink of water".

There was still time to visit another historic site, but of a much earlier century. From Tilly-sur-Seulles the D13 took us to Balleroy and through the forest to

CERISY-la-FORET, which is in the department of Manche. A commune with about 1,000 inhabitants; the area has been occupied since antiquity. The Ancienne Abbaye of Saint Vigor was founded in 1032 by Robert the Magnificent for the Benedictine Order, on the site of the hermitage of Saint Vigor, Bishop of Bayeux. It was remodelled in the 13th and 14th centuries and the nave was separated from its western façade in 1812. Only a small section of the original building remains. We reached the Abbaye at 16.20 and spent nearly an hour walking around the leisure grounds, including a lake, and photographing the Abbey and various pieces of modern sculpture. It was all very pleasant – 22°C – and enjoyable. At 17.55 we returned home to "think about le diner!" Tonight, it had to be AU 6 JUIN! We arrived at the restaurant at 18.35 and our last meal was croque madame and fruit salads. Lovely! was the verdict. A most enjoyable evening of two hours and a quarter, leaving at 20.50. We were home at 21.10 and it was still 18°C.

A very interesting and enjoyable day!

(62 miles)

Day 38 – Thursday, 6 October 2011

We have reached the end of our final sojourn at Les Châtaigniers and indeed the final day of our final journey. We have so much enjoyed our many stays at the farm in Vienne-en-Bessin, particularly in the gite with George and Samuel; the rural environment and the cows just the other side of the fence reminding us of our home at Camerton for so many years. We bid a fond farewell and very grateful thanks to Fabienne for our 'home' on so many occasions and, at 11.30, we sadly drove away for the last time. The temperature was 16°C.

We did not head for Bayeux and the N13 direct route to Cherbourg. No, we must make a final visit to Arromanches. In fact, we spent almost two hours in the little town which has become a favourite. It was 13.45 when we finally left the car park in Arromanches to drive along the interesting coastal route – D514 – through Tracy-s-Mer to Longues-s-Mer. Just inland from Longues-s-Mer is the little village of Vaux-sur-Aure with a population of about 300. An objective of the 2nd South Wales Borders on D-Day was the bridge here over the Aure – by midnight they had captured the bridge. Vaux was Fabienne's father's home! Next, to Commes (twinned with Brampford Speke) and Port-en-Bessin. At St-Laurent-s-Mer we faced a route barrée sign and we were directed along the D517 to FORMIGNY. We were pleased to have done so, when we discovered that it was the site of the penultimate battle of the Hundred Years' War, on 15 April 1450. Unfortunately, the Office de Tourisme was not open, but we spent a little time walking around the site and took a photograph of the impressive memorial to the French victory, which was created early in the 20th century. We also photographed the memorial to the dead of the Great War.

From Formigny we then joined the N13 for Cherbourg. At 15.00 we were passing St-Mere-Eglise and at 15.35 we saw the sign for Tourlaville and 'Car Ferries'. On reaching the ferry port at 15.45 we were very disappointed to discover that, instead of returning to Poole on the Barfleur we would be crossing to Portsmouth on a 'fast craft' type vessel! Subsequently, we realised that we had been booked to return on the Normandy Express at 17.30. However, while happily driving around France for five to six weeks we had given little thought to our return to England – it would simply happen in due time.

I have described our outward journey on 30 August as a wonderful crossing. The return journey did not promise to be anything of the kind – in fact, we anticipated stormy weather and we were warned straightaway to remain seated. For nearly two and a half hours we were tossed about by the winds and alarmed by the waves crashing against the windows near us. As we neared the entrance to Portsmouth harbour, Margaret decided that she should attempt to reach the toilettes not far behind us – she succeeded, by using the various structures for support. As I realised how long she had been away I frequently looked behind to see if she was returning. A lady sitting behind me obviously recognised my concern and came and asked if I would like her to check that Margaret was alright. It was just at that moment that Margaret reappeared to make her way back to her seat; but what a kind thought it was of a complete stranger! It was with great relief that we eventually docked. The diary record reads, "10 to 8 off Ferry after horrific crossing – really frightening." It was indeed the worst crossing Margaret and I had experienced in some thirty years. We spent some time in a queue for security checks before leaving the port and joining the M27; the continuing stormy weather made the journey very unpleasant all the way to Trowbridge where we encountered a most unwelcome scene.

As we left home on 30 August, we were well aware of extensive road works in the vicinity, but we assumed they would have been completed by the time we returned. That was certainly not the case as when we drove down the West Ashton Road towards Trowbridge and past the Service Station, there was much evidence of continuing works. When we reached the entrance to Green Lane, we were shocked – it was closed – completely. We could see our gates, but there was no means of reaching them. We simply sat in the car speechless; we did not know what to do. Although we had lived here for nearly 15 years, we had always used this entrance to Green Lane, and we were not familiar with an access from the opposite direction. However, we had to find a way and we began to explore the area further until we found a way into Green Lane from the opposite direction. What a relief it was when we eventually drove through our gates at about 22.30. Margaret recorded, "Green Lane at last!" and even found the energy to record the temperature – it was 13°C - and our mileage.

(154 miles)

At the moment of leaving France we had had a wonderful journey, and we travelled a total of 2,544 miles! Indeed, we regarded it as the pinnacle of our *'France – A Journey'*, and we hoped that the descent would not be too steep or too sudden. Unfortunately, our return to England was in complete contrast.

I had recorded the first 25 days of this journey by April 2013 and, I am sure, Margaret would have read much of it. However, on 24 July 2013, the Consultant Psychiatrist diagnosed that she was suffering from Mixed Alzheimer's and Vascular Dementia. At that point our lives took a different direction, although I had experienced instances of unsound memory during the two preceding years, even during the journey I have been describing; also, friends in France had suspected dementia in September 2011. Nevertheless, Margaret had continued to maintain her usual comprehensive record of our travels. It is now, when preparing a narrative of her diaries, that I have realized that some of her neatness and orderliness had left her, although her determination to continue the task clearly remained.

It has been a great pleasure for me to review Margaret's diary and what I had written about our first 25 days and to relive the final 13 days of a truly memorable journey. Those 38 days with 15 different stopovers and 2,544 miles were indelibly imprinted on the memory. I hope this record will be of interest and pleasure to others.

AUGUST/OCTOBER 2011

Congratulating our 'chauffeurs', Suzi and Kastor,
after an exhilarating tour through
the narrow streets of ancient Cahors.

By TGV to L'HERAULT

JUNE 2013 (Tuesday, 28 May – Friday, 21 June)

Our first family holiday in France was in 1979 and is recorded in my *'A Miscellany of Writings'* and in Part 1. It is still well remembered for, towards the end, our car (Hillman Minx FHW 11D) broke down in Herbignac, Brittany; we had to abandon it and we returned home via a hired car, the ferry from Cherbourg to Weymouth, a train to Frome and a taxi to our home in Camerton. The problem was relatively minor, but it was not possible to obtain a replacement part in the time available; the car was returned some weeks later and the necessary repair was so insignificant that I never received a bill. It was in no small measure due to the kindness and help of the local garage proprietor in Herbignac, Monsieur Cloarec, in taking us to temporary accommodation, as well as his continuing efforts to effect a repair, that we have had the confidence and trust to return to France every year until 2011.

In 1981, we made our first foray into the southern Languedoc-Roussillon Region. From the moment we experienced the warmth emanating from the buildings in Pézenas in the late evening of 11 August 1981 and, on the following day, setting foot on the shore of the Mediterranean, we developed a lasting fondness for the Hérault Department. We liked the southern climate, the temperatures, the vineyards, the boules and the pattern of daily life – the three-hour lunch periods, shops open till 8.00 pm, the somewhat relaxed, casual, easy-going way of life and the warmth of the red roofs! There are also many historic and interesting sites in the area.

We would like to experience it for a final time, but after our long and unforgettable journeys of 2011 we did not contemplate a further such car journey. Perhaps we could do so, travelling by train to Agde and sojourning again in the apartment at Cap d'Agde which had been our 'summer home' in 10 consecutive years until 2011. We could not only relax and enjoy life in a Mediterranean environment, but also 'observe' life and events in the region we know, as recorded in the excellent daily newspaper, *Midi Libre*.

At the beginning of 2012 we had reserved accommodation for a period in June. However, the regular dressing of Margaret's ankle ulcer, the unrelenting arthritis in her feet and legs and then the onset of her memory problems early in the year, regarding which we were kept waiting very many months for an appointment with a consultant, cast constant doubts on the wisdom of attempting such a journey – we cancelled the arrangements made.

Cometh 2013, we made similar plans except that we could not return to our 'summer home', but we could have an acceptable alternative. During the ensuing months, amidst frequent and considerable doubts, we took successive steps towards another and more

JUNE 2013 (TUESDAY, 28 MAY – FRIDAY, 21 JUNE)

demanding 'adventure'. We renewed our passports and later booked seats on trains and made a reservation at Hotel Lille Europe. But still the doubts and uncertainties kept recurring; I simply did not know if we were acting sensibly; in particular, whether we would be able to meet the physical demands involved in boarding and disembarking from trains in view of Margaret's disability and the amount of luggage we would need. However, as we were advised, the only certain way to find out would be simply to go; we were also assured that "people are very kind".

It was, therefore, with a measure of relief that the appointed day – Tuesday 28 May – arrived!

We had ordered a taxi to collect us at 09.00; it was waiting at the gate at 08.55 – a good start, but it was raining! The taxi driver was very helpful and pleasant. At Trowbridge Station we were able to keep dry in the small shelter on the platform. Our train was due at 09.27 and, although not on time, it was not unduly late. We succeeded in boarding without help and found our seats, or so we thought. It was not long before the conductress arrived and pointed out that we had booked first class travel and she assisted us into our seats in the appropriate compartment. Opposite us was a lady, sitting alone and reading. Inevitably, there was soon communication between us, firstly by facial expressions, soon followed by verbal contact which developed into interesting conversation and indeed some very wide and varied conversation which continued throughout the journey. Our train was due to reach London Waterloo at 11.49 and for all I know it may well have arrived on time for we had found the subjects of our conversation so interesting that we had barely noticed the towns we had passed through, Salisbury, Basingstoke, etc., etc. Ann, from Bradford-on-Avon, had told us that she was on her way to Colchester to meet a cousin who was visiting this country from Australia. Before we said farewell, she made a note of our e-mail address and promised to contact us after our return from France. We could not have had a more welcoming introduction to our journey, which we had undertaken with some trepidation.

As it was the terminus, and as we had ample time, we did not rush to leave the train, but as we began to do so we noticed a 'young' gentleman looking in from the platform; he came in to meet us and asked if we required some help. Without waiting for an answer he took some of our luggage and led us off the train; when hearing that the next stage of our journey was to find a taxi to take us to St Pancras, he said, I will take you to the taxis as I am going in that direction to visit a friend. What a kind spontaneous gesture that had been! Soon we were at the head of the queue, but before being assisted into the taxi we were able to say a final good-bye to Ann who had followed us to the taxis. I do not know what my image of a London taxi driver had been; I doubt if I had ever travelled by such means, but it certainly did not match our driver. He was young, well-spoken, courteous, polite, friendly and helpful and our 20 minutes or so journey was another enjoyable experience. He took us as near to the entrance to St Pancras Station as he was able to do and told us what we would find inside, particularly how much of the original station

June 2013 (Tuesday, 28 May – Friday, 21 June)

had been preserved during the course of its conversion to meet the needs of an international terminus. As we left him, we mentioned to our driver that we would be making the reverse journey on 21 June and said, jokingly, perhaps we might meet again, to which he replied that it did once happen to him.

We had never been to St Pancras Station before and we felt in awe of its spacious grandeur, but where was the station? First, we followed the sign for 'Toilets', but we found no toilets. Enquiries at two commercial premises revealed the probable location of temporary toilets; we found them, but the gentlemen's department was 'Out of Service'. There were many travellers seeking the same facility and, ignoring the sign and the barrier, we found that they were only being cleaned; the work had to be temporarily suspended. Yes, this is an international rail terminus! Whilst waiting outside we had been confused with a queue for taxis! On returning to the main foyer, seats were in short supply but as soon as two were vacated we took possession. We were glad to have the opportunity to sit, to have some refreshment and to collect our thoughts.

I had understood that there were some services for the disabled available here, although they could only be requested when making train reservations by phone – I had booked our seats online! However, I began to reconnoitre the area and soon noticed some premises referring to the 'handicapped'; we both made our way to this 'office' and enquired if it would be possible for us to have some assistance in boarding our train, etc. We were relieved to hear that, of course, we could have their services and all the details of our journey were taken and we were invited to sit in the waiting area. Well before the time of our train we were accompanied and helped through the border controls, etc., to a waiting area and, at the appropriate time, led the considerable distance along the platform to the entrance to our compartment. We were assisted on to the train, our luggage placed on the racks and our escort did not leave us until we were safely in our seats. This was a very welcome and helpful service which was much appreciated. As we sat expectantly, how nice it was to receive a text from Ian in Bath informing us that our train would leave on time; it did, at 15.04.

EUROSTAR services between Waterloo and Paris and Brussels began on 14 November 1994 and the London terminus was transferred to St Pancras International on 14 November 2007. The 18 coach trains are 394 metres long and run at speeds of up to 186 mph. In July 2003 a Eurostar train on a test run reached a record top speed of 334.7 kph (208 mph).

We moved imperceptibly from the platform, but soon began speeding through the outskirts of London. We did not find the journey of 69 miles from St. Pancras to the Channel Tunnel particularly interesting, as much of the route seems to be underground.

The CHANNEL TUNNEL was formally opened by Queen Elizabeth II and President Mitterrand on 6 May 1994. It comprises two train tunnels and a service tunnel. It is 50.5 km. (31.4 miles) long and is the longest undersea rail tunnel in the world and the second longest rail tunnel in the world. The deepest point below sea level the tunnel reaches is 195 metres.

After travelling through the tunnel at 100 miles per hour, mainly under the sea, for 20 minutes one is conscious of a stirring, a reawakening, as we break into the open countryside of France and our speed increases. We reached Lille Europe at 17.26, after a journey of only 82 minutes from the centre of London. As we approached la Gare, along with a number of other passengers, we had to arouse ourselves and make our way to our luggage and the exit. Obviously struggling somewhat as we disembarked, willing hands were instantly offered, simultaneously with our name being called from the platform; it was our escort from SNCF who had been advised of our arrival details by the staff at St Pancras. It was very comforting to be then assisted to a lift and then to the reception area of the handicapé centre. To our amazement this was not the end of the service. We were asked what our plans were; were we continuing our journey on another train or did we require a hotel for the night? On being told that we had made a reservation at Hotel Lille Europe nearby, they immediately said, "We will take you there" and, in fact, our escort remained with us until we were clearly in the care of the receptionist at the hotel. This was a remarkable service which we had no idea existed; in our circumstances it was a great relief to have this kind of help and support; what is more, we were told that, providing we returned to the centre in the morning at least 30 minutes before our train was due to leave, they would see us safely on our journey.

We had, in fact, unknowingly experienced the 'Accès Plus' service which, I have since been assuredly told, is available at every station throughout France. It is a free service for travellers of reduced mobility but <u>should</u> be booked 48-hours before the departure time of the train.

We have stayed at HOTEL LILLE EUROPE on a number of occasions; it provides very convenient, satisfactory and comfortable accommodation when travelling into France by train and for visiting the city of Lille itself. It is situated about 200 metres from both Lille Europe Station and Lille Flanders Station; in fact, midway between them. Close by is the entrance to a station on the Lille Metro; incidentally, this underground rail system is operated by driverless trains, which run on rubber tyred wheels and all stations have doors between the platform and the trains. Hotel Lille Europe does not have a restaurant but provides a wide-ranging choice for petit déjeuner extending over a long session and each room is equipped with a cold drink's cabinet.

Our room was on the third floor and the view was of the rear of other tall buildings, but we are here for one night only. After settling into our room, we enjoyed the 'all-day breakfast' sandwich purchased from Tesco on the previous day, together with drinks from the cabinet; fortunately, it was followed by a welcome good night's sleep. We look forward to petit déjeuner here and this was no exception. It is served on the first floor in the glazed corner of the building with views of both stations, the park and of prominent buildings of the city beyond. We enjoyed a very adequate petit déjeuner before returning to our room to prepare to leave.

JUNE 2013 (TUESDAY, 28 MAY – FRIDAY, 21 JUNE)

Although only a short distance, the walk to Lille Europe Station and negotiating the lift with our four cases was difficult without the assistance we had had on the previous evening. However, it was with a feeling of relief that we reached the handicapé centre with ample time to spare before our train was due to leave at 11.02; we felt we were then in safe hands. Whilst waiting we noted that our train originated in Boulogne and would terminate its journey at Perpignan, a very long journey from the north coast to the south coast; our train journey would end at Agde. At the appropriate time we were assisted to the lift and down to the platform and, what is most helpful, to the precise spot where the door to our compartment would stop. Margaret was helped to board by two SNCF staff and our luggage was put on the racks and we were accompanied to our seats. For all this, we were profoundly grateful, and we thanked our escort.

We were then very glad that we had chosen to travel in the first-class compartment, for it provided us with very comfortable reclining seats with ample leg room, arm rests, drop down table, power point and, most importantly, it was a wide window seat. We could now relax and look forward to enjoying the next five and half hours viewing the changing scenes as we speed smoothly and quietly through the countryside of France. We have travelled on a TGV before, but it is still a rare and exciting experience for us.

The idea of a TRAIN à GRANDE VITESSE rail system in France was first proposed in the 1960s; it was developed during the 1970s by Alstom and SNCF.

Construction of an electric high-speed line from Paris to Lyon began in 1976 and the first TGV service with paying passengers left Paris on 27 September 1981. Since then the service has expanded to connect 220 cities and towns across France and into neighbouring countries. There are now some 550 TGVs operating over about 2,000 kilometres of track at speeds of up to 320 km/h (200 mph). By 2013 total passengers had reached 2 billion; the network in France now carries about 110 million passengers a year. Remarkably, in three decades the TGV has not recorded a single fatality due to accident while running at high speed; what is more the system makes a profit – in 2007 the SNCF generated profits of 1.1 billion euros! On 3 April 2007 a test train set a record, reaching 574.8 km/h (357.2 mph).

Many of the TGV routes run on dedicated track and do not pass through recognisable places served by the conventional system. Sometimes the link with large cities is situated at new stations in the suburbs or in open countryside. Consequently, although we have a miniature atlas, it is often impossible to identify exactly where we are; a plan of the route would, therefore, be interesting! However, we are familiar with the landscape for the first part of the journey.

After leaving Lille (at 11.02), TGV Nord soon begins to run alongside the A1 Autoroute for a considerable distance, passing between Lens and Arras on one side and Douai and Cambrai on the other; names which remind us that this is a region which witnessed the horrors of the Great War. We then pass close by

June 2013 (Tuesday, 28 May – Friday, 21 June)

Bapaume, and we are in the area of the 1916 Battle of the Somme. We have visited Bapaume and we have a Christmas card sent by my father to my mother (she was then 17 and they were not yet married) from this town in December 1918. A little further on, we are near Rancourt which was our base for tours of the Somme Battlefield in the years 2000 and 2001. We have stood on the bridges which cross the autoroute and the railway, to watch the traffic and the trains below, when on our way to Combles and Guillemont. Further south, at Ablaincourt-Pressoir about ten kilometres from Péronne, on 21 December 1993, a TGV derailed at 190 mph at the site of Haute Picardie TGV Station before it was built. Rain had caused a cavity to open up under the track; it dated from the First World War but had not been detected during construction work. The front power car and four carriages derailed but remained aligned with the track. Of 200 passengers one was slightly injured. After lying side by side for some 120 km (75 miles), the A1 and TGV Nord go their separate ways near Compeigne. It is an interesting part of the journey and while travelling parallel with the Autoroute, the relative speeds of the train and fast-moving road vehicles appear to give the impression that vehicles being overtaken on the road are travelling backwards! During past centuries this area saw much mining activity and we pass close by a familiar slagheap.

Now we head into less familiar territory, though still in the Région de Picardie. The weather is bright and generally sunny, but with some clouds; excellent for identifying features of the landscape. It is generally flat agricultural land with crops of colourful rape being prominent; there are a number of fermes d'éoliennes (Greek *Aiolos* – the god of the winds) producing energy, we hope. At 11.55 we reach Charles de Gaulle Aéroport and, as we are about to descend underground, an aircraft comes in to land ahead of us.

AEROPORT CHARLES de GAULLE (also known as Roissy Airport) is situated 25 kilometres north east of Paris and it extends over an area of 32 square kilometres. Its planning and construction began in 1966 and it was opened in March 1974. It is France's largest airport and in 2012 it handled more than 61 million passengers (equivalent to the total population of the country) and nearly 500,000 aircraft movements. It is the world's seventh busiest airport and Europe's second busiest after Heathrow.

We spent all of five minutes here before continuing our journey at 12.00, but not for long. At 12.10 we stopped at Marne La Vallée – Chessy. MARNE LA VALLEE is a large new town, developed since the 1960's, in the eastern suburbs of Paris, and CHESSY is a commune therein, in which is located Disneyland Paris. We then begin the longest and, no doubt, the fastest run of our journey, approaching 200 miles per hour. The countryside is more undulating, with small villages, churches, farmsteads and herds of grazing cattle and, noticeably, more trees. There are the inevitable pylons distributing essential energy – to enable us to travel in this mode of transport, for instance. As we continue to 'glide' silently and smoothly, and yet at a speed of more than three miles per minute, the scene is changing constantly and rapidly, as is the

JUNE 2013 (TUESDAY, 28 MAY – FRIDAY, 21 JUNE)

weather – now we see storms over distant hills, and moments later the horizon is bathed in sunshine. The distance from Paris to Lyon is about 300 miles and, at 14.00, after less than 110 minutes we arrive at Lyon Part-Dieu; what an exhilarating experience!

LYON, capital of Rhône-Alpes Region, is the third city of France; its conurbation is second to that of Paris and it has an overall metropolitan population of more than two million inhabitants. It is a UNESCO World Heritage Site and one which we have long hoped to visit. East of the Rhône lies modern Lyon and the urban centre of PART-DIEU, incorporating the shopping centre and rail terminal and dominated by the Tour Swiss Life. GARE PART-DIEU is the city's main station; it was constructed from 1978 and opened in 1983 and has 11 platforms; in 2010 it served 51 million passengers. We see many of the monsters – the power units – which operate the transport system and also double-decker trains of the TER Rhône-Alpes regional rail network. TER (Transport Express Régional) is a part of SNCF but is heavily subsidised by the State. Here, it is evident that SNCF is a huge organisation providing a vast network of services.

After leaving Lyon, we cross the Rhône and the scenery becomes a little more 'southern', often flat, but with dark distant hills in the direction of the Alps. VALENCE is the capital of the Drôme Department; it is on the left bank of the Rhône and 100 km. south of Lyon. However, the TGV Gare, which was opened in 2001, is 10 km. north-east of the town; we reached it at 14.40. Valence marks the northern band of olive cultivation and, apparently, there is a local saying that "At Valence the Midi begins". Certainly, as we continue, the scenery has a distinct 'southern' flavour; it becomes more mountainous and rocky – the Vercors plateaux and mountains lie to the east. We are clearly heading south as vineyards and warm red roofs become a feature. I was disappointed not to be able to identify the spectacular Pont du Gard, before reaching Nimes, as we did some years ago; are we now on new track? The Pont du Gard was built as part of the aqueduct carrying water from the hills to the city. We arrive at Nimes at 15.30.

NIMES, capital of the Gard Department in the Languedoc-Roussillon Region, has a rich history dating back to Roman times. The Amphitheatre dates from the end of the 2nd century; we recall walking around it some years ago. Although served by the TGV network, our journey now is not on high-speed track and this route is unlikely to be upgraded for some years to come. Our next stop is at Montpellier at 16.00.

MONTPELLIER is the capital of Languedoc-Roussillon Region and also of the Department of Hérault; it has a population of about 255,000. Significantly, it has no Roman or Greek history, having been founded in the late 10th century by the combination of two hamlets; however, it is a very interesting city and has been a major centre for the teaching of medicine. Our recollection of a visit many years ago was being in the Cathédrale while an organist was preparing for a recital that evening. We were invited to attend, but as it did not begin until 21.00 we were not able to do so.

June 2013 (Tuesday, 28 May – Friday, 21 June)

At 16.20 we arrive at the penultimate stop on our journey, at SETE. Sète is a port and seaside resort and is built upon and around Mont St Clair; it is known as a centre of water jousting, which we have witnessed! The route from Sète to Agde is most certainly not high speed, for it is along the narrow strip of land between the salt water lake of Bassin de Thau on our right and the Méditerranée on our left; it is very attractive.

We were due at Agde at 16.36; I am not sure exactly at what time we arrived, but in view of the time we left Sète our arrival could not have been more than a few minutes late. Again, we were met as we descended from the train; after it had left we were assisted across the tracks and around the side of the station to the waiting taxi, which had been arranged for us. Our journey of some five and half hours had been excellent, trouble free, enjoyable and interesting.

AGDE is a port on the Canal du Midi and is one of the oldest villages in France, dating from 525 BC. In the 5th century it was the centre of a Greek colony. The distinctive black basalt used in its local buildings, such as the 12th century Cathédrale, is a particular feature. At the present time, Agde holds the unenviable record of the highest rate of unemployment of any commune in Metropolitan France.

Yes, a taxi was waiting for us and it was to be another experience of care, concern and kindness. It is remarkable how the recognition of someone needing assistance ignites a particular attribute in human character; it is certainly not restricted by national frontiers, as we have experienced and welcomed on many such occasions in France; as well as being a natural instinct, the requirement to assist is inscribed in French law. As Margaret was having some difficulty in entering the taxi the driver insisted on moving his car to a position where the pavement was lower so that it would be easier for her. As we set off for le Cap we were in exclusively French speaking company for the first time since leaving home. Our driver was interested to know what we were able to tell him about our journey and in no time, it seemed, we reached our destination. We were then instructed to wait in the car until the driver had visited the reception office to advise them of our circumstances and that we would need transport to take us to our apartment. The fare for the journey amounted to €20.30, but we were told to pay €20.00 only. We were very grateful for the 'service' we had received, and we thanked the driver with the customary handshakes. Perhaps we shall see him again.

We were very pleased and relieved to have arrived and to renew our acquaintance with staff. There was one essential matter to be attended to; they had not yet collected the balance of the charge for our apartment as authorised. We were soon very much aware that the weather here in the south of France was no better than that we had left at home; indeed, there were complaints of the unpleasant and persistent northerly winds. However, we were quickly transported in a small 'vehicle' and escorted to our apartment, which, fortunately, faced in a southerly direction; of course, it was not the one we had occupied in the past, but it was

June 2013 (Tuesday, 28 May – Friday, 21 June)

roomy, comfortable, satisfactory, and had a view of the sea. We would be happy here for the next three weeks!

My first priority was to obtain some food and drink and, leaving Margaret in the apartment, I set off on the short distance to the shops to purchase the essential items for the next day or two; it was a great pleasure to be greeted by familiar commerçants. Unfortunately, when I returned with our shopping I realised that, in my anxiety to obtain some supplies quickly, I had forgotten to take the key enabling me to regain access to the building – I then had to continue, with my bags of shopping, all the way back to the office to obtain a second key. Fortunately, when I reached home all was well. After our usual first meal of cold ham, etc., etc., there was the bed to prepare, etc., but we were comfortably established and more than ready for a good night's sleep by midnight.

Life is inevitably restricted physically nowadays, and our somewhat mundane routine is centred around regular medication, ulcer dressing and meals, but we are relieved, for the time being, of the multitude of other tasks and responsibilities we have left at home. Shopping is a matter of, as and when, according to our needs; it is an easy exercise and is quite a pleasurable experience. However, a visit to the patisserie every morning is essential, to purchase croissants and fresh bread for breakfast and often a delicious pain-au-raisin, well endowed with custard and sultanas; this latter is delightful later in the morning. While on this expedition I must, of course, purchase each day's edition of *Midi Libre*.

Petit déjeuner is always an enjoyable meal as, in addition to the freshly baked items, we have our favourite marmalade, jam and cereals. Evening meals are certainly varied if not ambitious. There is always a plentiful variety of excellent fresh vegetables and fruit in the supermarket, including potatoes (still clothed in soil), carrots, beans, tomatoes, cucumber, peaches, etc., etc. Occasionally, we have fresh meat from the boucherie. On two or three evenings we bought a ready cooked meal of roti de porc or poulet, together with frites. Of course, a cold meal of pre-packed ham together with tomate and concombre is always acceptable; the customary tin of red salmon from Tesco provided a meal to enjoy. However, our favourite meal is of fried lardons and potato with eggs; we must admit that this was our meal on four evenings, including Friday 7 June, which was our 55th anniversary and my 83rd birthday!

To occupy us for much of the day there was the *Midi Libre* with, from time to time, associated publications; we did, or almost did, a crossword (French) and there was the television. We were pleased to be able to watch Le Journal every evening, as we do at home; there were a number of very interesting programmes such as the annual selection of the favourite village of the French, out of the 20 which are featured and described; there was a programme, presented by Elise Lucet – well-remembered for her seemingly endless commentating on the events of 9/11/01 – on the banking crisis; also, a number of the football matches of the Confederation Cup, taking place in South America, were broadcast.

June 2013 (Tuesday, 28 May – Friday, 21 June)

Normally, I like to go for a walk and run along the shore early in the morning and, as Margaret was happy to be left, I did so on several days. The sun rises at about 6.00 at this time of year and I have witnessed that special sight on several occasions in past years, but not this time. I was there at about 7.00 on the 7 June, however. As often happens, I met a gentleman on successive days, and we stopped for a greeting (in French); it is a unique situation and time of the day where the only sound is that of the sea.

Unfortunately, Margaret was not able to walk very far, but she did visit the shops with me two or three times and walked by the beach on a couple of late afternoons.

The weather, yes, the weather is an important feature of each day when we choose to be away from home. It may be the shores of the Mediterranean, but past experience has been that during a period of two or three weeks there is usually quite a variety of conditions, although during the months of July and August the sun would be expected to predominate. When we arrived, the northerly wind was unpleasant and keeping temperatures disappointingly low; these conditions continued, but with periods of sunshine, for a few days. We had the inevitable thunderstorm and, on occasion, misty conditions. When the winds veered to the south-east it caused the sea to become very agitated, a sight we could witness from our apartment. Gradually, as the sun exerted its strengthening influence, temperatures rose to the upper 20s and lower 30s and for the last 10–14 days of our stay the weather was very comfortable and acceptable. In particular, I noted that on Wednesday 12 June, Margaret wrote 'Le temps est parfait'; however, on the following Wednesday, 19 June, there was a heavy mist, the sea was very agitated, but it was warm and we could see there were many people on the beach.

Although we were not able to revisit familiar places in the Hérault and make new discoveries we gained much pleasure and interest in reading about happenings in villages and towns we have visited in years past, in the daily *MIDI LIBRE*; I record a selection of those articles.

<u>Vendredi, 31 mai 2013</u>

A cassette of the well-known recording by Maurice André and Jane Parker-Smith of music for trumpet and organ has often accompanied us on our journeys in France. The renowned trumpeter, MAURICE ANDRE, was born in 1933 at Alés in the neighbouring Department of Gard; he died in 2012 at the age of 79 and was buried in the tiny village of Saint-André-Capcèze deep in the Parc National des Cevennes. We recall that, some years ago, we drove along the D906 from Langogne to Alés, a distance of about 90 kilometres; for some 20 km. the road lies along the valley of the Allier and then, after Villefort, it passes very close to Saint-André-Capcèze; it was a most memorable journey through unforgettable scenery.

On Saturday evening, at the Theatre of the Cratère à Alès a concert was held featuring 'Cent trompettes pour un homage à Maurice André'. Among the 100 trumpeters taking part were the two sons of Maurice and former students; they were all accompanied by an orchestra of 80 musicians. The 900 seats of the theatre had been quickly booked and a giant screen was to be installed in the Cathedral Square to accommodate another 400 spectators. Such a concert had been anticipated to celebrate the trumpeter's 80 years. However, surely, this was a very fitting tribute and a most joyful occasion.

Dimanche, 2 juin 2013

EN JUIN, ON SKIE DANS LES PYRENEES. Yes, some ski stations have reopened.

Mardi, 4 juin 2013

About 30 kilometres north of Pézenas, is the medieval village of SAINT-GUILHEM-le-DESERT in the heart of the Gorges de l'Hérault. It is one of the Plus Beaux Villages de France and its Abbey of Gellone is a World Heritage Site. Close by is the Pont du Diable, also a World Heritage Site. Work on this bridge began in about 1030 and for approaching 1,000 years it has resisted the floods of the river, although when we have been there the river level has been very low and appearing quite harmless. However, a tragedy has occurred nearby when three women and one man, all of Bulgarian origin, were celebrating the birthday of one of the group. Apparently one of the women slipped on a rock and fell into the river, pulling her friend with her. It seems that one of them could not swim and that the water was very cold and the currents dangerous and, despite the efforts of rescue services, they both died.

The village of ADISSAN, with a population of some 900, is about 10 kilometres north of Pézenas. At the recent annual parish meeting attended by more than 20 citizens, le maire presented the annual budget; he explained the main items of receipts and expenses. For this year, income will remain stable and expenses will be controlled. (familiar words!); projects include a new electricity pole and improved lighting in a street and in the car park. The main task is the construction of a new water purification station, etc., which should commence in September and be completed by March, providing the weather does not delay the work. The cost of this station will be met by the Départment and l'Agence de l'eau (52%) and by a 25-year loan. The meeting ended with questions on the proposed works and the explanations by le maire; informal conversation followed, assisted by a glass of wine. An interesting insight into parochial life!

Our special interest in Adissan relates to its vineyards. Having read about it previously, a few years ago we visited a particular vineyard. In 1914 all the young men of the village received orders to report for military duty. However, one of them, Maurice, was very busy grafting his vines; he was determined to complete the task and delayed reporting for service. Eventually, he journeyed to Marseille, but found that his regiment had already left. Without, it seems, being severely punished, or even executed, for not complying with the initial orders, Maurice eventually joined another unit. When Maurice returned home at the end of the Great War, he found that all his friends had perished and yet he, miraculously, had survived. Consequently, he promised that he would never sell or dig up this vineyard which had saved his life; a promise which was honoured by his family. A few years ago, it was decided to hold an annual celebration at the site to commemorate this remarkable record.

To find this One-Hundred-Year-Old Vineyard and to walk between the vines was a moving experience and one we will never forget; in fact, we still have a piece of one of the vines which had broken off. We had parked nearby and there was one other car there at the time. In fact, the gentleman driver was there to exercise his cat, which was on a lead. We exchanged a few friendly comments and as he left, he exclaimed "Vive la Reine", to which we appropriately replied!

Mercredi, 5 juin 2013

The Cévennes are a range of mountains forming part of the Massif Central. It is a fascinating area of many and varied natural features and diverse landscapes, of winding rivers and deep gorges; much is wild and remote and sparsely populated; the highest point is Mont Lozére at 1,702 metres. In the past we have visited such differing sites as the Cirque de Navacelles, Grotte des Demoiselles, Corniche des Cévennes and Mont Aigoual. MONT AIGOUAL, at 1,567 metres, is the highest point in the Gard Department and we reached the summit by car.

We were particularly interested to read, today, a vivid account of the felling of two trees in the arboretum on Mount Aigoual – the sound of the chain saw, then silence, the onlookers and foresters hold their breath, the tree begins to wobble, the cracking intensifies and, finally, the roar of the crash of the giant, followed by applause from the spectators. United in life and in death, these two firs, from Vancouver, planted in 1906, had reached a height of 62 metres and were probably the tallest trees in France. Sadly, they had been attacked by a tiny insect, the pityokteines spinidens, which blocks the circulation of the sap.

Midi Libre may be a regional paper of the South of France, but it did not fail to recognise an historic date in the United Kingdom – "Un régne de 60 ans". It reported on the service to celebrate the 60th Anniversary of the CORONATION of QUEEN ELIZABETH II, which took place in Westminster Abbey yesterday and included a photograph.

<u>Vendredi, 7 juin 2013</u>

The PONT du GARD is the aqueduct bridge which crosses the Gardon River; it was built by the Romans in the 1st century. The aqueduct was constructed to carry water from a spring at Uzès to Nimes, a distance of some 50 km. The bridge is a Historic Monument and a World Heritage Site and is a very popular tourist attraction. However, it appears that many people are objecting to the entry charges, which, from now on will be: – pedestrians €10, cyclists €12 and cars €18.

This is the day of St Gilbert. SAINT GILBERT was born in about 1100. He participated in the failed Second Crusade from 1146 to 1148. When, on their return to France a number of crusaders were suffering from leprosy, Gilbert decided to devote his life to the poor and to the sick. He founded two religious establishments, one at Aubeterre and the other at Neuffonts.

We are reminded that, on 23 June 2010, we were travelling along the D6 after leaving the outskirts of Vichy and in the direction of Moulins when we noticed on our map that we would be passing close to the Ancienne Abbaye de St Gilbert in the commune of Saint-Didier-le-Forêt; we decided to make a detour. Although it was then after 17.00 the 'abbey' was still open and we were able to walk around quite freely. After a while we were spotted by the propriétaire (?) who soon called his wife and we had a long and most interesting conversation; even their two goats joined us. It was almost one and a half hours later that we left to continue our journey to Coulandon near Moulins. Incidentally, what remains of the abbey is now a very inviting centre for receptions, conferences, etc; chambre d'hôte is also available. This is a Monument Historique du XII siècle.

Samedi, 8 juin 2013

A few years ago, we found it appropriate to pause at the little village of CAUX, near Pézenas, for a cup of tea. Afterwards, we made a short tour of the village and we noted how clean and tidy it was. A number of older buildings were undergoing restoration work and it was interesting to read the descriptions of the work on the explanations displayed.

This is not an area where one would expect to find any reference to the practice of TRANSHUMANCE, the custom in mountainous areas of moving livestock to higher pastures in the summer months and bringing them back to the lower valleys for the winter. However, tomorrow 9 juin, between 18.00 and 20.00, the shepherd, Nicolas Saudadier, will take his herd of 400 ewes from Caux to graze at Le Travers at Alignan-du-Vent, a distance of perhaps five kilometres. The herd will extend over about 40 metres and motorists are asked to be vigilant. The return journey will probably take place next Sunday.

ALIGNAN-du-VENT too is eagerly awaiting this special occasion. Anyone wishing to assist should equip themselves with a yellow jacket and a bottle of water and meet behind the old station at Caux. After the transhumance there will be a pique-nique in an assuredly convivial atmosphere. How nice it would be to witness this exceptional event! Alignan-du-Vent is adjacent to the village of Margon.

Lundi, 10 juin 2013

L'Appel du 18 juin 1940 by GENERAL de GAULLE is one of the most important speeches in French history and is widely commemorated. The mayor and council of CAUX invite the 'population' to attend the commemorative ceremony of laying a wreath at the Champs Blancs and at the memorial in the cemetery, at 18.30 on 18 juin.

Mardi, 11 juin 2013

An update on the proposed high-speed rail line between Montpellier and Perpignan! At present not a centimetre

JUNE 2013 (TUESDAY, 28 MAY – FRIDAY, 21 JUNE)

has been built and pessimists are beginning to believe that the project will be buried. Happily, this is not necessarily the case. The commission charged with the task of classifying the various projects of LGVs in order of priority is preparing to submit its report to the Minister of Transport. Apparently, an independent expert has concluded that this high-speed link would not be the most expensive and, as it would provide an international link, it could benefit from European financial aid.

JEAN MOULIN is one of the most significant figures of French 20th century history. He was born in Béziers on 20 June 1899. After the German occupation of the country in 1940 he became very active in resisting the suppression and, in September 1941, he was smuggled out of France to meet General de Gaulle in London. In January 1942, he was parachuted back into his homeland and commenced to organise the Resistance movement. He set up the National Council of the Resistance in May 1943, but shortly afterwards, he was betrayed and was captured on 21 June. He was interrogated by the Gestapo, but despite being tortured, he consistently refused to disclose information about the organisation of the Resistance. While being taken to Germany by train he died, before crossing the border, a martyr, on 8 July 1943.

BEZIERS will commemorate the 70th anniversary of the death of Jean Moulin with a series of events beginning with an exhibition of photographs, etc., celebrating the life of the hero of the Resistance in the house in which he was born; this will begin on Thursday and continue until the end of October. The 'Presence' of Jean Moulin is everywhere in the town – that familiar figure in a long coat, fedora and scarf.

It was about 30 years ago, in 1983, when we visited Béziers and, particularly, the Cathédrale St-Nazaire. We recall looking down upon the River Orb from the top of the tower, when visitors alongside spoke to us in English. In fact, they were from Holland and were interested to know where we came from; having told them, we were amazed to learn that they had a relative who lived in Wellow, a village very close to our own. On that same occasion we purchased, in the Flower Market, a cactus which survived for many years.

Béziers is one of the oldest cities in France, perhaps older than Agde. The town was a stronghold of Catharism, which was condemned as heretical by the Catholic Church; it, and especially its Cathedral, is known for the massacre of perhaps 20,000 people in the course of the Albigensian Crusade in 1209. The Abbot of Citeaux, leader of the crusade, is reputed to have said, "Kill them all, God will know His own".

Mercredi, 12 juin 2013

Because of the storms and rain on Sunday afternoon the shepherd had decided, with much regret, to cancel the planned transhumance from Caux to Alignan-du-Vent. It is hoped to rearrange this event in October.

In the course of several journeys from Cap d'Agde to Castelnau-Montratier, near Cahors, we have driven

JUNE 2013 (TUESDAY, 28 MAY – FRIDAY, 21 JUNE)

from Pézenas to Albi, passing along the D908 between Hérépian and St-Pons-de-Thomières. Midway along this picturesque route, in the valley beneath the Monts de l'Espinouse and in the Parc Naturel Régional du Haut-Languedoc, is one of the 'Plus Beaux Villages de France' – OLARGUES. It lies just off the D908 and on a couple of occasions we have made a detour to spend an hour here to have our 'lunch'. This village site was occupied by the Romans but, in addition to its ancient buildings, it has some of more recent times – the Hôtel de Ville of the 1930s and the Collége Alexandre Laissac, (we parked nearby) of the present century. We were interested to read that, following a visit and inspection by the Commission, it has been confirmed that Olargues retains its coveted status.

When making a similar journey (Cap d'Agde to Castelnau Montratier) some years ago we planned a route via Béziers and the D14, to join the D908 before Olargues. Much of this route is very attractive also, as it follows the valley and the gorges of the Orb and passes through the village of ROQUEBRUN, where we spent an hour or two. About 10 years ago we read an article about Roquebrun. Although high above sea level it is sheltered by surrounding hills and is said to be one of the sunniest places in France – le petite Nice. In fact, it has a Mediterranean Garden and oranges can be picked at Christmas.

At the time of our visit it was, indeed, very sunny and warm; there was little activity other than by some musicians preparing the setting for a festival in the evening. We read today that the village post office, which is only open for specific periods of the week and is, apparently, under threat of permanent closure, has again been closed unexpectedly; the reason being the loss of the internet connection. It is 'la goutte d'eau qui fait déborder le vase!'. Perhaps it is its sheltered position, which provides its favourable climate, which also causes this problem.

Jeudi, 13 juin 2013

Today's saint is SAINT ANTOINE de PADOUE. St Antoine was born in Lisbon in 1195 and died in Padua, Italy in 1231. He was a Franciscan priest, an exceptional orator and is the saint of finding lost articles or people. We have visited very many churches in various parts of the country and so often we have found a statue of St Antoine within its walls.

Vendredi, 14 juin 2013

The photograph of Dany et Henri Subias celebrating their 50 years of marriage at SAINT-THIBERY, reminds us of our visit to the remains of the Roman Bridge over the Hérault River and the old water mill nearby, a couple of years ago. We don't forget the visitor who arrived on a bicycle with his cat on his shoulders; the cat was on a lead!

La Diane de MARGON invites members to attend the general meeting of the Hunt tomorrow evening. The minutes: – report of the year, balance sheet, followed by questions. At the end of the meeting, "le verre de l'amitié sera servi." We have very happily sojourned

June 2013 (Tuesday, 28 May – Friday, 21 June)

several times at the Auberge du Chateau in Margon, where we have always been warmly greeted by Fabienne and Florent, often with the question, "Only two nights?" and we have always enjoyed the meals prepared by Florent.

The French language, like most, is constantly evolving and the latest edition of *Le PETIT ROBERT de la LANGUE FRANCAIS* (Cost €60) includes a number of new words and phrases which can, from now on, be spoken or written; they include *street art* and *low cost!*

Yesterday, we saw on *Le Journal* reports of the DISRUPTION OF RAIL SERVICES because of the strikes by staff; we were glad we were not travelling home on that day. According to the SNCF, the overall rate of participation in the strike among the 150,000 employees was only about 33%, but it was considerably higher among drivers and controllers. However, it seems that about 40% of services were operating. The reasons for the strikes are the conflicting policies of the unions and the government regarding the accepted need of reform of the rail system; the unions being anxious to defend the public monopoly.

Samedi, 15 juin 2013

We are very familiar with such supermarket offers as 'buy one – get one free', but I was not aware that such policies had extended into the motor trade. However, we read that Hyundai Nimes are offering up to 10 purchasers of a SUV Hyundai iX35 (€29,678), a second new vehicle (a petite Citadine i10) for €1. The purchaser's car of eight years or more is taken in part-exchange. Three offers have been taken up.

Dimanche, 16 juin 2013

SAGA d'une MISSION IMPOSSIBLE. By a decree, signed by General de Gaulle on 18 juin 1963, the largest building site seen in France during the previous century was inaugurated. At that time, it was probably one of the most ambitious construction operations contemplated anywhere in the world. It was the mission of one Pierre Racine; the development of the coast of Languedoc-Roussillon, the creation of a beautiful amphitheatre facing the sea. Thus, was born the resorts of La Grande-Motte, Port-Camargue, Carnon, le Cap d'Agde, Gruissan, Port-Leucate and Port-Barcarès. After 20 years the project was largely completed and in 2007 the new resorts attracted some 10 million holidaymakers.

Lundi, 17 juin 2013

MINERVE – a nocturnal stroll on the causse (limestone plateau)! Would you like to walk by the light of the moon, listen to the stealthy presence of animals and the song of the nightingale, see the countryside under a new light and discover the causse and its inhabitants on a summer night with a different eye and a different ear? If so, meet at the car park at the dolmens near Minerve on Saturday, 22 June at 20.00. Walking shoes, a torch and a pique-nique are recommended. At the beginning of the 13th century, Minerve would not have presented such a tranquil scene. After the massacre at Béziers, many Cathars took refuge here, but during the siege (1210) by Crusaders led by Simon de Montfort, access to the well, the only water supply, was destroyed and the village surrendered. The majority of the Cathars then threw themselves on to the flames of a pyre. Minerve, with a population of little more than 100, is situated in the Hérault Department to the west of Béziers; it is a Plus Beaux Village de France and the centre of a well-known wine region. However, it was an interest in the locations and events relating to Catharism in Languedoc and the Albigensian Crusade initiated by the Pope to eliminate it, that prompted us to visit Minerve. Access to the village by the bridge over the river is only available to vehicles owned by residents and, having parked, we walked into the village; we visited the well and then decided to purchase some wine. We had a long conversation with le commerçant; it was in September 1992 and the day following the French Referendum on the Maastricht Treaty, in which a small majority had voted in favour. We asked Monsieur how he had voted, and he replied that he had voted Yes, as the Treaty will mean, "No more wars in Europe". Before we left the shop, he invited Margaret to stand with him behind the counter to be photographed. Sadly, that and other photographs of the village we have never seen, as the film was lost in the post. Following correspondence, the Royal Mail sent us one or two books of stamps as compensation!

Mardi, 18 juin 2013

We have driven many thousands of miles in France and we have never encountered a serious accident or been delayed by one; we have, in fact, passed a couple of minor collisions. However, we know that, every year, there are many fatal accidents in the country and we have passed a succession of black silhouettes indicating fatal accidents on a particular section of road. Many accidents involve motorcyclists. Yesterday, on the Autoroute A75 near Paulhan, north of Pézenas, a motorcyclist crashed into the rear of a campervan and suffered fatal injuries. He was travelling north with two friends; he was 39 years old and from London!

Jeudi, 20 juin 2013

Although it will not be presented to the minister of transport until next Thursday, it is understood that the report and proposals of the commission Mobilité 21 do not include the construction of the high-speed rail line from Montpellier to Perpignan before the year 2030. Apparently, the commission has had to place some 78 projects in order of priority. Not good news for the region!

As we approached the day of our departure, we exercised careful control over our shopping, endeavouring to avoid having food, etc., we would not need. On the morning of Thursday, 20 June I made a final visit to the patisserie to buy our needs for breakfast and to say farewell; I was advised to return in September! I also bought a copy of *Midi Libre*. We had contrived to preserve sufficient bread, ham and cheese for me to make a few sandwiches which we would eat when we arrived at Lille. Preparing to depart and our packing was a fairly straightforward exercise, simply returning

JUNE 2013 (TUESDAY, 28 MAY – FRIDAY, 21 JUNE)

possessions to the case, haversacks, etc., in which they came. In some respects, there was a little less, but there were a few small items we wished to take with us; nevertheless, the task was completed without much difficulty. However, there was one special item to be included. I had purchased the magazine *Planète Cyclisme* containing the excellent and detailed 'Le Guide du Tour 2013'; this would enable us to be transported back to France while watching the wonderful three-week spectacle next month on TV.

We have been very comfortable here, in this 'beautiful amphitheatre facing the sea', for the past three weeks. The roomy well-equipped apartment and the private terrace providing a peaceful, relaxing and enjoyable period of relief from the domestic routines of home. Of course, it is, most certainly, the last time that we reach the shores of the Mediterranean, which has been regarded as the ultimate horizon of our 'France Journey'.

The agency had kindly arranged for a taxi to meet us at the entrance to the building at 12.00 and, indeed, was waiting for us when we emerged. We were taken direct to Agde station, but during the journey of about 20 minutes, the lady driver was very interested to know of the places in the area with which we are familiar. As we arrived at the station, suddenly a gentleman (perhaps the driver of another taxi) was at the car to assist with our luggage; he took us into the waiting area and established us in seats while our driver presented our tickets and explained our circumstances at le guichet. When I mentioned that we must composter (punch) our tickets, she immediately said I will do it for you. All we now had to do was to sit and wait to be collected by a member of the staff; it would be a long wait as our train was not due to leave until 14.26!

Eventually we were beckoned by a gentleman in a peaked cap and, together with a number of other passengers, lead out on to the adjacent platform. However, this was not the platform for our train, and we had to walk along a narrow uneven pathway alongside the rail track for some distance and then over a boarded route across the tracks to the appropriate platform. It was quite a large group of generally elderly travellers, but we found it especially difficult trying to manage our four 'cases', particularly that on wheels, as the surface was uneven. Our escort simply lead the group and did not and, we must say, was not able to individually assist such a number of passengers carrying a considerable volume of luggage. Unfortunately, we got left behind the group and the SNCF man had to return to offer us some assistance. However, once on the platform we were all abandoned.

We studied the plan of our train and decided where we should wait to be at the appropriate entrance. In fact, I asked a gentleman if we were in the correct place and he agreed that we were. When the train arrived, on time, there was the usual urgency to board, but some passengers had particularly large suitcases and access to the carriage was blocked for vital seconds. Eventually, we managed to get inside, placed most of our luggage on the racks and found the numbered seats in accordance with our tickets.

June 2013 (Tuesday, 28 May – Friday, 21 June)

We settled down in the comfortable first-class seating and looked forward to the long journey; conveniently, our seats were again on the right-hand side of the train and, therefore, we had a view in the opposite direction to that on our outward journey.

After Nimes we were travelling very fast and the scenery was changing rapidly; there were areas of purple lavender and of yellow gorse; sometimes rugged and sometimes rounded mountains in the background and tunnels to pass through. We reached Valence TGV at 16.10 and Lyon at 16.50. At the latter, a large number of passengers boarded. Some were obviously having difficulty in finding their reserved seats; we were asked to check our tickets and it was suggested that we were not in the correct seats. I pointed out that the conductor had already inspected our tickets and had made no comment, but a certain lady seemed convinced that we were occupying their seats. I could not face having to move along the train with all our luggage and I made that clear. Mercifully, they left us where we were and moved on. Were we in the wrong coach and, therefore, occupying seats reserved by other passengers? We shall never know, but it emphasises the importance of joining these trains at the appropriate entrance in the correct coach.

We stopped at all the same stations as on the outward journey and, again, there was quite a lot of activity at Charles de Gaulle Aéroport. We hoped that when we reached Lille at 19.57 we would be met by our friends from the handicapé centre, but we recognised no one.

We realised that we had not advised the kind lady taxi driver who registered our tickets at Agde Gare that we should request the 'accès plus' service there and, particularly, at Lille.

Once on the platform, with the help of other passengers, we decided to let the large numbers disperse before making our way alone up to the reception level. This may not have been very wise as, very quickly, we were completely alone. First, we dismissed the staircase as inappropriate with our wheeled case; then we decided that we would not be able to make use of the escalator; finally, there must be a lift. I walked a long distance along the platform to locate the lift and then returned for our luggage. When we both returned to the lift with our luggage, we found that it was not working! We felt trapped with no obvious means of escape. We did not know what to do and exclaimed that we needed – Help!!

Fortunately, by then we were not alone, and a French couple heard our pleas and came to our aid. They helped us back to the escalator and, not having to control our luggage, we then managed to cope with the moving staircase. We were so grateful for their help and as they left us they explained that they were there to meet a cousin from Australia; this reminded us of how our journey had started in Trowbridge.

It was with great relief that we reached the handicapé centre, to find it open and willing escorts ready to assist us to the Hotel Lille Europe; however, this time there was no hesitation, a wheelchair would be employed. As we made our way the short distance to the hotel our young man emphasised that we should have had much more help at Agde and that Lille should have been alerted to our impending arrival as, according to him, the service is universal throughout France. Perhaps our lady taxi driver, who introduced us to the station staff, was not herself aware of this facility! We were assured that, providing we return to the centre at least 30 minutes before our train to London was due to leave tomorrow afternoon, we would be assisted to the train.

However, we were now in the safety and comfort of the Hotel for the night and in the same room as on the outward journey, albeit somewhat later than anticipated. Now, we much appreciated the time spent earlier in the day in preparing our sandwiches and we had cold drinks available in the cabinet. We would not be leaving Lille until mid-afternoon tomorrow and so we would be able to enjoy a more leisurely petit déjeuner.

In fact, we found that we were able to occupy the table in the very corner of the building, which provides a wide-ranging view. The weather was certainly not inviting, but we were able to watch the busy activity in the streets below. We were due to vacate our room by 11.00 and, indeed, we were still there to receive a reminder call. Fortunately, room was found to store our luggage until it was time to make our way to Lille Europe station.

We had hoped that, having several hours to spend in Lille, we would be able to walk into the city. However, the weather was quite unpleasant, damp and cold and unseasonal, even though it was 21 June and the summer solstice; also, we were clearly not going to be able to walk very far. We got no further than the couple of hundred metres to Lille Flanders Station, where we decided to rest for a while and watch the comings and goings of the TGVs, etc. Unfortunately, the only seating available was in a waiting room where we spent about an hour.

Knowing that, after 13.00, the hotel 'breakfast room' would be available for use, but with no refreshments, we returned to spend another hour there. At about 14.00 we decided that it would be sensible to begin to make our way back to la Gare. It was quite a struggle without any help, particularly in negotiating the lift up to the reception level and we were much relieved when we reached the security of the handicapé centre; we were assured that we would be accompanied to our train, which was due to leave at 15.35.

In fact, we quite enjoyed being able to relax and to watch on the screen, with interest, the many train movements and all the activity around us. In particular, we were impressed by the way in which all the staff went about their various tasks, preparing and leaving to meet new arrivals, etc.; the atmosphere of camaraderie was impressive, and it was an uplifting experience.

When the time came for us to be taken down to the platform, we were especially pleased to find that our escort was to be the same young man who assisted us to the hotel on the previous evening. Margaret was seated in a wheelchair and I was relieved of most of our

June 2013 (Tuesday, 28 May – Friday, 21 June)

luggage. We set off on the quite long journey, on both levels, making use of the lift, and on the request of an 'excusez moi!' from our uniformed escort the dense crowds separated and we were allowed a priority passage; my only problem was trying to keep up with them. We were guided through the ticket control, passport control and UK border control without delay and then taken to the spot on the platform where the door to our compartment would stop. We have never before received such priority treatment. When the train arrived our escort (I wish I had asked him his name) helped us on to the train, put our luggage on the racks and made sure we were seated in our correct seats. It was a wonderful service and we could not thank him enough, but he had to then force his way against the oncoming passengers to get off the train.

As we moved quietly and smoothly away from Lille at 15.35 there was not the same atmosphere of anticipation and excitement as on our outward journey; it was more of a commuter journey, perhaps because most of us were on the return leg. However, sitting near us at a table were a family of four, including a teenage boy and a younger girl; they had, most certainly, boarded in Brussels. Perhaps they were making their first visit to London as they were studying, with much interest, a guidebook of the capital.

The 82-minute journey seemed to pass very quickly and, as we entered into the seemingly unspectacular approach to London, we began to wonder if we would receive the same kind of welcome and assistance at St Pancras as we had enjoyed at Lille. However, we were, perhaps, not especially anxious as it would be the terminus for the train, and we had allowed more than three hours to reach our train at Waterloo.

Fortunately, we were not to be disappointed; having arrived at 15.57, we were among the last passengers to disembark and we were very relieved when our name was called; yes, another young man, equipped with a wheelchair, was there to assist us. Although it was quite a long way to a taxi, there were no formal checks to pass through; they had all been completed in Lille. We said how valuable and helpful this service had been, especially the liaison between Eurostar and SNCF, but our escort explained that it was, at times, difficult for them to meet demands, particularly at this time when some three trains carrying about 2,000 passengers were descending upon them within an hour. We were seen safely to the taxi rank and we thanked the escort for his help and, indeed, for all the help we had received.

We were quickly assisted into a taxi; it was not the friendly young man who had taken us to St Pancras on 28 May, but an equally friendly and kind gentleman. He made our car journey very interesting; he told us how he became a taxi driver a few months earlier; how he purchased a motor scooter and spent many months preparing for the role, riding all over London and getting to know the city well. Consequently, he was able to point out various landmarks, including the Shard, as we travelled to Waterloo; this must be a very important asset when transporting visitors in the capital. On reaching Waterloo Station he took our luggage from the car to a convenient place for us to continue. Our taxi

JUNE 2013 (TUESDAY, 28 MAY – FRIDAY, 21 JUNE)

services in London had been of an outstanding level. Once again, we were now left to our own devices.

It is several years since we last travelled this route and, as always, Waterloo is a vast and very busy complex. We recall that, on previous occasions, the indication of the platform from which the train for Bristol would depart was delayed until a matter of minutes before it was due to leave. We recall standing for a considerable time, with eyes fixed on the large screen, until that number appeared; it was then a desperate dash to the train and, particularly, to that part which would continue beyond Salisbury to Bristol.

This was a situation which we were very anxious to avoid, and we first visited a ticket office to explain our situation. We were advised to make enquiries at a travel office nearby, where I spoke to a gentleman who assured me that, if we returned about 30 minutes before our train was due to leave, he would provide assistance for us. We felt reassured and decided that the next priority, after visiting toilets, was to obtain a cup of coffee.

We had hoped that we could find a convenient café on the same level and where we could comfortably sit outside at a table with ample room to look after our luggage. Such a place was difficult to find, and we eventually resorted to the interior of a Starbucks café and on a slightly raised level involving two or three steps. However, we found this to be very comfortable and we spent a considerable time there, both enjoying a large cup of coffee and a chocolate cookie and another chocolate cookie – the assistant agreed that they were very nice; at the same time observing the various comings and goings.

Eventually the time came for us to return to the travel office. Unfortunately, the gentleman I had talked to earlier was no longer there, but after explaining our needs once again to a lady assistant she spoke to someone on the phone and assured me that help would soon be at hand. Indeed, it was; there was no wheelchair available, but we were duly helped to the appropriate platform by a very friendly gentleman. On our way we noticed the lift to the upper level of the station where, on an earlier occasion, we had found the refreshment facilities that we had had in mind today; however, we had been quite happy with Starbucks, even if they are noted for not making a very large contribution to the British Treasury!

We were taken to the correct carriage of the train and established in seating reserved for handicapped passengers, where we had ample room to store our luggage in front of us; it was extremely roomy and comfortable accommodation, probably more so than in first class travel! We were very grateful for this help.

The train left on time at 19.20 and we relaxed to look forward to a rather different kind of train journey, an English train journey of two hours and 11 minutes! We were on a South West Trains service to Exeter and Bristol and we had been assured that we were in the section which would continue to Bristol! There were a lot of passengers, some standing, but it was a friendly atmosphere. However, we did not have an absorbing conversation as we had had on our outward journey; instead, we paid more attention to the places and landscapes we passed.

Our first stop was at Clapham Junction, where a number of passengers left the train, but no one joined. CLAPHAM JUNCTION is actually in Battersea; it has 17 platforms and some 2,000 trains pass through every day, more than through any other station in Europe. It is difficult to imagine that, before the railway came, it was a rural area where fields of lavender grew.

At WOKING we are in Surrey but, although a 25-minute journey from Waterloo, it is part of the Greater London Urban Area. This now large town was the site of a monastery in the 8th century and its name appears in the Domesday Book. The Shah Jahan Mosque in Woking was the first purpose-built mosque in the United Kingdom; it was completed in 1889.

Our next stop, at Basingstoke, is in Hampshire. BASINGSTOKE, situated in a valley through the North Downs, has a population of about 85,000; it was a market site in the Domesday Book and a regular weekly market has been held there since 1214. The town was expanded in the 1960s and is now an economic centre with various industries; it is the UK headquarters of Sun Life Financial of Canada and the Automobile Association.

From our forward-facing spacious seats alongside a wide window it appeared that the longest day of the year was ending with a pleasant evening, compared with the morning weather in Lille; the broken clouds and the still bright sun in the western sky creating a golden image, as we continued through the attractive countryside of Hampshire and then into Wiltshire.

Still in Hampshire, we stopped at OVERTON, a large ancient village of about 4,000 inhabitants and first mentioned in the 10th century. It is situated in the Test Valley; the stream rises about a mile east of Overton and reaches the sea at Southampton.

WHITCHURCH lies on the River Test and, by virtue of the wildlife in or near the river, is the centre of a Conservation Area. It is an interesting ancient town with a population of about 4,800 and it shares a distinction with Chinon, in the Indre-et-Loire Department of Central France, in that it has no traffic lights!

Next, we come to ANDOVER, a large town of some 52,000 inhabitants, situated on the River Anton. It was recorded in Anglo-Saxon times and in 994 it was the site of the baptism of Viking King Olaf. The Domesday Book (1086) records 107 male inhabitants; the total population may have been about 500. At the present time the largest employer is the Ministry of Defence; other industries include the Twinings tea and coffee firm and the producers of Pitkin Guides; of lesser significance is Schaefer Ltd., the company which produced our garden waste bin!

In the north-west corner of Hampshire and shortly before the border with Wiltshire, lies Grateley. GRATELEY is a small village of about 600 inhabitants;

June 2013 (Tuesday, 28 May – Friday, 21 June)

it comprises some 250 dwellings and has two shops, two pubs and a 13th century church. That sounds rather mundane; however, it has a rich history, which goes back 2,000 years. Its name derives from Old English, meaning a 'great wood or clearing'. Farming has been the main source of income for parishioners for most of that period but is now very much less so. The Romans were here and it was here that King Aethelstan enacted the first official code of laws in about 930. During the First and Second World Wars, Grateley was the site of ammunition stores. In addition to its ancient church there are 16th century farm cottages and 17th and 18th century manor houses. Grateley is, of course, a station on the main line from London to the West of England and is served by frequent trains. Grateley Parish Council website provides an excellent historical record of the village and a fascinating insight into life in past times. About 15 minutes after leaving Grateley we received a text from Judith saying that, according to the internet timetable, we should now be in Salisbury – we were.

The city of SALISBURY was established in 1220, but there had been a settlement here since prehistory; it now has a population of about 40,000. It is noted for its Cathedral of Early English Gothic style, the construction of which began in 1220 and much of the building was completed in 60 years. Its spire, at 123 metres, has dominated the skyline since 1320; it is the tallest in the United Kingdom. Remarkably it is all built on only four feet of foundations. The crossing point of the West of England Main Line and the Wessex Main Line is at Salisbury; consequently, there was a short delay as the forward section of the train was detached from the remainder and then headed for Exeter; our coaches then continued towards Bristol; while at Salisbury I telephoned to order a taxi to meet us at Trowbridge.

The route then passes along the valley of the River Wylye and to WARMINSTER. This town was first settled in the Anglo-Saxon period, but its prosperity followed the growth of the wool trade in the Late Middle Ages; it has strong military associations.

Our penultimate stop was at WESTBURY, a town of some 17,000 inhabitants. Probably, its name can be explained as – 'west' being near the western edge of the county, the bounds of which have been much the same since the Anglo-Saxon period and 'bury' a market town or village centre, as 'bourg' in French! Westbury is known for its "deliciously creamy butter" – Anchor.

We were due to arrive at Trowbridge at 21.31 and, although I did not check the time, I am sure that our train was on time.

Immediately after leaving Westbury our thoughts turned to the matter of disembarking. We need not have been concerned, for soon the conductor arrived to check our luggage; he was to assist us to disembark.

On emerging into the car park, we were a little surprised to find that there was no taxi waiting for us. However, it was only a matter of a few moments before a taxi arrived, immediately followed by a second taxi. As they drew up side by side, we heard the comment,

June 2013 (Tuesday, 28 May – Friday, 21 June)

"How did that happen". We were quickly ushered into the first vehicle and were soon on the final leg of our journey. The driver was interested to know where we had travelled from during the day, but there was little time for conversation and well before 10.00pm we reached Green Lane and our driver kindly deposited our luggage in the gateway.

We were home with a feeling of accomplishment and satisfaction and gratitude.

Despite my doubts, we went, we stayed, and we have returned, without regrets. However, had we not received such unexpected and unbelievable assistance and help from so many people, many in the course of their work and others as complete strangers, the conclusion could have been somewhat different. We remember particularly, when all other passengers had left the train at Waterloo, the young man who returned to offer us his help; also, when we felt helpless, isolated and trapped on the platform at Lille, the couple who offered us assistance and helped us to reach the comfort and security of the handicapé reception centre above.

During the course of the journey, we exchanged many text messages, some trivial, with family and friends; they were all very much appreciated. It all contributed greatly to making this expedition – successful. Yes, "people are very kind". THANK YOU ALL.

At the end of the day, when sitting comfortably in the sitting room, Margaret said, with some emotion, "I have had a lovely holiday". That was most gratifying to hear!

LILLE AND ARRAS

OCTOBER 2014 (Tuesday, 21 October – Thursday, 30 October)

This year, 2014, has been marked by the special anniversaries of two momentous events in European history – the 100th anniversary of the commencement of the Great War and the 70th anniversary of D-Day. Television has provided us with memorable pictures of numerous poignant commemorative events which have taken place in many historic locations but, of course, it is even more deeply moving to visit relevant sites in person. However, the year was now passing so quickly and we were approaching the Autumn Equinox; with the days rapidly becoming shorter it was too late in the year to plan a visit by car to Normandy. In the circumstances, we decided to travel by train and spend a few days in Lille and Arras in the Nord-Pas-de-Calais Region; this would be quite a challenge involving six separate train journeys. I contacted Eurostar and SNCF and I was assured that services for the handicapped were still available. In fact, the Accès Plus service is apparently provided at virtually every station in France.

Following exploratory internet visits to hotels and rail services, we concluded that we could make an outward journey to Lille on 21 October and return on 30 October, also a convenient onward journey to Arras and return, whilst reserving acceptable accommodation at hotels in both cities. As all the pieces of the jigsaw fitted together we made firm reservations straightaway.

As the date of our departure approached it was essential to give careful consideration to the matter of luggage, etc. In particular, should we take with us Margaret's three-wheel-walker and/or walking stick. Both would be useful at times and I had been assured by Eurostar that the former could be accommodated on their trains. However, when not in use I would have responsibility for handling it, particularly the folding and opening, in addition to our general luggage. Although we could rely on assistance at the stations, it was clearly most beneficial and practical for escorts to employ a wheelchair and we could not expect them to take responsibility for another piece of equipment. We decided to make do with a stick! We had to restrict our luggage to three items, a case on wheels, a bag which could be attached to it and a haversack, all of which I could carry or control and still have a free hand. All was prepared by the previous evening – essential documents, clothing, vital medications, etc., etc. However, overnight I recalled that on the previous journey a bag attached to the case had become somewhat uncontrollable and I decided that a second haversack would be more manageable – one on the back and one over the shoulder, which would still leave me with a free hand. Therefore, in the morning there was some urgent repacking to be done. Nevertheless, and quite remarkably, we were more or less ready by the time we planned to leave.

Day 1 – Tuesday, 21 October 2014

Shortly before 09.00 our taxi appeared at the gate and with the driver's help we were quickly aboard and on our way to Trowbridge Station. This station provides very easy access to the trains and we were deposited adjacent to the platform. We had quite a long time to wait as our train, to Waterloo, was due at 09.27 and it was a little late. Although it was not a pleasant morning it was dry. When the train arrived a couple nearby realised that we had our hands full and offered their help. Unfortunately, they were travelling second class and we had booked seats in the first-class compartment. We had to scramble on board as quickly as we could, and we were relieved to find two empty seats at the end of the carriage with ample room for our luggage; although the seats were facing the wall, we were quite content to remain there. We sent a number of text messages to family and friends to let them know that we were on this stage of the journey. It was generally an uneventful journey with the usual stops but, compared with the same journey last year, there was no one to engage in conversation with.

When we reached London Waterloo, no one, staff or passengers, offered assistance, except that, when on the platform, one gentleman did show his concern. However, we had ample time and our plans had been based on the assumption that, at times, we might have to manage without help. We know where the toilets, particularly the disabled facilities, are situated and we decided to make use of those before continuing. Afterwards we slowly made our way to the taxi rank – again it was very helpful to have made this same journey last year. When our turn came for the next available taxi we were assisted into the vehicle by a very polite and friendly driver. However, we were separated from the front of the vehicle by a screen and it was not possible to carry on a conversation with the driver or to have the route explained to us as we did last year.

When we reached St Pancras we were taken as near to the entrance as possible, for which we were grateful. When inside we found that the handicapped reception centre was no longer where it was last year; in fact, it is now immediately inside the building on the right and consists of no more than a desk and a computer. We were received straightaway, our details taken, a wheelchair provided, taken through border controls and to an area in the departure lounge which was for the specific use for passengers such as us, without any delay whatsoever. Margaret was allowed to remain in the wheelchair and we were assured that, when the time came for boarding, someone would come and assist us to and onto the train. It seemed that, within minutes of arriving at St Pancras, we had, I suppose, legally left the country; it was a remarkable experience!

Of course, we had a long time to wait, but it was a relaxing and interesting situation and the usual facilities, refreshments, etc., were available. We observed the variety of activity and we noticed, in particular, quite a number of men passing in front of us very casually in

OCTOBER 2014

twos and threes; they were not formally dressed but were all wearing a casual type of 'blazer' and each carrying a small 'haversack'. Obviously they were all part of a large group, a club perhaps, even a football club. Eventually, the time came for us to be taken to the train and as we were passing along the side of the train our escort said, "We have the Arsenal Football Team travelling with us today – they have reserved two complete coaches". We were quite excited and as soon as we had been installed in our seats we sent text messages to say how privileged we were. George, in particular, exclaimed, "You're not!" The team was, in fact, on its way to play a Champions League match in Belgium on the following evening. As we sat patiently, or impatiently, we received a text from Ian saying that we would not be delayed and at the precise appointed moment of 15.04 we began to move, silently and very slowly at first, but we quickly gained speed. These moments bring a special sensation, of achievement and of the adventure of setting off on an international journey. No doubt many who make this journey frequently find it simply a very routine experience. In any case, the route to the Channel Tunnel does not have many scenic virtues and then for 20 minutes we are under the sea, but after emerging in France we are welcomed to a very pleasant tranquil rural landscape.

How different it would have seemed to the hundreds of thousands who travelled in this direction in 1914–18! On time, of course, we approached Lille and we had to arouse ourselves and struggle towards the luggage racks and the exit. Fortunately, there often seems to be someone who recognizes that one would welcome a little help and here was no exception. However, as soon as the train drew to a halt, there again was 'our man' waiting at the door with a wheelchair. What a welcoming, comforting, reassuring sight it was; all our concerns and worries evaporated; we are truly in France. As we made our way up from the platform and towards the handicapé centre our escort asked us where we planned to spend the night and on being told that we had a reservation at Hotel Lille Europe, he said, "I will take you there straightaway". Remarkably, about 100 minutes after leaving London we were established in our room (512) at the hotel in Lille. As it was now approaching 18.00 and as we had accomplished our task for today, we decided to remain in our room; it is small, with a view of other uninteresting tall buildings, but it is comfortable and quite acceptable. Time now to relax, to send some messages and, in particular, to enjoy our excellent Tesco sandwiches, together with a drink from the cold cabinet. Unfortunately, we found that we had forgotten to bring our travel clock and so we had to arrange for a wake-up call. Having done so, we could now take advantage of the opportunity of a very early night.

Day 2 – Wednesday, 22 October 2014

A varied and generous petit-déjeuner is available here over a long period, to meet the needs of guests who have early morning appointments in the city and those who may be leaving early by train or car. Also, it suits the arrangements of those, like ourselves, whose timetable is somewhat more leisurely. Towards the latter end of the session there is usually an opportunity to choose a table which provides a grandstand view of the busy activity in the streets below, with a comfortable feeling of detachment. However, we too are continuing our journey today and, therefore, we are required to vacate our room by 11.00. We returned our keys to the reception desk and confirmed that we will return to the same room on Monday next. It is only a short distance to Lille Flanders, but it involves crossing a very busy route; there is a lights-controlled crossing and in such situations we always wait until the lights change to green to allow ourselves the maximum time for crossing; we had allowed ample time for the journey.

At the station there were many staff in evidence, but we found an office where we were advised, quite informally, to wait in the nearby waiting room where someone would meet us with a wheelchair and accompany us to the platform for our train to Arras at 12.02. Indeed, a gentleman did so and he led us to the train and kindly assisted us into suitable seats with adequate room for our luggage; the train left on time! The journey took about 40 minutes with one stop at Douai; it took us across very flat countryside with numerous level crossings and much evidence of mining in earlier years; this was, of course, a battlefield and we noticed a military cemetery close by a level crossing. As we drew into the platform there was a uniformed SNCF man, with a wheelchair, waiting for us. Our exit involved travelling down in a lift, along a subway and up to street level by another lift. He led us out into the station car park and directed us to Hotel Mercure just ahead of us. What a great help this service had been. By 13.00 we were at the hotel, a very modern building; we were received by a very friendly receptionist and given the keys to our room – 304. As we emerged from the lift there was our room, just opposite; as we entered we were very pleased with what we found – it was spacious and welcoming and the bathroom, in particular, was designed and equipped for use by handicapped guests. On opening the curtains, there was the view! In the immediate vicinity there was a fairly busy road leading to Amiens in one direction and to Cambrai in the other, but the streets were lined with buildings which displayed a variety of façades and, notably, and not too distant, two towers – on the left the famous Beffroi and on the right, the tower of l'Eglise St Jean Baptiste. It was all very enticing; we had made a good choice!

The city of ARRAS is the capital of the Pas-de-Calais Department and has a population of about 43,000. Its long history and its architectural inheritance, attracts many visitors. The Romans were here, in 1430 Jeanne d'Arc was imprisoned here and Napoléon visited the city in 1804. The squares – Place des Héros and Grand Place – date from the year 1000 and the surrounding houses from the 12th and 13th centuries. The Beffroi and Hôtel de Ville date from the 15th and 16th centuries and were built over a century from 1463; built in flamboyant Gothic style it is a World Heritage Site. During the Great War Arras suffered terribly; being less than five kilometres from the front line, it was shelled relentlessly by the Germans. Architectural heritages such as the Beffroi and the Hôtel de Ville were virtually destroyed; the Cathédrale and the Abbaye Saint-Vaast greatly damaged and, in fact, some 95% of the buildings of the city were either destroyed or severely damaged. My father was in Arras in 1918; it must have been a scene of great destruction and desolation at that time. However, in 1919 an ambitious programme of reconstruction was commenced, and it took 12 years to identically rebuild the Place des Héros and the Grand Place; this time the new town hall was built on concrete foundations!

The afternoon was dry and still young and we decided to, at least, attempt to walk to the centre of the city. Crossing the Boulevard de Strasbourg by carefully observing the crossing lights was not difficult; passing La Poste on our left to another crossing in Rue Gambetta, continuing along a pedestrianised street towards the church of St Jean Baptiste and a short street took us to the entrance to the Place des Héros. This is an arcaded square formed by splendid buildings with a great variety of baroque façades. On the far side is the magnificent Hôtel de Ville crowned with its wonderful 77 metre high Beffroi; this building houses the Office de Tourisme. When we made a short visit to Arras in April 2000, we spent time in the tourist office; we will make it our first port of call again today as these offices are an important source of information, advice, etc.

We are pleased we did so as our attention was quickly drawn to an interesting exhibit displaying information, pictures, etc., relating to the experiences of Arras in the Second World War. By the end of 1939 Commonwealth armies were deployed in Northern France, the British Army GHQ was established at Saint-Vaast Abbey, troops were arriving at Arras station in large numbers and the Artois countryside became a vast training centre. All this was barely 20 years after the end of the Great War and, as we know, it was all to no avail. At 11.00pm on 14 May 1940 Arras suffered its first bombardment and on Sunday 19 May at 3.17pm the station and surrounding neighbourhoods were bombed by 18 enemy aircraft, killing more than 110 people. The Germans were at the gates of Arras and many civilians left. Overnight on 23/24 May the British evacuated the city which was then occupied by the Germans on 24 May. The Town Hall was requisitioned to accommodate the Kommandantur and four long years of German occupation began. On 1 September 1944 British tanks entered Arras without opposition; it was the Regiment of the Welsh Guards which liberated Arras, the Regiment which had been the last defender of the city in May 1940. This was a very interesting exhibition. Also, one cannot avoid being attracted to three giant figures – 'Les Géants d'Arras – Colas (4.6m), Jacqueline (4.3m) et Dédé (3.8m)', dressed as 18th and 19th century local peasants; they have a most interesting background. In Northern France and Belgium the tradition of giants goes back to the 16th century; it was revived in the 19th century as towns and cities identified themselves through huge figures representing a founding hero, a brave protector, or which embodied a trade symbolic of the town's history. The late 20th century saw a further revival of the tradition; new giants were created and a number of baptisms and weddings held at that time. The Giants of Arras are market gardeners of a nearby village; in fact, the Place des Héros is a market square where, several times a week, growers have come to sell their produce. Colas and Jacqueline existed in song from 1812; in 1891 they appeared in the form of giants. Destroyed during the bombardments of the Great War, they made a comeback in the 1920s only to be obliterated again in the Second World War. They were reborn in 1981 and the family expanded in 1995 with the birth of Dédé. The guardians of the giants are the Jouteurs d'Arras, who provide an entourage for Colas, Jacqueline and Dédé during Arras's festivities. We took photographs of the interior of the 'town hall' and we bought an excellent little book *'Balade au Coeur d'Arras'*, which includes pictures of beautiful facades, gables and sculptures which adorn so many buildings.

It was now time we began to make our way slowly back to the hotel and as we did so we took further photos of the 'square' as well as of l'Eglise St Jean Baptiste and, particularly, of a plaque recording the bravery of two sapeurs pompiers who fought a fire at this church during a violent bombardment on 10 July 1916. We looked forward to spending a pleasant leisurely evening in the hotel restaurant and to an enjoyable meal; we were not disappointed. We wasted no time and made our way to the restaurant, on the ground floor, shortly after it opened at 19.00. We were warmly welcomed, and the young waitress suggested that we might like to sit at a table for three or four situated in a corner a little detached from the main area, but with a view of the whole restaurant, as well as of the activity in the streets beyond the far windows of the building. Although we were quickly joined by quite a number of other guests, including a very large group, we were continually shown much personal concern, attention and friendly interest by, on this occasion, Estelle. Our meal, yes; for our main course we had gigot d'agneau, but I cannot recall our chosen dessert; it was all certainly enjoyable, but the lasting memory was of the convivial atmosphere. Before we left, after some three hours, the hardworking young waitresses, Estelle and her colleague Melody, were preparing the setting for the next day and petit-déjeuner. Time now, for us to wish them goodnight and return to our room. We had had a good day!

Day 3 – Thursday, 23 October 2014

Needless to say, the waitresses supervising petit-déjeuner were not those making the preparations on the previous evening, but they were equally welcoming and helpful. The menu was very comprehensive and the proceedings informal and leisurely. After enjoying a very adequate breakfast, and before making plans for the remainder of the day, we made use of the shower and how convenient it was to use – an open area in the corner of the room with no restricting screen, no tray to negotiate and a seat fixed to the wall, but foldable when not in use. It may be designed specifically for disabled but is very practical for many others. Some years ago we visited the France Exhibition in London where we found an exhibit of the Arras Tourist Office particularly interesting. Talking to one of its representatives we were told that a further aspect of the town's history had recently been revealed to the public; it was the ancient quarries under the town. We were told that we should make a point of visiting them; well, now is our opportunity.

It was at the Chantilly Conference on 16 November 1916 that the plans of General Nivelle for an offensive by the British in the Artois Region, followed, a few days later, by an attack by the French at Chemin des Dames (near Reims), were adopted; amazingly both Petain and Haig were not in favour. Chalk quarries had existed beneath Arras since the 16th century and the decision was taken to develop these quarries as a holding point for the troops; in fact, actually beneath no man's land. The work of linking and adapting the quarries by a series of tunnels was done by about 500 New Zealand tunnellers, who named them the WELLINGTON QUARRY. Facilities incorporated included electricity, running water, railway lines and the exits for the day of the battle. Kitchens were required as the provision of adequate meals, etc., was essential in maintaining morale; the British soldiers were particularly demanding regarding hygiene and sanitation and latrines, showers and water tanks were installed; the arrangements for sleeping provided little comfort in the cold and damp conditions; all the time, walking around was banned. The total underground network stretches for 12 miles and, ultimately, the Quarry accommodated 24,000 British soldiers. It was Easter Sunday on 8 April 1917 and, with an improvised altar, a service was held in the Quarry; it is still possible to see the black traces on the walls, left by the candles.

At 5.00am on 9 April 1917 a better than normal breakfast was provided, even a glass of rum for some; the last letters home, the last goodbyes, were posted. Ordered to leave great coats behind, at 5.30am these brave young men climbed the steps to burst out into the early daylight and the field of battle; the Germans had been taken totally by surprise. The great Artois Offensive stretching from Vimy Ridge to Bullecourt Plain mounted by British and Empire soldiers, preceded by a lengthy bombardment, had begun; initially it was a great success, but German counterattacks from 14 April halted the offensive. The British had gained some 12km, but at what a cost; during a period of two months 4,000 men died every day. Many of the 24,000 soldiers who climbed out of the Quarry early on that Easter Monday morning would not return to collect their great coats; the goodbyes had, indeed, been the final goodbyes. As Laurence Binyon wrote:-

> *"They shall grow not old, as we that are left grow old,*
> *Age shall not weary them, nor the years condemn.*
> *At the going down of the sun, and in the morning,*
> *We will remember them".*

Although we were told that the quarries were not far away, behind the station, we felt that it was not a likely walking distance for us; the receptionist ordered a taxi and within minutes we were at the doors of the entrance. We did not have to wait very long for the next tour and after being provided with the obligatory tin helmet and an optional personal hair net, we were taken to a lift. We descended about 20 metres into this amazing subterranean world. It has been made accessible to the public by the construction of a wooden walkway with a rail on each side; it is dimly lit, reminiscent of the times of its original use. As we proceeded, our well-informed guide pointed out various areas and features by the use of a torch; we noticed the graffiti on the walls, the drawings, inscriptions, messages, names and prayers engraved by the soldiers as they awaited the battle. I had noticed that the temperature in the Quarry was 11°C; one cannot imagine what it would have been like, living, eating and sleeping and unable to move about, in these conditions for any length of time. This is a very moving experience. Towards the end of the tour, our guide was very interested to know that my father had been in Arras in 1918 (not at the time of the Battle) and I wonder if he had been in this Quarry; it is possible. Our visit concluded with a short film realistically simulating the battle into which the young soldiers were instantly thrust. Of all the very many places of evidence of the Great War surely this must be unique and one of the most poignant. We spent a while surveying the items for sale and we bought a souvenir book; it contains two verses:

The General

"Good morning, Good morning!" the General said
When we met him last week on our way to the line.
Now the soldiers he smiled at are most of 'em dead.
And we're cursing his staff for incompetent swine.
"He's a cheery old cart," grunted Harry to Jack
As they slogged up to Arras with rifle and pack.
But he did for them both by his plan of attack.

Siegfried Sassoon, wounded at the Battle of Arras.

All of the night was quite barred out except
An owl's cry, a most melancholy cry
Shaken out long and clear upon the hill,

*Speaking for all who lay under the stars,
Soldiers and poor, unable to rejoice.*

Edward Thomas, killed in action on 9 April 1917.

The Battle of Arras continued from 9 April to 16 May 1917. The British casualties numbered nearly 160,000; what a terrible price to pay for so little gain. Nearly 100 years afterwards, at 6.30am on 9 April of every year, a tribute is paid to the soldiers of Britain and the Empire at the foot of the Battle of Arras memorial wall.

How shall we spend the remainder of the day? Firstly, we need a taxi. Once again help was willingly offered at the desk; a taxi would meet us in a matter of minutes. As we were driven away, we asked the driver to take us to the centre of the city where, perhaps, we could find somewhere to eat; he took us to the Place des Héros. The cost of our two taxis had been €5.60 and €9.00. Unfortunately, it was still too early for evening meals, but at Café Leffe we were able to have Crepes au Sucre and, at the same time, to savour a typical busy early evening setting with lively friendly background conversation. When we left, we first walked the very short distance into that other, and larger, magnificent square the Grand Place. Darkness had now descended and, back in the Place des Héros, we spent awhile absorbing its captivating scene and atmosphere now that natural light had been replaced by the gentle light of the street lamps and the interior lights of the buildings, all silently guarded by the towering Beffroi; this is the Place of Heroes which, in years gone by, has presented very different scenes – of destruction and desolation.

We had little alternative but to return to our hotel on foot which we did very slowly and with not a little discomfort and complaining. Back in the comfort of our room and after a short rest we felt sufficiently refreshed to spend an hour or so in the 'bar' area adjacent to the restaurant and to enjoy a cup of coffee. We found one sole gentleman there enjoying a glass of beer. We suspected that he was a coach driver and, after a while, he was joined by a number of ladies. We could not avoid overhearing their animated and excited conversation and we were in no doubt that they originated from the South Wales area; they did not appear to be conscious of our presence. Our small cup of coffee kept us occupied for a long time but, eventually, it was time for us to retire and, as we left, we wished the group "Goodnight". They were a little surprised to discover that we were English and a short conversation ensued. They told us that they were members of a choir and were on their way to visit a twin town in the west of Germany beyond Strasbourg; yes, the gentleman was the coach driver! How nice to end a memorable day sharing the anticipation and joys of others.

Day 4 – Friday, 24 October 2014

Today, we will endeavour to visit l'ABBAYE SAINT-VAAST and la CATHEDRALE. What an interesting saint Saint-Vaast is! As a priest, he was called upon by the Bishop of Reims to teach the catechism to Clovis, King of the Franks (509–511) and he moved to Arras to evangelize the Artois Region. According to legend, he miraculously healed two sick beggars and he was also known for his ability for taming the bears that had terrorised the region; the museum possesses a fragment of the tapestry depicting St Vaast and his bears. When Saint Vaast became Bishop of Arras; he erected a chapel and he repaired the church in which he was buried, when he died in 540. In about the year 650 St Aubert, Bishop of Cambrai and Arras, founded an abbey on the site of the chapel and decided to transfer to this place, on the banks of the river Crinchon, the relics of St Vaast. Although the abbey was razed by the Normans in the ninth century and successively burnt down and rebuilt, a Benedictine monastic community became established; it was to be one of the most prestigious north of Paris and continued until the Revolution. The original abbey church was built between the 11th and 14th centuries; by the 18th century it had fallen into disrepair and the monks decided to renovate and rebuild all the abbey buildings. When the Revolution broke out in 1789 the work had not been completed; the abbey was taken over by the forces of Revolution, desecrated and partially destroyed; the monks were forced to leave. In 1804, Emperor Napoleon I decided that the remains of the once beautiful Gothic cathedral should be demolished and a new Arras Cathedral constructed, "limiting the work to the requirements of solidity and decency"; it was completed in 1834. The remainder of the abbey was bought by the town and now houses the Musée des Beaux-Arts and a library. During the Great War the Cathedral was almost destroyed; on 26 June 1915, it was ripped open by a massive shell and from 5–10 July both the Cathedral and St. Vaast were in flames.

Reconstruction began in 1920 and it was reopened in 1934; it was damaged again by a bomb in 1944. In fact, the Cathedral has never been completed, as the planned bell tower was never constructed. Therefore, the building is only 75 feet tall at its highest point.

Our interpretation of the street plan suggested that it might not be a practical walking distance from our hotel to the ABBAYE SAINT-VAAST. Hence, the receptionist promptly booked a taxi and we were soon set down at the entrance gates. Inside, the spacious courtyard is enclosed on three sides by an impressive three-storey building. On the far side, in the centre and raised above the level of the courtyard, is the entrance to the Musée des Beaux-Arts. It is not a particularly auspicious entrance and there was little sign of activity. However, we found a door which was open and we were pleased to find that the museum was, in fact, open. Once inside we were instantly enveloped in the atmosphere of a museum richly endowed with its many treasures, testimonies of Arras's history, sculptures, porcelains and tapestries, in addition to paintings by significant artists. Also, at this time and for a period of eighteen months, the museum is displaying 100 masterpieces on loan from the collection of the Château de Versailles; they include the bust of Louis XIV (1665), the Dauphin's writing desk (1745), the sculpture Latone and her children (1670) from the Latone fountain and the remarkable sculptural group, Apollo Served by the Nymphs (1675).

Altogether, this was a wonderful exhibition of many and varied treasures and works of art, appropriately housed in this superb eighteenth century monastic complex. Although spread over a considerable area, we succeeded in viewing all parts; however, we were grateful for being reminded that there was an occasional chair placed at certain intervals! During the course of our tour we were able to see and photograph, through the windows, the splendid cloisters. We left through the 'shop' and, as we did so, we enquired how we could reach the CATHEDRALE most directly; we were told to go left after passing through the gates and then to take the next turning to the left and go straight ahead.

With these straightforward instructions we set off; however, as we walked along close to the side of the buildings it became evident that this complex was, indeed, one of the largest religious sites in France. With no 'cathedral' in sight I decided to go ahead to reconnoitre to ensure that we were going in the right direction. It was quite a long walk before I saw what appeared to be a large individual building; it was not impressive, with scaffolding implying that it was undergoing some much-needed maintenance. Of course, there was no tower or spire to distinguish it! Indeed, I was still not convinced that it was the building we were seeking and I descended a set of aging stone steps to a door – surely this is not the entrance to a cathedral! I opened the door and then I was in no doubt. I hurriedly retraced my steps to meet Margaret who had continued to make slow progress. Together, we were finally inside this huge and impressive church and yet it is of remarkable simplicity. It was constructed in ancient temple style from plans by the architect who, later, built La Madeleine in Paris. There is much of interest in this cathedral; we looked at the Chapelle de la Vierge in the apse; we noted, particularly, the magnificent organ, the work of Roethinger of Strasbourg, which was inaugurated in 1964; it is said that, in the Choeur are relics of Saint Jacques le Majeur, Saint Vaast and Saint Thomas Becket. In the transept there is a small shop and we talked to a gentleman there; in fact, he produced a chair for Margaret's use. I talked to a lady and asked her if la messe would be celebrated here on Sunday; she replied, "non, fini" and promptly found a street plan and highlighted the churches where there is a service regularly and noted the times.

We purchased a small book *La Guerre 14–18* and collected one or two information leaflets. Although we had spent some time here, it is a building which deserves more attention. However, we felt that we should begin to make our way back to our hotel. Firstly, we would head for the Office de Tourism but, by now, it was becoming dusk and difficult to read the street plan. We returned along the road back towards the museum and then turned left in what we hoped was the right direction. After some distance we asked a lady if we were going towards the Office; she assured us we were – she was going that way herself and suggested that we follow her. Her speed was somewhat superior to ours and after a while we lost sight of her. At one point we found ourselves alongside a taxi, but we soon realised that he was already responding to a call and our hopes quickly faded.

Eventually, to our relief, we recognized the rear of the Hôtel de Ville. We could not contemplate walking the further distance to the hotel and we asked an assistant at the Office de Tourism to order a taxi for us. However, most taxi drivers appeared to be very busy and it was only after many calls that a taxi was contacted which could collect us in a matter of minutes – we could meet him outside the fish shop, we were told. Unfortunately, the fish shop was closed and I didn't recognise it and, while searching for our taxi on the further side of the Place des Héros, the taxi driver had found Margaret and was looking for me near the Tourist Office. Eventually, we were all united and, somewhat relieved, safely delivered to Hôtel Mercure. The fare for this taxi was €8.50; however, this cost and the physical efforts required to enable us to visit these wonderful buildings and their contents were well justified.

After a period of recuperation in our room we did not find it difficult to make our way to the restaurant, anticipating a relaxing and enjoyable couple of hours. We were welcomed again by Estelle and Melody and we were pleased to find that we could occupy the same table as on the previous occasion. This evening was a fairly busy one, but we were again given generous attention by, in particular, Melody. Both waitresses speak commendable English and Melody clearly enjoyed exchanging brief comments with us as she busily went about her work. When speaking to Estelle, she said that she felt she needed a holiday; in fact, she is going away next week, to Chinon. We were pleased to be able to tell her that we know Chinon well and we wished her, bonnes vacances! Perhaps it is surprising that, although we recall such aspects of the evening, we cannot remember the details of our chosen menu. However, it was certainly enjoyable as, indeed, was the entire evening; an appropriate conclusion to a very interesting day.

Day 5 – Saturday, 25 October 2014

Of the numerous battlefield sites of the Great War perhaps few are more widely known and visually recognisable than VIMY RIDGE. In fact, The Ridge extends over some fourteen kilometres, while the memorial stands on Hill 145, the highest point. As at Arras, the Artois Offensive began here at 05.30 on the morning of 9 April 1917, when thousands of Canadian and British soldiers emerged from tunnels and trenches and, preceded by a heavy artillery bombardment, stormed the Ridge. They achieved all their objectives with the exception of Hill 145, which was captured on the following day. Although out of 10,602 casualties 3,598 Canadians died, it was a significant victory of the War and it brought honour and pride to the young Canadian nation.

We have visited Vimy Ridge on previous occasions, but we felt we would like to do so once again. We obtained a Salient Tours leaflet detailing minibus tours from Arras hotels; unfortunately, neither I nor the hotel could obtain a telephone response. In the circumstances, we decided to make the journey by taxi. Again, the hotel arranged a taxi for us. When driving in this area many years ago we had discovered an orientation table showing the disposition of the various armies during the war; one of these units was the 51st Highland Division of which my father was a member (the Machine Gun Corps, in fact). I cannot remember where exactly it was;

I had hoped that we might locate it again, but we did not spot it on this journey. Nevertheless, it was good to travel over this historic landscape again, even though we did not have the independence to stop or take diversions whenever we felt it might be interesting to do so. Our driver took us to the Visitor Centre of Vimy Ridge, a situation we did not readily recognize for we could not see the massive monument.

We spent some time in the Centre, looking at photographs, exhibits, etc., and we talked to the supervisor, a young Canadian gentleman – perhaps he was a student or a member of the military. He told us that a new Visitor Centre was to be constructed nearby during the next two years to commentate the 100th anniversary of the battle in 1917. We realised that we now had some walking to do and there was no doubt as to the direction we should take. There is a clearly defined route for pedestrians at the side of the road and one must not stray from this path. The area is now reverentially forested and the very uneven surface neatly grassed, for, no doubt, it still conceals human remains. The area is pock-marked with shell holes from artillery bombardment and mine craters from the fierce underground war. Here, the earth's surface has been turned over and over again by the tunnelling, the trenches, the shelling and the underground mines; one cannot imagine how human life survived amidst such a hell. As we walked and walked, albeit very slowly, we still could not see the Monument. Quite suddenly and remarkably we found ourselves talking to a couple going in the opposite direction. Perhaps it was the use of the walking stick which attracted their attention and prompted them to make some comment. However it was, we had quite a long and very friendly conversation – they were aged 80 and 81; they live in Vimy and they told us that they walk this way every day. They clearly have much respect for this site. We spent quite a few minutes talking and, I think, we said 'goodbye' three times. What an uplifting encounter.

Eventually, we continued on our way and, after a while, we saw the first glimpse of the towering Monument standing on Hill 145. After reaching the open area and the car park it is still quite a long way to the base of the Monument and suddenly a buggy drew alongside us; it was the young Canadian gentleman we had been talking to earlier. He asked if he could take us the remainder of the way; we thanked him, but we felt that the appropriate way to approach this revered site is slowly and on foot. However, he did offer to come and collect us in 30 minutes or so; this we accepted.

The MONUMENT stands on land ceded by France, in perpetuity, to Canada in 1922 – it is the Vimy Ridge National Historic Site of Canada. It was designed by a Canadian sculptor and architect, Walter Seymour Allward, who said that the design came to him in a dream; his aim was to produce 'a structure which would endure, in an exposed position, for a thousand years – indeed, for all time'. The work began in 1925 and it took eleven years to complete; the memorial was unveiled on 26 July 1936 in the presence of King Edward VIII. Some facts relating to the construction of the Monument are, in themselves, awe-inspiring – the foundations are formed of 11,000 tonnes of concrete reinforced with hundreds of tonnes of steel; the pylons and sculptured figures consist of almost 6,000 tonnes of limestone transported from a former Roman quarry in Croatia; the figures were carved where they now stand from huge blocks of this stone, the largest being of a sorrowing mother (representing Canada) mourning her dead; one of the massive twin white pylons bears the maple leaves of Canada while the other bears the fleurs-de-lys of France; carved on the walls are the names of 11,285 Canadian soldiers who were killed in France and who have no known grave. Barely three years after the unveiling, France and Germany were at war again and when the German Army occupied France, there were fears for the preservation of this priceless treasure. However, there was one person who had admired it, as a monument to peace rather than a celebration of war. Incredibly, that man was none other than Adolf Hitler and he assigned special troops from the Waffen-SS to guard Vimy Ridge. About 70 years after its construction major restoration work was carried out on the Monument with particular care and craftsmanship, including repointing the two massive pylons and cleaning the twenty statues; work which took two years to finally complete in 2007.

Although the Monument is not a building, and is in a very exposed situation, its huge presence pervades an atmosphere of sacrosanctity. It was a lovely warm afternoon; there were many visitors – we had noticed a coach of Glovers of Ashbourne – and people were silently appreciating the experience; however, as we have found on earlier visits, some felt they wanted to express their emotions – one man turned to me and said, "this is the most beautiful place". Indeed, a visit here is a deeply moving experience. Nearby, sheep are grazing peacefully now. Looking beyond the Monument and across the Douai plain to the east we can see symbols of a different kind, slag heaps; a reminder that this was a mining area in bygone years. We had spent quite some while at the memorial when our buggy duly arrived to take us back to the nearby car park He enquired how we were continuing our journey and, when we told him that we required a taxi to return us to our hotel in Arras, he was able to telephone a taxi driver. The response was, 'would we be willing to share a taxi with another couple', to which we readily agreed. It would be some while to wait, but the weather was still good and we spent the time sitting on the wall near the flags of France and Canada and with a more distant view of the Monument. When the taxi arrived for us it still had to collect the other 'couple'; however, we soon discovered that it was, in fact, two young Canadian men. Our journey back to Arras was, therefore, very interesting; they told us that they are backpacking around Europe by train and so our taxi delivered them to the station at Arras before taking us to our hotel. The cost of our return journey to Vimy Ridge was €26.60 and €15.00; this was well justified. We are now grateful that, with the benefit of the nearby lift, it is only a few short steps from our room to conclude the day with a very pleasant evening in the restaurant. However, tonight is l'heure d'hiver, which means that all clocks move back one hour!

Day 6 – Sunday, 26 October 2014

Sunday, in towns and cities, is regarded somewhat differently in France than in Angleterre. Generally, no shops are open and we have often found petrol stations closed. It is a day more for leisure, for pleasurable activities, sightseeing, visiting museums, etc., a day for recreation and relaxation. Leisurely, was how we intended to spend our day and, appropriately, petit déjeuner is available until 11.00. When we were ready to do so we set off to walk into the centre of Arras again. How nice it was to enjoy this unique atmosphere; the shops were closed and one focused more on the facades of the buildings. Our first stop was at the EGLISE St JEAN BAPTISTE. The first church on this site was constructed in the 12th century; it was demolished in 1564 and rebuilt as the church of Saint-Nicolas-des-Fossés. This was the only church in Arras to survive the Revolution, when it became known as the Temple of Reason. In 1803 it became the Cathédrale St Jean Baptiste and until 1833, when the present cathedral was completed. On 10 July 1915 the church was bombarded and destroyed by fire; two firemen gave their lives, and their names to the street on which the church stands. Reconstructed in 1918–20 in neo-gothic style, it was consecrated in 1927. There are some noteworthy features of this church such as: a painting by Reubens 'Descent from the Cross', a retable of the 17th century, sculptures and beautiful stained glass windows dating from the 1920s and 1930s and also of the 1950s, notably that of the four evangelists. This is a beautiful and much used church where there is to be a messe at 18.00 today; I took some photographs. In the Place des Héros there were many visitors, but we eventually found a seat in the inviting and very busy, pâtisserie of Pâtissier/Chocolatier, Sebastien Thibaut, where we enjoyed pain-aux-raisins and cups of coffee.

Afterwards, we visited the Office de Tourisme in the Hôtel de Ville again, mainly to browse over the many items in the shop and we bought some cards and an interesting book, *Arras – Pas à pas*. It was approaching the end of the day for the office as we left. We lingered awhile in the Place des Héros for the last time and continued past the Church we had visited earlier, before setting off for our hotel. It had been sunny and warm for a while during the afternoon, but daylight is now fading, for it is the first evening of 'winter time'.

Back at the hotel, we welcomed the evening which we could spend in the friendly atmosphere of the restaurant. It seems that many visitors spend no more than one or two nights here and clearly the waitresses very much appreciate and enjoy having guests for a longer period and creating a friendly relationship. This evening Melody gave us her attention and, before we left, we had a longer conversation with her; she told us that she has served three years of a five-year apprenticeship at the hotel and she would like to have a career in the hotel business. At present she works from 14.00 to midnight, when she has a 10-minute walk to her home. We had told her that we planned to spend a few days in Lille after leaving Arras, to which she replied, "Be careful in Lille, it is a big city". What a kind thought! As we said "Goodnight", we thanked her for the attention and concern that both she and Estelle had shown to us and we wished her success in the future. Once again I have no record or recollection of our actual meal, something which I will not have to admit in respect of the three subsequent evenings! In fact, our overriding happy memories of our evenings here have been of the general conviviality and the warm personal friendliness of the staff.

Day 7 – Monday, 27 October 2014

We leave Arras today, but not until this afternoon! It is a sunny morning and we are able to appreciate once more the view from our room, particularly of those two magnificent towers which dominate the city. We have time, also, to enjoy an unhurried further petit déjeuner before preparing to vacate our room by 11.00. Eventually, we took our luggage down to the reception desk, where it was kindly accommodated while we spent another couple of hours in the nearby bar and enjoying a cup of coffee. Our train was due to leave at 16.24 and we must allow ample time to get to the station and to arrange for assistance on the journey. Before we left the hotel we expressed our very sincere thanks to all the staff for the help, kindness and understanding they had showed; our comments were much appreciated. There are no busy roads to negotiate between the hotel and la gare and, once in the foyer, we quickly found some vacant seats. Nearby, there was an enquiry kiosk, periodically manned by a gentleman who from time to time would don his peaked cap, his symbol of authority, and rush off to perform other duties. As soon as there was an opportunity I told him of our situation and our need of assistance; without any formality, he told us to remain in our seats and someone would come to assist us in good time. There was a vacant seat alongside us; soon it was occupied by a young lady, probably a student; when the time came for her to leave, she turned to us and wished us "bonne journée". Next, we had the company of an older man. We exchanged a few comments; regarding our respective nationalities, for instance; I told him that we were English and he said that he was French, but significantly, he added "European". These exchanges were typical of our stay in Arras; everyone had been so friendly; perhaps the presence and the sacrifices of so many British soldiers in bygone years have left a lasting gratitude. While we were waiting for our train I walked across the square for a closer look and a photograph of the monument 'ARRAS – á des Enfants MORTS pour la defense du DROIT'. This stands in front of Hotel Angleterre!

Our visit to Arras has been memorable; apart from the tenuous personal link, it has been a wonderful opportunity to see more and learn more of this ancient city, with such a long and interesting history; a city which saw so much of its treasured past devastated and destroyed in the horrors of the second decade of the 20th century; a city which rose again, a phoenix, from the ashes to recover its previous beauty, as we see it today. Also, we remember the kindness, helpfulness and friendliness of everyone we have come into contact with.

Before we began to think that the time for our train was approaching, a lady, yes, in a peaked cap, arrived with a wheelchair to take us to the appropriate platform. This involved using the lifts which were not large enough for all of us; consequently, I had to be sent ahead with the luggage to be followed by Margaret, in the wheelchair, and our escort; a rather amusing episode! Again, she was a very friendly communicative person and she kindly established us in our seats with our luggage. I do not know where this train originated, but there were not many passengers when we joined, but many boarded at Douai for Lille. It was about 17.00 when we arrived at Lille Flandres, and, as we did so, there again was an SNCF man waiting at the door with a wheelchair. This is a terminus and no lifts are required, but it is a large station. He took us to an exit which was in the direction of Hotel Lille Europe. Yes, as Melody said, this is a big city and it was a very busy time. However, we reached the hotel safely and we were promptly given the key to return to room 512. In this immediate area, we have not found a restaurant providing evening meals; however, immediately underneath the hotel is a cafeteria, Brioche Doree (it is part of the vast Centre Commercial Euralille) which is open until 19.00. Here, we were able to have a large baguette ham and salad sandwich and a cold drink; it provided an adequate meal and, afterwards, we had only to walk a few yards to the door of our hotel.

Day 8 – Tuesday, 28 October 2014

We have visited Lille many times; even for a day trip from our home in Camerton, soon after Eurostar services were inaugurated in 1994. In the past, we have explored much of the city on foot and we are particularly fond of the area known as, Le Vieux Lille (Old Lille). Where better to spend a few hours, as in its midst stands the cathedral. To limit the amount of walking involved, we first walked the relatively short distance to Lille Flandres where taxis are always available. We asked to be driven to Vieux Lille and the driver set us down, very conveniently, at the junction of Rue de la Monnaie and

OCTOBER 2014

Rue d'Angleterre. Le VIEUX LILLE is full of history and interest. It holds great charm in the wonderful diversity of the flamboyant architecture of its restored 17th century buildings; the variety of façades, gables and of colours is amazing. Rue de la MONNAIE runs through and forms the heart of the old town, where the city was born many centuries ago. Previously called Rue Saint-Pierre, it took its present name in 1685, when a Hôtel des Monnaies was created in Lille by Louis XIV and installed in the former house of the 'lord of the manor' of Lille, situated in this street.

We slowly walked along the street until we came to a little café; how appropriate – it was time for a cup of coffee. It was at Le Porthos, 53 Rue de la Monnaie and we were served by Juliette. As we continued along the street, we photographed (again) the striking remains of the mill, Saint-Pierre, of 1649. On reaching the end of Rue de la Monnaie, and at the junction with Place du Lion d'Or and Place Louise-de-Bettignies, we came to the building which has attracted our attention whenever we have passed, either on foot or in a vehicle; it is 'Le Lion'. It has a remarkably picturesque façade with a variety of colours and is the office of estate agents; it dates from the late 19th or early 20th century. I had to photograph it again, as one which I took some years ago had been installed on my 'desktop', until, unfortunately, it was lost when the computer was replaced. A little further along Place Louise-de-Bettignies, I photographed another interesting building. Retracing our steps, we joined a passageway from Rue de la Monnaie which leads to the rear of the cathedral. There is a gift shop underneath the building which has an entrance at the side and then is reached by descending a flight of stairs. While standing at the top and wondering if we would find it worthwhile to proceed, a lady noticed us and insisted on activating the goods lift to enable us to reach the shop. It was a kind gesture and we did, indeed, buy a small standing monthly calendar, which has been a focus of interest. Our memories of this cathedral are of when, in 2007, I fell on a step approaching the entrance and had to receive hospital treatment before continuing our visit. Safely inside this time, we were pleased to be able to sit for a while in this magnificent church.

La CATHEDRAL NOTRE-DAME de la TREILLE is not an ancient building. The blessing of the cornerstone took place on 1 July 1854 and construction began on 9 June 1856. Built in the gothic style, the building grew, bit by bit, between 1854 and 1953. With the erection of the translucent marble front wall, the cathedral was finally completed in 1999. The Cathedral contains notable works of art in the form of sculptures, stained glass, frescos and mosaics; we noticed, in particular, the fine statue of Saint Pierre. It is described as a 'living cathedral' as we have witnessed, having attended an office and a concert. Our particular interest today is the organ. When we were here in 2007 a Cavaille-Coll choir organ had been in use since 1869 and we were told about the instrument which was about to be installed; it consists of more than 7,000 pipes and had been donated by Radio France. It is now lofted high in the south transept and the console, with 106 stops, is near the choir. We read that this organ was originally built between 1957 and 1966 for studio 104 Olvier Messiaen at Radio France, Paris, by Danion-Gonzales and has been reconstructed here by Orgelbau Klais of Bonn. It was formally inaugurated and blessed on 1 June 2008. We did not expect to experience the sounds of the organ in the acoustics of this building, but we hoped to be able to purchase a recording. We recognized a gentleman we had seen in 2007, who was, from time to time, at a small kiosk and also acting as a guide and providing explanations to visitors. When I noticed an opportunity, I asked him if we could purchase a CD and a DVD. We are pleased to now have an excellent recording by the Organist of the Cathedral, André Dubois, of music by composers whose lives spanned from 1657 to 1998. We also have a documentary film recording the process of the dismantling, transfer and reconstruction of one of the finest organs in France; it was an immense task, involving 40 tons, 7,600 pipes, 20 km of cables and 28 metres of height. Having completed our visit to the cathedral we hoped that we could find an appropriate eating place nearby. There is a restaurant in the square in front of the Cathedral, but we found that they would not be serving meals until 19.00. However, we were welcome to use the toilets and they willingly ordered a taxi to take us back to our hotel. We were more than happy to resort to another baguette ham and salad sandwich at Brioche Doree.

Day 9 – Wednesday, 29 October 2014

Earlier in this book I wrote about the tradition of the presentation of a weekly religious magazine programme, *Le Jour du Seigneur*, incorporating the live broadcast of la messe, every Sunday morning on the main state television channel, France 2, since October 1949. Back in July, the broadcast from the village of Bouvines was particularly interesting; it marked the 800th anniversary of the BATTLE of BOUVINES.

Early in the 13th century, the wretched King John, in conflict with his barons, planned to invade France determined to recover lands lost in Normandy and Anjou, and thus to regain some of his prestige at home. However, the barons refused John's summons to accompany him and he went without them. He created an army of mercenaries and formed a coalition with some allies, including – Emperor Otto IV of Germany and the Counts of Dammartin and Flanders. John himself went to Poitou, landing at La Rochelle but, despite some initial success, he made little progress. The key confrontation was in the north, in Flanders, where the army was led by Emperor Otto and the English contingent commanded by William of Salisbury, John's half-brother. The armies, comprising about 40,000 men, confronted each other on marshy land near the village of Bouvines on 27 July 1214; it was a hot Sunday afternoon and the battle lasted four to five hours, during which some 2,000 men died; the result was a decisive victory for Philippe Auguste of France. Otto fled, the Count of Flanders and William of Salisbury were captured and the Count of Dammartin surrendered, while John was still in the south. His hopes of re-conquest utterly crushed, John returned to England, defeated, humiliated and deeply in debt, to face the angry barons. Consequently, he was compelled to submit, unconditionally, to the demands of the barons. Hence, on 15 June 1215 he set his seal to Magna Carta – thus forming the basis of English democracy. John died in 1216 and was buried in Worcester Cathedral. Meanwhile, the victory at Bouvines was a very significant event in French history; a 'gift of God', it is said!

It would be interesting to visit Bouvines and we estimated that it may be about 10–15 km. from our hotel. Obviously, the only practical way to reach it would be by taxi. We talked to one of the receptionists, who kindly ascertained an estimate of the cost. It would be quite expensive, but it was our only opportunity and as we were already prepared to leave; we decided to go ahead. It was only a matter of minutes before the taxi arrived and we were on our way through the extremely busy environs of Lille and out into pleasant countryside. Not knowing where exactly it would be best to be taken, we headed for the village church which was easily located. We arranged for the driver to collect us in an hour or so.

L'EGLISE-SAINT PIERRE, a 'mémorial national', was constructed on the site of an 11th century chapel between 1880 and 1886, in neo-gothic style inspired by the architecture of the 13th century. The most notable and remarkable feature of the church are its 21 stained glass windows. Created by master glassmakers at Bar-le-Duc, the windows are eight metres high and 3.2 metres wide. Each window is composed of three parts; at the top is a picture of angels, at the bottom is the coat of arms of the donor and the centre depicts a moment of the battle according to the chronicle of the chaplain of Philippe-Auguste. The cost of 350,000 francs was five times the cost of the church. In addition to these fascinating windows the church contains other information regarding the battle, including a map showing the disposition of the armies at the time. Another feature of the church is the splendid Cavaille-Coll organ and we also noted the statue of St Pierre. Before we left I went outside to photograph the exterior of this 'Monument Historique'. Interestingly, we have learned that the celebrations on 27 July 2014 were attended by descendants of King Philippe-Auguste, including Louis de Bourbon, heir to the throne of France.

Our taxi duly arrived to collect us and, as we left the village, I noticed a sign which may have indicated the direction of the actual site of the battle. However, I could not translate my reaction into French quickly enough to suggest a diversion; in any case it was beginning to rain. We asked to be taken to the OFFICE de TOURISME in Lille; this is housed in the notable Palais Rihour which was constructed in the 15th century and has been classified as a monument historique since 1875. It was now raining very heavily and we had to hurry into the shelter of the Office. In the circumstances, we decided to book one of the city bus tours, which takes 50 minutes and costs €24. While waiting, we talked to two ladies from the USA, who had travelled from London but, having failed to leave the train the first time at Lille, had been returned from Brussels free of charge! It was still raining as we left on our tour and, unfortunately, the windows soon became steamed up. However, we had excellent pictures on a large screen in the front of the bus, showing the varied places we were passing. Despite the unfortunate weather, it was a very interesting experience and no less so, having taken this excellent tour on a previous occasion!

Back at the Office de Tourisme, surely there must be somewhere nearby where we could have a light meal regardless of the time! Yes, we are in the Place Rihour and here is Le Rihour's – we have eaten here before. Without hesitation, our suggestion of a croque-monsieur received a positive response. We were pleased to be able to relax and to enjoy it, unhurriedly, with cold drinks followed by a cup of coffee. Anxious to make good use of our last available hours in the city, we went for a short walk. We first noted the large monument 'Aux Lillois victimes des guerres' at the side of Palais Rihour; then, to experience the flavour of life and activity this early evening in the busy centre of the city, which has a large student population, we continued into the impressive Place Charles de Gaulle or Grande Place. This has been the living centre of the city since the Middle Ages; its notable features include – the tall column of la Déesse, erected in 1845 to commemorate the siege of 1792, the Vieille Bourse, the bookshop Furet du Nord where we spent a while browsing and, next door, the Grand Hôtel Bellevue where Mozart stayed in 1765. Back in Place Rihour we hoped to find a taxi, but none were evident, except, that is, for a couple of three-wheel 'taxi bikes'. We have never travelled by such means before and so it would be a novel experience. We decided to accept the offer and, with our 'driver' pedalling furiously, weaving through the busy traffic and waving to his friends as we went, we reached our hotel safely; the fare was €5. Well, despite being physically limited there are alternative ways of getting around and, now, we are not too late for a final visit to Brioche Doree for a cup of coffee!

Day 10 – Thursday, 30 October 2014

The final day of this journey; the day of our return! In fact, until leaving Waterloo for Trowbridge at 19.20 we shall be travelling for no more than 27 minutes of the day; however, the times of our trains are the most convenient as they allow a generous three hours in London, to make the transfer and allow time for refreshments, etc. Unfortunately, having to vacate our room by 11.00, we have more than four hours to pass before our train leaves for St Pancras. We are able to store our luggage at the reception and there is an available rest area adjacent to the 'breakfast room'. As on previous days, we had time for interesting conversation with the receptionists. We allowed ample time to proceed to the handicapé centre at Lille Europe. Once there, and having registered our details, we felt completely in the care of Eurostar and we could relax. On the platform, waiting for our train, I told our guide how much we appreciate this service; he seemed a little embarrassed – after all he was only doing his job. Our train was on time at 15.36, the journey very pleasant and as we drew into St Pancras there was a gentleman waiting with a wheelchair.

When our turn came for a taxi we were greeted by a friendly cockney character – "Where are we going then?" he asked. I replied, "Waterloo – do you know where it is?" I promptly added "I'm sure you do". This set the tone of our journey. Our driver asked us where we were going from Waterloo. When I told him,

Trowbridge in Wiltshire, he clearly had a picture of a typically English market town. When I told him of the various nationalities living in Trowbridge and that we have public notices on the streets in Polish he was amazed. Then, he boldly stated, "I'm a UKIP man myself," he obviously favours this country's exit from the European Union. An interesting conversation followed in which I said that the founding fathers of the Union had experienced a period of history of ghastly turmoil which we have since been spared and they had the benefit of greater wisdom than most of us; I feel that we have more to lose than to gain by leaving the Union. As we parted company at Waterloo, our driver said that he likes such a conversation; he shook hands and wished us well. Entering the station, it was another world. The usual continuous announcements of train information, was accompanied by an enthusiastic military band; it was an incessant din.

Our first priority was to arrange for assistance when the time came to board our train. Next, we needed some refreshments; we used the lift to reach the upper level; everywhere was so crowded and so busy and it was difficult to move around and control our luggage. Eventually, we found somewhere to sit, not very comfortably, and to purchase something to eat and a drink. We felt we should not move until it was appropriate to check that our help was, in fact, now available. Indeed it was, and a very friendly gentleman helped us to the train and installed us in seats for the handicapped with our luggage. Fortunately, the train had just arrived and was yet to be cleaned of the rubbish left by the previous passengers, for rapidly it began to fill. Soon, passengers were sitting on luggage racks, our luggage was moved to allow sitting on the floor and some were sitting in the doorway; one lady, sitting on the floor, said, "One does not want this kind of journey after a long day's work". The circumstances did not ease for much of the journey, perhaps not until we reached Salisbury. As we approached Trowbridge, we were relieved to hear from the conductor that our request for assistance had been passed on when the crew changed at Salisbury; he came and helped us to leave the train with our luggage. Having booked a taxi during the journey, we were pleased to find a car waiting for us at the station and, after emerging from the taxi at our gate, we were surprised to be told, "I have put your large case outside your door". Yes, another friendly and very helpful driver. We were home before 22.00.

We have successfully accomplished another 'France Journey'. It was an experience we shall not forget, walking when it was practical to do so and using taxis at other times, we have been able to recall past journeys and to visit historic sites for the first time. We are most grateful for the help and assistance we received from so many on so many occasions. I am not sure how many journeys we have made since the 1950s, but they probably represent a total period of some two years. Throughout that time we, as English visitors, have been extended a warm welcome and much respect, courtesy, consideration, kindness and help and not least during these past ten days. We too consider ourselves – European!

Margaret, equipped for the tour of the ancient quarries at Arras.

THE FINAL INSTALMENT

A FOND FAREWELL TO NORMANDY

SEPTEMBER – OCTOBER 2015 (Tuesday, 15 September – Thursday, 1 October)

It was on 6 October 2011, but only just, that we reached home at the end of the second of two near six-week journeys in France during that year. It had been a long, interesting, enjoyable and memorable journey – a wonderful experience, visiting Burgundy, in particular, and all our friends in France – that is until we reached Cherbourg. To our surprise and disappointment we found that, instead of returning to Poole on the cruise ship *Barfleur* as we had expected, we must travel to Portsmouth on the 'fast-craft' *Normandie Express*. It was a stormy evening and we were warned straightaway to remain seated. As it turned out we had little desire to do otherwise as the little vessel was tossed about by the sea with large waves frequently crashing against the windows. We had never been more relieved to enter into the relative calm of the entrance to Portsmouth harbour. However, the wind and rain certainly extended inland and the drive along the M27, amidst all the traffic, was difficult as we concentrated on remaining on the motorway and not to be enticed onto one of the many slip roads, until reaching the exit for Salisbury. Once heading for the cathedral city we felt a little more secure, although there was little improvement in the weather. The 'final straw' of this journey was saved until we reached the entrance to Green Lane from West Ashton Road; it was closed – closed completely and it was almost midnight! We could see the entrance to our home, but how were we to get there. Feeling like strangers in our own land, we tried one option and then another before finally entering Green Lane from the opposite direction and eventually driving through our gates with a great sigh of relief.

Perhaps 2011 would have been a not inappropriate concluding instalment of our *France – A Journey*, at least by road. Indeed, at that time we did not contemplate a further journey by car. However, we soon had thoughts of returning to the Hérault Department in the Region of Languedoc by train and come the end of the year we had made a reservation for a period in June 2012. Unfortunately, Margaret's continuing ulcer, unrelenting arthritis in her feet and legs, coupled with the onset of memory problems early in the new year, cast constant doubts on the wisdom of attempting such a journey; in particular, we were kept waiting very many months for a planned appointment with a consultant. In the circumstances we eventually cancelled the arrangements made. However, 2012 passed and the situation had changed little – what should we do? We made plans for 2013 similar to those cancelled in the previous year; this time we succeeded in fulfilling our hopes. Then, in 2014, we were grateful to be able to travel to the north-east of France, once again by train.

SEPTEMBER – OCTOBER 2015

It is now 2015 and our love of France and its people remains undiminished and there is no better way of visiting the country than independently with one's personal transport; we continued to cherish the prospect of doing so – could it be this year? Unfortunately, Margaret's ulcer, which had remained healed for six months, recurred at Easter and again necessitated weekly visits to the Hospital and, subsequently, thrice weekly dressing. However, the nurse who has been tending the ulcer over a long period helped us to be optimistic and said that she would be willing to provide us with an adequate supply of dressings to enable us to make the regular changes. Also, Margaret's mobility limitations remain a considerable handicap. My eyesight was still an important consideration. Although the consultant to whom I had been referred last year had been reassuring, I was aware that I was not recognizing and identifying road signs and obstructions as readily as is desirable; in any case I was due for another test in the middle of this year. Fortunately, after a seemingly thorough examination by the optician, I was not subjected to any further consultation or, particularly, to any comments or reservations regarding driving.

There was now no apparent reason why I should not give serious consideration to once again driving in France. However, it was by no means an easy decision; although I had driven many thousands of miles in France over many years with no difficulties or problems whatsoever, I had had no such experience during the past four years. Most importantly, I had driven so little in this country either, with little desire to do so – driving only in the environs of Trowbridge with the occasional slightly longer journey over familiar routes. In fact, did I now have the confidence to contemplate a journey of perhaps several hundred miles over largely unfamiliar routes? I was concerned of the possibility of failing to observe important road signs, messages and directions, of making errors of judgement, mishaps and of possible breakdowns, etc., and of the likely consequences. The journey would require considerable concentration. We wrestled long and hard with the question – do we plan a further France Journey by car – quite probably our last – or, particularly in view of Margaret's health and our increasing years, do we abandon such a project at this stage. Eventually, we concluded that the latter alternative would leave us with the permanent uncertainty of what we might have been able to achieve – the disappointment of perhaps an opportunity missed. I felt that, for a while at least, we should lift ourselves out of the humdrum routine of daily life to an experience which we could recall and reflect upon long into the future. We began to make positive plans.

We would love to again visit familiar places and friends in the Indre-et-Loire, the Corrèze and the Lot, but that would involve extensive journeys and we must not be too ambitious. In any case the Départements of Manche and Calvados of the Region of Normandy hold so much of interest to us and we could visit friends in and near Bayeux. Fortunately, we find that Brittany Ferries will be operating their cruise ferry service between Poole and Cherbourg, with the *Barfleur*, throughout the year and through the winter. However, the timetable is not as inviting as we would like. The daily sailing from Poole leaves at 08.30; sailings from Cherbourg, from

September, are at either 18.30 or 22.15, arriving at Poole at 21.45 and 07.00 respectively. As the year is passing rapidly towards autumn the journey from Poole and a return journey at 18.30 could well involve travelling from and to home during the hours of darkness; this we wish to avoid. The options appear to be to drive to Poole on the previous day and spend a night there and to return on an overnight ferry; this would be our plan.

So far as accommodation is concerned, we would like to spend a couple of nights at Valognes, perhaps three nights at Grandcamp-Maisy, four nights at the farm in Vienne-en-Bessin, then four nights in Bayeux, returning to Grandcamp-Maisy for a final night. We then successfully made bookings for just a few weeks in advance as follows: Brittany Ferries – from 16 September to 30 September; Holiday Inn Express, Poole – 15 September; Le Relais du Louvre, Valognes – 16 and 17 September; Hôtel Le Duguesclin, Grandcamp-Maisy – 18, 19 and 20 September; La Ferme des Châtaigniers, Vienne-en-Bessin – 21, 22, 23 and 24 September; Hôtel Campanile, Bayeux – 25, 26, 27 and 28 September; Hôtel Le Duguesclin, Grandcamp-Maisy – 29 September.

Arranging essential travel insurance gave me little encouragement; it was not a straightforward matter, particularly in view of our respective ages, regular treatments and medications, etc. Having virtually completed the process, as I thought, 'online', my screen suddenly disappeared and I had to start again. After finally completing the task a second time, I realized that this time I had failed to refer to Margaret's ulcer condition. I then sent an e-mail explaining my omission.

I promptly received a telephone call and I was required to complete the application for a third time. The outcome was that the cost of covering Margaret's various conditions became prohibitive and I finally accepted full cover for myself alone. This is what I had hoped for in the first place – as I explained to Staysure, I particularly required cover for the possibility that I could suffer an accident and be unable to drive, for instance. Having completed these formal arrangements, we could now relax and look forward to the day of departure? Most certainly not! There is little time left and there are all the personal arrangements to complete. I have to arrange for the car to receive a reassuring check and also to be cleaned and washed and, importantly, to arrange to temporarily extend breakdown cover to apply in France. We must ensure that the numerous essential items, particularly medications, dressings etc., are taken with us and, having the benefit of the facilities the car provides, such items as might be useful. No doubt there will be occasions when some additional revitalization might be welcome in the car, if not elsewhere, and I filled a large cool box with a varied and plentiful supply of cereal bars, biscuits, bottles of fruit shoot, water, etc. One piece of equipment which we most certainly wish to have with us is Margaret's three-wheel walker as, hopefully, there will be opportunities for its increased use.

Day 1 – Tuesday, 15 September 2015

I had already placed in the car much of our 'luggage', etc., and, this morning, we are well advanced towards being ready to leave. Finally, after a lunch of sandwiches, purchased the previous day, we left home at 14.05, feeling reasonably well prepared for the journey, but with some apprehension! Heading eastwards in West Ashton Road for the first time for a number of years we soon encountered the new roundabout; then on to the busy A350 before passing slowly (that was familiar) through Westbury; the fast-moving traffic along the A36 section (the Warminster bypass) became more intimidating and we were relieved to resume on the A350 towards Crockerton. Although there was quite a high volume of traffic, village names such as Longbridge Deverill and East Knoyle give this road a more rural flavour. It is attractive countryside, but I must not take my eyes off the road ahead.

Following my examination by the Consultant Ophthalmologist last year he wrote to the optician saying that there are 'corneal guttata' and I was finding that my Marciac Jazz cap (a souvenir of a visit to the town of Marciac in the Gers Department and the Region of Midi-Pyrénées, where the world famous jazz festival is held for two weeks in August of every year) was being very effective in combatting the effects of the problem by excluding the background light (the sky) and assisting in focussing on the surfaces. Soon we reach Shaftesbury and we remember to take the Salisbury direction and then, almost immediately, the road through the village of Melbury Abbas with its severe speed restrictions. The route across Cranborne Chase affords excellent views; it is not a main road, but it is fairly straight and many motorists are impatient and driving uncomfortably fast.

At the outskirts of Blandford Forum we rejoin the very busy A350. From now on the route requires much attention and care, particularly the speed restrictions through the villages of Charlton Marshall, Spetisbury and Sturminster Marshall. At the roundabout link with the A31 it is important to take the correct exit, for Poole, and at the junction with the A35 to join the B3068 through Hamworthy. We are now on the last part of this journey and it is fairly familiar. However, we were suddenly alarmed to notice an illuminated sign which said 'Poole Bridge Closed'; we were not able to read the entire message – probably containing directions for an alternative route – and we were very concerned; we are not familiar with this area and we had no idea what alternative route to the hotel was available and how we could then reach the ferry terminal in the morning. Soon we passed a second sign, but again we failed to read more. As we continued, we thought we must find a convenient place to turn around so that we could take a careful look at these signs, but we found nowhere. However, quite suddenly there was the bridge ahead of us and vehicles were moving over it – what a relief! What we had not been able to read was the dates of closure!

We were now in the area of Poole which Paul had guided me through on the internet two or three weeks earlier. Although I still had a general idea of the directions we should take – follow West Quay Road; get in the right-hand lane to return in the opposite direction along West Street keeping in the left-hand lane, then turning left into the Quay – I did not recognize the surrounding buildings as my attention was focused so much on the moving traffic, but we did reach the Quay successfully. We found it difficult to read the street names, but we probably entered Ballard Road correctly, continuing in the direction of the hotel. However, we felt we had gone too far as we were now entering a more residential area; we stopped to ask a gentleman the way to the Holiday Inn Express. We were pleased to hear that we were then only about 200 yards from the hotel, although we could not see it. He kindly directed us to a car park where we could turn round and then, if we turned to the left a short distance ahead, we would find the hotel. In a matter of a few minutes, there it was standing at our left at the intriguing address of Walking Fields Lane! We parked in a 'disabled' parking place near the entrance, which we learned afterwards we were welcome to use. We had arrived! The journey had been completed successfully with a good degree of attention and care and, consequently, with no particular difficulties. It was 16.30 and the journey had taken two hours and 25 minutes; the distance travelled so far is 55 miles. In August 2011 the journey to the ferry port took 1 hour 30 minutes!

I was anxious to report our arrival and to complete the check-in formalities and to know that the arrangements had been completed satisfactorily. This is a very modern hotel; I had read that both English and Polish is spoken here and the smart and very polite young man who welcomed me could well have been Polish, for English was certainly not his native tongue. While I had the opportunity, I enquired if he could offer directions for driving to the ferry terminal in the morning. He gave me a sheet of directions, but he pointed out that it was for travelling from the port to the hotel. When I enquired if there were any one-way streets on that route, there was clearly some uncertainty – perhaps we shall discover! How curious to be given instructions for finding the hotel (from the ferry-port) when one is already there! I had mentioned when booking that facilities for the handicapped would be appreciated and we were allocated a very comfortable room conveniently on the ground floor. This was very helpful for the purpose of transferring our luggage from and to the car. The hotel does offer a 'restaurant' and, although we had had some lunch at home, something to eat would now be appreciated. The menu was somewhat limited, but we chose to have a crepe – after all we should be in France tomorrow! After a long delay we were advised that crepes were not available. We turned to the menu again and chose 'apple crumble'; after a while we were told that that was available, but it was some time before we were served; however, it was satisfactory and enjoyable.

There was another couple on a nearby table and they, particularly the husband, joined in conversation with us. They had had a particularly difficult time. They were on their way to their home in Jersey after returning their daughter to her University in Winchester, but they had been delayed for two days in Poole. On one day their crossing had been cancelled because of weather conditions and on the other it was cancelled because of technical problems; they were now hoping to leave at 05.30 in the morning. Although they had been able to be accommodated here for tonight, on the previous night they had had to go into

Bournemouth to find a room. Surprisingly, the husband said to me, "What do you think of Jeremy Corbyn's election – I think it is terrible – I was a Labour Party supporter, but not now". What a note on which to end such a day – a day which had been reasonably successful for, with much diligence, we had accomplished the first stage of our journey; we must not prolong it unduly for tomorrow is to be another challenging day and it begins early!

(Today 55 miles)

Day 2 – Wednesday, 16 September 2015

Our room at the Holiday Inn Express was quite acceptable with comfortable beds and we enjoyed a restful, but short, night. Of course, our sole purpose of being here is to catch the ferry for Cherbourg which sails at 08.30 and we are advised to arrive at the port no less than 45 minutes before the scheduled departure time; we decided that we should aim to be there by 07.30! The early morning routine is a very slow process these days and we felt we should set our alarm for no later than 06.00. We had been informed that breakfast would be available from 06.30; however, my attention was now focussed entirely on leaving the hotel and, as the minutes passed alarmingly quickly and, in view of the tardy service we had experienced in the restaurant during the previous evening, we decided to forgo the breakfast which we had already paid for. I am not sure exactly what time we left the hotel, but it was later than we had planned. When handing in the key to our room I hurriedly asked the receptionist which way we should go from here.

However, it was by now a very busy time in Poole with much traffic. We had not driven very far when I felt unsure that we were going in the right direction. We interrupted a lady who was hurriedly making her way to her work; even so, she kindly gave us some further directions; at one point we found ourselves in what appeared to be the rear entrance of commercial premises, perhaps a supermarket. Gradually, we moved forward with the general traffic in, hopefully, the right direction. It was certainly a relief when we recognized that bridge ahead of us; after that we knew we had to turn left towards the ferry port. As we entered territory we recognized we were intercepted by a Brittany Ferries man who would point us in the right direction. As he looked inside the car, he must have spotted the walking stick and he asked if we required any assistance – would we be able to negotiate the stairs. We responded that we thought we could manage.

However, on reaching the border control and Brittany Ferries checkpoint I asked what help was available. I was told that I should have requested assistance when making the booking; however, the lady kindly enquired if it was still possible to implement the appropriate procedure; I was pleased to see the thumbs-up signal. We had a label stuck on the windscreen and I was told to keep my hazard lights switched on and follow the directions. As the boarding continued, we were set aside until we were perhaps the final car. We were then invited to drive on to deck five and we were positioned just outside the entrance to the staircase and the lift. That was indeed most helpful and, taking no more than we were likely to need, we made our way, by lift, to deck seven without too much difficulty.

During the preceding days we had been led to believe that the weather today would be rather unpleasant, with references to the tail-end of a hurricane reaching the English Channel by Wednesday! There were a number of empty seats and we chose a reasonably comfortable one by a window and conveniently near the cafeteria. This was a very significant stage in our adventure; perhaps we could now relax for a while, that is providing the sea did not make us feel too unwelcome. After some minutes into the crossing we were pleasantly surprised to realize that the ship remained fairly steady; we felt sufficiently confident to walk the short distance to the cafeteria for the breakfast we had left behind in the hotel. We bought Fruit and Fibre cereals, etc., and the assistant, seeing that we were going to have difficulty in carrying what we had purchased, immediately abandoned her duties and, as well as carrying our tray, assisted Margaret to a convenient table. What a helpful spontaneous gesture! However, sitting in the chair at the table was not going to be the most comfortable way of spending a large part of the four and a quarter hour journey.

As we entered the lift after leaving the car I had noticed the large area of reclining seats on deck five and I ventured to the enquiry office from the cafeteria to ask if it was necessary to book those seats; I was surprised to hear that they were, in fact, free and we were welcome to use them. Returning to Margaret, we summoned up enough energy and courage to make our way to the lift using available fixtures for support as the ship was now rolling somewhat more. Even at the lift it was difficult to control our movements until, suddenly a gentleman left his seat to come and give us his support. Leaving the lift at deck five was less difficult, but we were relieved to sink into the nearest available reclining seats; there we stayed until the end of the voyage. On reaching Cherbourg we were advised, with apologies, that the ship would dock at 14.00 hours – 15 minutes late because of weather conditions in the Channel. In fact, the crossing had certainly not been as stormy as we had anticipated. Bringing the ship to a standstill and linking it to the port facilities requires no little skill on the part of the captain and members of the crew, for it has a gross tonnage in excess of 20,000 tons and the sea is by no means calm; yet the manoeuvre was accomplished almost imperceptibly.

We were now pleased to be just a few steps from the door to the car deck and there was our car, with ample space around it, waiting for us. Being, probably, the last car to board, we were now perhaps the last vehicle to disembark. Most other vehicles have now disappeared ahead of us and, as we left the cosiness of the car deck and drove onto the expansive port area, there is some feeling of loneliness; however, it was not to last for long, for we are now in France! I remember that we must go to the left to leave the port and, ahead of us, we noticed a small group by a kiosk – it was the border control point. After a friendly welcome, a brief look at our passports and a glance inside the car we were allowed to begin our journey – it was all very informal. Soon we reach the roundabout and the direction sign for Caen.

SEPTEMBER – OCTOBER 2015

Driving on the right-hand side and giving way to traffic from the left just comes quite naturally again. This excellent new road is the eastern bypass of Cherbourg; it must be close on 10 miles of mainly dual carriageway – through Tourlaville – then climbing up the N13 to reach the roundabout junction with the direct route from the centre of Cherbourg, at the top of the hill. Here we take the exit for Caen. There had not been a great volume of traffic, nevertheless, I had driven cautiously, keeping in the right-hand lane and resisting being enticed into any of the slip-roads. Soon after the junction we had to begin to keep a very watchful eye for signs for the exit for Valognes for it is no more than a further 10 miles. Fortunately, we spotted the advanced sign for the junction and so we were prepared for it. The N13 is not an autoroute, but it has most of the characteristics of a motorway with, naturally, fast moving traffic – it is the main route to Caen and beyond. It had not been an easy journey from the ferry port as, apart from the need to be very watchful of traffic, road signs, etc., the weather conditions added to the difficulty with heavy storms alternating with bright sunshine.

It was with some relief, therefore, that we entered into a much more relaxed kind of road system. Now, we must find Le Relais du Louvre; I had printed a street plan, but we did not find it particularly useful – the latitude and longitude references were of no practical help; so we drove around for a while asking a couple of people for directions. The address of the hotel is 28 Rue des Religieuses and so we assumed it would be somewhere near the church. Of course, this is a building which is not normally difficult to locate in any town or village. Having found the church, we drove down one of the ancient streets leading from it. Margaret thought she had seen a reference to a hotel, but we had now gone some distance beyond it and we are in a one-way street. We found a way to enter the street again and this time drove very slowly and, yes, it was Le Relais that she had seen. There was a direction to a guest's car park through an arch in the buildings. I made several attempts to position the car in line with the arch; while doing so I was obstructing other cars, but no one expressed any irritation or impatience – yes, this is France. I could see that the 'car park' was quite small and the access was very narrow. Eventually, I abandoned the attempt; in any case, if I managed to get in, I would probably have difficulty getting out. There was, in fact, space for one car immediately in front of the entrance. It would be partially on the pavement, but other vehicles were parked similarly. I made use of this space with relief to me and to other drivers! It was now about 15.30 and we had travelled a mere 20 miles from the ferry port.

I was pleased to find that the door was not locked, and I was even more pleased and relieved to find that our reservation was confirmed. Madame then offered to take me to our room. However, I was somewhat less pleased as she led me up the stairs – a spiral staircase of 17 steps. How was Margaret going to be able to negotiate such an access, not once, but many times; how was I going to be able to carry all our necessary luggage up – and then down – such a staircase. The room had the necessary facilities, but the bed was rather small. Had we made an unwise choice? I mentioned that I had parked the car outside the entrance, not knowing what parking regulations apply; the reply was reassuring – pas de problème – and I decided there and then that the car would remain there throughout our stay. I took the opportunity of asking if the restaurant would be open in the evening and I was pleased to hear that it would be open at 19.00, but I was told there would be one menu only – pork!

Fortunately, we had ample time in which to establish ourselves and eventually, and with some difficulty, Margaret reached our room and after many journeys I felt that we had all that we would need at least for the remainder of this day. There was now time for a welcome hour's rest. We made our way down to the restaurant shortly after seven o'clock, and we were pleasantly surprised. After passing through the kitchen, the dining room is quite large; it is on a slightly lower level than the street outside, which is viewed through large windows; this image is projected to the opposite side of the room by the use of large mirrors; indeed, it has 'the charm of bygone times'. We learned that, in fact, Le RELAIS du LOUVRE is an historic building – a 17th century Coaching Inn; it incorporates a tower at the rear which accommodates the spiral staircase; the 'car park' is a cobbled courtyard adjacent to former stables. A notable guest of the 19th century was the writer Jules Barbey d'Aurevilly. Perhaps we were a little surprised by our meal for it was excellent and the service was good. There were a number of other diners present and it was a very friendly and pleasant atmosphere. We were happy to spend a couple of hours there before deciding it was time to summon up the energy and courage to make the ascent to our room. Well, concerns and worries there certainly have been, but with appropriate application we have successfully reached the end of the second day of this adventure. We feel reasonably pleased with our progress.

(Today – 20 miles)

Day 3 – Thursday, 17 September 2015

The first sounds we are aware of are those of the occasional vehicle travelling along the street, rue des Religieuses, below our window – we had had a good night. Petit déjeuner did not disappoint; it was generous and nicely presented. The ascent and descent of the ancient spiral staircase is a laborious and stressful process, but with much care and attention we have avoided any mishaps – myself, going first and backwards, when descending, but following when ascending, hopefully available to offer any necessary assistance!! However, we feel privileged to spend some time in this old part of the town. From our window we can appreciate the great variety of designs, styles and heights of the buildings opposite; there is certainly no uniformity. Fortunately, this part of this street did not suffer the degree of destruction which was inflicted upon so many others in June 1944.

Many times have we driven down the N13 heading south and hoping that one day we would visit this nearby ancient and historic town. In the first century the Romans established the town of Alauna and the ruins of hot baths and the site of the theatre are still visible. It was abandoned in the third century and the inhabitants resettled nearby, at VALOGNES. Although destroyed by Viking invaders in the 10th century, as Normans, they rebuilt the town and castle and, none other than William the Conqueror spent part of his youth here. When Edward III invaded France early in the Hundred Years' War, which began in 1338, one of the first towns he took was Valognes; he spent one night here before destroying it. The château suffered sieges and occupation during the war, but survived to be finally demolished in 1689. However, the rebuilt town continued to grow and with the establishment of various administrations it took on a role of 'capital' of the Cotentin region. At the same time it attracted many distinguished families who constructed aristocratic mansions; social life among the nobility was very strong and the town became known as the Versailles of Normandy. Some of these town houses remain to this day.

Following the Revolution in 1789, Valognes lost much of its status and prestige, but survived and its recovery was assisted by the arrival of the railway in 1858. However, much of the town centre, including the parish church and many of the grand town houses, was destroyed in the course of the bombardments of 6, 7 and 8 June 1944 and following days, by the United States Air Force; the purpose of which was to prevent or disrupt the movement of German reinforcements. Sadly, so much of Valognes' heritage was destroyed by its liberators in a matter of hours; its citizens who survived, having lost their homes, faced many months without water, electricity, coal, food and clothing – a life of misery, of cold and of mud! In time, temporary barracks and other facilities were erected, but it took some 20 years to rebuild Valognes! In 1992 its rich heritage earned it the title of 'Ville d'Art et d'Histoire'. The population of the town now is about 8,000.

It seems that the existence of a church was recorded in a charter at the time of William the Conqueror, but Christianity was probably established in this area, centuries earlier. After the Hundred Years' War, the church was rebuilt on the ruins of the roman chapel. It was constructed in the flamboyant Gothic style and was decorated with additions during the 16th and 17th centuries to become a most beautiful church; its cherished Renaissance dome was early 17th century work; from 1574 the square tower contained five bells and in 1866 the spire was raised to a height of 47 metres. An old drawing shows what a splendid building it was; in utter contrast, a photograph after the bombardments of June 1944 depicts a 'horrible carcass'. However, after the war the CHURCH of SAINT MALO was rebuilt; the choir was reconstructed in its original style on what remained of the original building, but the nave was rebuilt in a boldly contemporary style. This church, "symbolizes both the permanence of faith throughout the ages and its constant adaptation to its times."

It was a dry morning, if somewhat 'maussade', and we decided to explore some of the town, aided by the three-wheel walker. First, I took some photographs of this street and then, walking slowly along the Rue des Religieuses, we noted some of its interesting features; a warning above No 20 – 'Attention à votre tête!'; the Ecole Sainte-Marie – the ancient Hôtel du Mesnildot de la Grille (XVII–XVIII Siècle), which became a school in

1895, but was requisitioned by the Germans from 1940 and became an internment camp for 300 prisoners – gypsies and homosexuals; the little Pont Sainte Marie over a little river – perhaps it is the Merderet or one of its tributaries – which reveals an interesting view of the backs of ancient houses. At the end of the Rue des Religieuses we join the Rue de l'Officialité where we are at the chevet of l'Eglise Saint-Malo. Some photographs! We continued to the right of the church, avoiding many steps to the left, into the Place Vicq d'Azir. (Félix Vicq-d'Azyr was born here in 1746.) Since leaving the Ecole Sainte-Marie we are now in a vast area which was heavily bombed and largely destroyed.

Our attention was soon drawn to one of those attractive pavement cafes, on the upper side of the Place – Le Versailles Normand – some refreshment would be welcome! It was an opportunity to make use of the toilet facilities and, recognizing Margaret's difficulty in negotiating the steps at the entrance, our waiter immediately came to her assistance. We had noticed a nearby road leading up to the Place du Château and we decided to explore. Of course, there is no château, but a very large surface car park. Before the war it was the site of livestock markets, fairs and public festivities. During the war the Germans constructed an underground telephone exchange here, but after the bombardments the square was the site of a provisional church, of prefabricated commercial facilities and of barracks for the homeless survivors. In the corner and raised above the level of the roads is the Office de Tourisme; we found that the office was closed, but it would be open later.

We decided to wait, despite it being a somewhat exposed and bleak location; there were no conventional seats, but some substantial concrete barrier pillars, standing about two feet high, were useful to rest on! When the staff eventually arrived, we were glad we had waited, as they were very helpful and provided us with much information about the history, etc., of the town. It was now time to make our way back to l'Eglise Saint-Malo. The entrance is through a long porch and the supporting pillars each bear the figure of a prophet. Once inside, we noticed a remarkable memorial – to an American airman who, although wounded on 6 June, he insisted upon flying and was killed on 8 June over Valognes; it is dedicated to him and to his comrades who made the, "sacrifice supreme pour liberer la France". An expression of forgiveness, also? Always ready to take the opportunity to sit for a while, we chose a pew which gave us a good view of this beautiful church; it is difficult to believe that it is only a little more than 50 years old. We noted the rather slender pillars. The organ certainly attracted our attention; the instrument is in an elevated position at the rear of the church, but the console is on the floor.

I was reading how the choir had been restored to its original style – I must take a closer look to see how the remains had been incorporated in the new. As I went step by step focussing on the structure rather than on the floor, I suddenly experienced the sensation of first one foot, then the other, meeting no resistance – I could not prevent myself falling on the hard floor. It was not a very dignified entry – first, I realized that my glasses were on the floor and I was very relieved to find that they were intact for, unfortunately, I had not brought a spare pair with me – I gradually struggled to regain my feet and was pleased to realize that I did not appear to have suffered any particular damage. Slowly I returned to the pew, where Margaret had heard my exclamation and was anxious to attract some attention, but there was no one else in the church. Then, suddenly, the door opened and a lady carrying a music case came in. Margaret immediately tried to explain to her what had happened; she was very concerned, and she looked at my left knee which had been grazed – it seemed to be sound! During our ensuing conversation she told us about her health; I'm not now sure whether she had recently had a major operation or was waiting to undergo one but, as she said, her situation is "very grave".

As suggested by the music case, our friend was, indeed, the organist and she was quite excited when I told her that I too had been an organist many years ago. With that news she was particularly pleased to proceed with the purpose for which she had come and, of course, it gave us much pleasure to hear the sounds of the organ. We enjoyed the music for some while, until felt that we should continue our tour of the town; however, before leaving, I must thank her for the 'recital' and for the concerns she had shown. Taking the most direct route to the organ I attempted to walk between the pews; it was not very wise for, suddenly, I somehow missed my footing and went crashing to the floor again. This time I had not only severely knocked my right thigh and shoulder, but scraped skin off the back of my right hand. Once again, Madame, l'organiste, came to assess the damage. She enquired where we were spending the night and she strongly recommended that I should either see a doctor or visit a pharmacie; we had to agree, as my hand needed a dressing.

We left the church rather hurriedly and were pleased to see the pharmacie sign not far distant. As soon as I asked the young lady assistant for some plasters, she invited me to the rear of the counter, where she proceeded to clean the wound, apply an antiseptic solution and carefully applied an appropriate dressing. When I asked how much I had to pay for this attention, she emphasized that the treatment was free. I was extremely grateful for the concern and care she had exercised.

As the afternoon was now passing, we did not consider attempting any further walking, but a return to Le Versailles Normand for a cup of coffee would be a good idea. We were received by the same waiter; he was sorry to hear of our misfortune and gave us his sympathetic attention. After some while of viewing the scene and activity of the Place and, not least, some relaxation, we set off on the fairly short distance to Le Relais. As we approached the hotel, we were surprised to meet Madame, l'organiste. She had called at the hotel to enquire how I was, but, of course, they knew nothing about our experiences; she was, therefore, very pleased to see us. We found it difficult to find the words to express our gratitude for the concern she had shown – what a gesture! The three-wheel walker had been exceptionally helpful today; however, after returning it to the car we now had to resort entirely to our 'unreliable' and unwilling feet to reach our room. There was still reasonable time for rest before making our way to the restaurant at 19.00. Again, there was no choice of menu, but the meal was excellent and the company very friendly. I am not a connoisseur of food and rarely remember particular menus; the test for me is the degree of satisfaction and enjoyment. Well, the day had not been wholly as we had hoped; however, we had explored the centre of Valognes and visited its church, we had learned something of its past, of life during the years of occupation and about its dreadful suffering at the hands of its liberators in 1944 and, once again, we had experienced much human compassion.

Day 4 – Friday, 18 September 2015

So much has been written about D-Day and the beginning of the Battle of Normandy with regard to the military operations; however, we have learned less about the consequences on the many towns and villages affected and the experiences and plight of the civilian population. After four years of brutal oppression they were then inflicted with death and destruction and, for those who survived, a long period of great hardship and deprivation – in the course of their liberation. We have long hoped to learn more of the experiences of those towns and villages and of their inhabitants. It has, therefore, been an opportunity and a great privilege to spend some time here in historic Valognes, just one of the many towns which suffered such experiences. Perhaps it was appropriate that our visit to Valognes should not be made without some particular personal experience and 'suffering' – certainly, thus it became even more memorable! Following yesterday's falls, thoughts of the wisdom of continuing the journey inevitably occurred; however, the prospect of cancelling all the remaining arrangements we had made, not least of having to arrange an early return to England, quickly nullified such thoughts. We would continue, certainly for the time being, from day to day.

Friday did not dawn with the promise of a lovely day; on the contrary it was maussade et humide. However, we have petit déjeuner to enjoy – a pleasant interlude before preparing to leave Le Relais. Before we leave we have one important task; after all her diligent care and attention during many months and her approval of us making this journey, we must not disregard the advice and instructions of Nurse Anna-Marie for dressing the ulcer and she had provided us with ample dressings, etc. However, it was not an easy exercise in the restricted facilities and poor light of an ancient inn and, at least once, the 'spider' dressing was more inclined to stick to itself than to the surround of the wound, until I felt the job had been done satisfactorily. Returning all our various items of 'luggage' to the car was a slow and careful process; having completed it successfully, we had a short chat with le propriétaire and we thanked him for the opportunity of un séjour at this ancient hotel. It was 11.50 and raining steadily as we sat in the car studying the map and considering which direction we should take. Our destination for tonight is little more than one hour's journey by the most direct and quickest route, via the N13, but in spite of the poor weather, we wished to explore a little of this area of the Cotentin Peninsula.

SEPTEMBER – OCTOBER 2015

The COTENTIN PENINSULA is wholly in the Department of Manche of the Region of Normandy; it is that huge piece of granite thrusting out into the English Channel. In fact, at one time the Marais, or marshlands, at its southern boundary, almost created an island. For many, ourselves included, its port of Cherbourg provides a very convenient and quick route to Brittany and far beyond and it often does not receive the attention it deserves.

We decided to continue along the Rue des Religieuses (we had no choice – it was a one-way street) and then head north-eastwards towards Quettehou. Unfortunately, we first took a right turn assuming that the opposite direction would lead us back into the town and we soon had no choice but to join the N13 which sweeps round to the south of Valognes; however, it was not for long and we escaped at the first opportunity – the exit for Montebourg. Here, it was not difficult to find the D42 towards Quinéville and then we joined the D14, the coastal road to Quettehou. Just a couple of miles further, on the D1, we are in St-Vaast-la-Hougue on the coast. Then we drove some distance towards Barfleur in the north-eastern corner of the Peninsular before returning to Quettehou. It was now time to begin travelling in the direction of our destination for tonight. We continued on the D14, past the junction for Montebourg – at the village of Fontenay-sur-Mer we could have visited the gardens of the Château de Courcy, but the weather was still rather inclement. At St-Marcouf – a reminder of the rural and peaceful nature of this countryside – cows grazing in the adjacent field and, then, two or three on the road itself! At Ravenoville the

D15 takes us very conveniently into Ste-Mère-Eglise. Here, it was time to pause, visit the church again and have something to eat – it was now 13.45.

Once again we are making a journey in our Saab 9-5 Auto Estate. We purchased this car in June 2004, having owned a very satisfactory Saab 9000 during the previous 10 years. On noticing its registration (Y304 UGF), Margaret commented that it suggested that this car would be Useful for Going to France. We noted from the Registration Document, that it had previously been owned by Great Percy Productions Ltd – John Smithson. Quite remarkably, and barely one month later, we read an article in *Le Monde* headed 'John Smithson, un producteur Britannique à Marseille'. It revealed that Darlow Smithson Productions had produced many documentaries for the BBC, Channel Four and Channel Five, but they had now decided to work with producers in France in producing documentaries for TF1, France 2 and Arte for instance and had, consequently, moved to Marseille. Perhaps, therefore, this car was destined to spend the subsequent period of its life traversing the roads of France! For us, 'UGF' has been more than useful; its size, its comfort – at times in temperatures of 30+ – and its reliability has served us well and has taken us safely over many thousands of memorable miles in France.

After well over 60 years of driving the physical aspect of managing and controlling the vehicle – it is an automatic – requires little effort and comes very naturally; however, for a number of years I have had little enthusiasm for doing so, without a very good reason and, exceptionally, when we have been in France! Remarkably, this quite short tour today has again recaptured for us the pleasure and the joy of motoring, which we had not experienced for the past four years.

Here, there is not spectacular scenery, nor exceptionally beautiful countryside views; it is not hilly and barely undulating; a rather ordinary paysage consisting of pastureland, of trees, of hedges, farmsteads and occasional dwellings and, of course, livestock. However, the adequately well signed roads are comfortably negotiated and one is able to leisurely observe the features of the landscape and associate with the quiet peace and calm of the countryside. Why? – because there is such a welcome sparseness of moving vehicles; one is not continuously distracted by having to pay constant attention to the movement, and anticipating the intentions, of other vehicles. Here are the 'quiet roads' we long for! This is France!

However, at times in centuries past this land has seen much activity – in the 11th century William the Conqueror's army preparing for the invasion of England – in the 14th century Edward III passed this way with his army, on foot and on horseback, beginning his invasion of France and the Hundred Years' War – in the 20th century it was occupied by the hostile German Army, much more mobile, to be removed some four years later by the Americans. Indeed, this journey has taken us through a region which encompasses much interest and historic significance from far back in the Middle Ages to the present day.

It was at SAINT-VAAST-LA-HOUGUE – we 'met' St Vaast in Arras last year – on 12 July 1346 that Edward III landed with an army of 12,000 men and proceeded to victory in that most decisive of battles, Crécy, on 26 August 1346. Its fortifications were constructed by Louis XIV's great military engineer, Marshal Vauban, and are a UNESCO World Heritage Site. In the 19th century its jetty and harbour were developed and it was the first harbour to be freed from German occupation in 1944. Today Saint-Vaast-la-Hougue has a population of about 2,000 and is known for its oyster farming and fishing; its large marina accommodates some 700 yachts.

In the year 1066, BARFLEUR was an embarkation port for William the Conqueror's army heading for England and the Battle of Hastings. A significant event in English history of the period occurred nearby in the year 1120. Prince William, the only legitimate son of Henry I, died when the *White Ship* sank outside the harbour. A period of civil war followed in England, known as the Anarchy, as Henry attempted to install his daughter, Matilda, as his successor. However, on his death in 1135, his nephew, Stephen, like Matilda a grandchild of William the Conqueror, seized the throne. When Stephen died in 1154, the crown passed to Matilda's son Henry II. The new king's father was Geoffrey of Anjou, who habitually wore a sprig of broom (planta genista) in his cap, a name which was adopted by the new dynasty. Thus, began the Plantagenet Dynasty which continued for more than 300 years until the death of Richard III in 1485. Barfleur today is a village of about 650 inhabitants; it is twinned with

Lyme Regis and, of course, it has given its name to the Brittany Ferries cruise ship we travelled to France on.

Immediately following his arrival in Normandy, on 12 July 1346, Edward III knighted his 16-year-old son, the Black Prince, in the church of QUETTEHOU; there is a plaque in the church commemorating this occasion. Quettehou dates from the period of the Viking invasions of the, perhaps, ninth century. Its name derives from that of chief Ketil who settled on the top of a hill and, in time, Ketil's hill became known as Quettehou. The population of the village is approximately 1,500.

The small town of MONTEBOURG (population 2,000) suffered a similar degree of destruction in June 1944 as Valognes. In their excellent *Battlefield Guide of Normandy* Major and Mrs Holt recount the experience of a 12-year-old girl who was living in Montebourg on D-Day, as she recorded it. Her father was the local doctor, but at Easter he was taken ill and was sent to a sanatorium in the Alps. On 5 June her mother received a telephone call to say that he was dying. Her mother called the ten children still living at home together to brief them as to how they were to look after each other in her absence. Each older child was given direct responsibility for a younger one. She was given responsibility for her seven months old brother. At about five o'clock in the morning of 6 June the replacement doctor was called out to tend wounded soldiers – Allied soldiers – the invasion had started. For a while they stayed in their own home, but it was terrifying. Bombs were falling and there were fires everywhere. A vehicle full of ammunition was hit by a bomb and exploded near their home. They were very frightened. They bundled as much as they could, including cans of milk and – most precious of all – a tiny burnous (a hooded woollen cape) which was kept in a pillowcase, into the baby's pram and took refuge in a nearby abbey. As the battle came to the very courtyard and there was fierce fighting they managed to get to a nearby farm, but it was already full of refugees. They had lost all their possessions – except the little 'burnous' still in its pillowcase. The first Allied soldier she met was an American, which surprised her as she had always expected to be liberated by the British. A poignant commentary of the experiences of a child of the Battle of Normandy!

RAVENOVILLE consists of Ravenoville Bourg and, about one and a quarter mile to the east, Ravenoville Plage; the population is about 250. Near St-Marcouf, are two prominent structures, the CRISBECQ BATTERIE and the AZEVILLE BATTERIE, which formed part of Hitler's Atlantic Wall. This defensive system was constructed by the Todt Organization using forced labour (slaves) recruited from the occupied countries of Europe. Despite one of these batteries being camouflaged to resemble ancient Norman cottages, with their obvious massive strength and extensive underground network, will they be allowed to remain and ultimately fall into a category similar to that of the fortifications built by Vauban in the seventeenth century? Prior to the war, Fritz Todt was involved in the construction of autobahns and also the Siegfried Line!

We have visited STE-MERE-EGLISE a number of times during the past thirty-five years and we have always found a large number of visitor cars in the spacious car park alongside the village church. Today was no exception, but we were able to park for a modest two euros. This town (present population about 2,500) had, remarkably, passed four years of relatively peaceful occupation; there had been occasional air raids and on the night of 5/6 June a house near the church was set on fire; it was not subjected to the kind of bombardment inflicted on many others. At about 01.40 on the morning of the sixth, some 13,000 American parachutists began to descend on to this area from about 900 aircraft and at 04.30 of that morning Ste-Mere-Eglise became the first town to be liberated. However, for one unfortunate soldier, JOHN STEELE, his parachute became hitched in the tower of the church; he hung there, pretending to be dead, until freed by the Germans; his life was spared and he was taken prisoner, but he soon escaped. In the succeeding years, until his death in 1969, John Steele often visited the town. Today, the experience of this one man is commemorated by his effigy suspended from the tower and by the nearby Auberge John Steele; there are also relevant stained glass windows in the church. Now, more than seventy years after the events, people still flock to this place. Although, during the 24-hours following l'aube du jour-J, some 2,500 French civilians perished at the hands of their liberators in such places as Valonges, Montebourg, Caen, Lisieux, Condé-sur-Noireau, Vire, Flers and Argentan and much of their heritage devastated par une pluie de feu et d'acier, there was, inevitably sorrow, but also such great relief, joy and deep and lasting gratitude felt by the liberated population, expressed by the creation of so many permanent memorials in the form of street names, etc. Here, we have Rue Eisenhower, for example, and, before we left Ste-Mere-Eglise, we enjoyed some welcome refreshment in La Libération!

It is now 16.00 and we must continue and complete our journey for today – to Grandcamp-Maisy. After returning to Ravenoville by the D15, we did not feel that we should spend the time to drive along the D421 to Utah Beach, and we turned right, re-joining the D14. We passed through the villages of Foucarville and St-Germain de Varreville each with a population of about 100. After Ste-Marie-du-Mont the D13 takes us to the N13, which here becomes the E46 as it skirts the bottom of the Marais and the Baie des Veys, a large estuary where four rivers (le Douve, la Taute, la Vire and l'Aure) discharge into the sea. It is a fast section of road, but soon after passing from Manche into the Department of Calvados, we are relieved to be at the exit for ISIGNY-SUR-MER. In no time we are passing close by that symbol of the lush fertile meadows of this area of Normandie – the impressive premises of the Isigny Sainte-Mère Cooperative. Milk processing began here at the beginning of the 19th century and the present Cooperative was formed by the merger, in 1980, of two cooperatives originating in 1909 and 1932. Apart from milk, its products of butter, cream, cheese and skimmed milk are known all over the world and more than half is exported. Isigny is no longer on the coast, but in past times coal from Littry was exported from its port and, following the D-Day landings, Dutch coasters used the port to bring supplies and equipment ashore from large supply ships out at sea. In June 1944 the town suffered much damage but was mainly rebuilt. Oysters are cultivated nearby in the bay. The town has a population of about 2,750 and is twinned with Kingsbridge.

It is about five to six miles to Grandcamp-Maisy on the D514. After Osmanville we pass, on our left, the access to the MAISY BATTERY. Now here's a fascinating site and experience – built with Russian, Czech and Polish forced labour, it was part of Hitler's Atlantic Wall; surprisingly, it did not appear on D-Day maps! After the war it was buried by the Americans, concealed by nature and lay unknown for some 60 years; that is until a British historian, Gary Sterne, acquired, by chance, an old map, which led to his discovery of the site in 2004. He bought the land and subsequent excavations revealed a vast complex, of buildings, gun platforms, two miles of trenches and even an underground hospital. It was opened to the public in 2007.

GRANDCAMP-MAISY (the two communes merged in 1972) is a fishing port with a population of about 1,800. Grandcamp is of very ancient origin being mentioned in records of 1082. It was heavily bombarded on 6 June 1944 causing enormous damage and suffering; it was liberated at 17.00 hours on 8 June and became a principal port for the supply of materials for the armies. As we approach the sea and bear left into the harbour we recognize the distinctive memorial to the two French bomber squadrons – Guyenne and Tunisie – which were attached to RAF Bomber Command on D-Day, for it incorporates a striking silhouette of one of their Halifax bombers.

Now we can see our hotel, Le Duguesclin, but – and I had forgotten this – there is a 'no entry' sign preventing us from reaching it. We must return past the harbour, turn left and continue through this little town until taking another left turn which takes us to the other end of the sea-front road – Quai Crampon. It was now 17.30 and, after parking outside the hotel, I found the door open, but no immediate signs of activity within. After operating the 'attention bell' a gentleman arrived and I was relieved to know that our reservation had been correctly recorded. I was advised that we could park in the private car park at the rear and that our room would be in the separate building at the far side of the car park – I was given the code for gaining access to the building and the key to the room. The vehicle entrance is narrow, but there was sufficient room in the car park.

Taking some of our luggage, we set off in search of our room. First, up one flight of stairs, then another, until, on the second floor, we found our room. After all the strenuous exertions in negotiating the 17-step spiral staircase at Le Relais, we were not greatly pleased to find that we now have to overcome 34 steps every time we will have to ascend or descend this staircase, while there is probably half of that number leading up to the restaurant level of the hotel itself. However, in our building, at least the staircase is wide, enabling side by side assistance, with a fixed handrail and we will be able to progress at our own speed! The room itself is satisfactory and comfortable with a view of the rear of the hotel and of the car park below! Having established ourselves we are looking forward to a meal and a pleasant evening in the restaurant. At about 19.00 we began to make our way down the staircase, into the car park and climbed the somewhat narrower stairs and then individual steps of the hotel and into the restaurant.

We have stayed at this hotel before and, as we entered the large and long room it was very familiar. It is a lovely setting, on the first floor well above the road level, its many and large windows providing a wonderful view of a large expanse of the sea. We were warmly welcomed and invited to take a seat alongside one of the windows. We noticed that, in the centre of the restaurant, a number of tables had been arranged together across the width of the room to form a single large table. Obviously, this was to be the scene of the celebration of a special event. Gradually, the guests, of at least three generations, began to arrive, greeting one another in that warm and affectionate manner in the way they do in this country. Soon it became evident that the occasion was the celebration of the birthday of the senior member of the family – the father. There was much animated and lively conversation – clearly a happy and joyful gathering. However, the group was not obtrusive, rather, the atmosphere it created permeated throughout the restaurant. How nice it was to be associated in this way with a French family occasion. Towards the end of their celebrations, fireworks attracted the attention of us all.

Yes, we did have a meal. So far as I recall it consisted of entrecôte, vegetables, including chips in a basket, accompanied with a small glass of wine and followed by une glace. There were quite a few other couples and groups in the restaurant all, no doubt, enjoying their own special occasion. In particular, we were conscious of a couple immediately behind me talking together quite a lot during the evening. Guests were beginning to leave and we too decided that, after perhaps about three hours, we should, at least, begin to make our way back to our room. As we did so, we felt it would be courteous to wish the couple behind us 'bonne nuit'. They were delighted that we did so and thus began quite a long conversation.

They were so pleased to know that we were English and that we love France and, as we have often experienced, were so interested to know that we have visited their country many times. The gentleman told us that he was previously in Paris, but emphasized, with pride, that he originates from Alsace. (Alsace is the small cultural and historical region in the far east of the country and borders Germany and Switzerland. Now, from 2016, it is part of the Region of Grand Est) On the other hand, his wife is proud of her Norman background. We were all somewhat reluctant to bring our conversation to an end, but we succeeded in doing so with a final 'bonne nuit'. While talking to this couple another couple sitting quietly in the corner were provided with a firework display – they too had something to celebrate!

By now more guests had left and we too, slowly made our way cautiously and carefully down the stairs, across the car park and successfully negotiated the entrance to our building, to climb the 34 steps to the comfort of our room. What a varied and enjoyable day it has been – awaking in an ancient inn to a maussade (gloomy) outlook, then a thoroughly pleasant and interesting drive, revealing so much history and reviving many memories, and ending in the light and warmth of the restaurant welcome and in the presence of a happy family gathering, followed by a most interesting and friendly personal conversation.

(Today – 70 miles)

A demain!

Day 5 – Saturday, 19 September 2015

'Tis le weekend here in France (and in England too!) – one of the words which have found their way into the French vocabulary. However, these two days, particularly Sunday, are experienced somewhat differently in France. For instance, there is a welcome absence of heavy goods vehicles on the roads – they are prohibited and we have often seen lorries parked on wasteland during weekends. Many petrol stations will be closed, particularly on Sunday and on D (departmental) roads and some N (national) roads. Many restaurants and hotels are closed, certainly during part of the weekend – we recall a number of occasions when, with the code of access provided, we have been welcome to spend a night in a seemingly otherwise empty hotel, accepting that there would be no service of food available! Also, here there is no widespread 'Sunday shopping'.

In France it is, rather, a time for re-creation – for relaxation, for leisure and pleasure; for visiting places of interest – on one weekend in September of every year (Les Journées du Patrimoine) all sites of historic and cultural interest are open to the public free of charge; it is a time for walking, for cycling – we have often seen families with young children cycling on the quiet roads. The contrasts are emphasized in the nature of television programmes too. On Sunday mornings the main state television channel – France 2 – broadcasts a programme entitled *Le Jour du Seigneur,* which, every week includes a live presentation of la messe. I have already explained that it was introduced in October 1949 and has continued to this day.

So, how are we going to spend this weekend in France? Well, from our window we see that it is a clear and sunny morning, and, in fact, we have a very minute view of the sea, just visible between the buildings which separate us from it. However, on reaching the restaurant and returning to the table we had occupied during the previous evening, we have a splendid panorama – a wide expanse of calm sea and to our left the eastern coast of the Cotentin peninsular and, in the distance, will be one of the D-Day landing beaches – Utah Beach. The atmosphere this morning is somewhat different, relaxed and informal, compared with that of the evening meal. Petit déjeuner is available in a buffet style over quite a long period during the weekend, although a member of staff is available to advise and assist if help is needed, such as how to operate the orange crushing machine and kindly carrying drinks, etc., to our table.

After leisurely enjoying our breakfast, we returned to our room and decided that we would spend our day in

Grandcamp Maisy. Making use of the three-wheel walker, we walked the very short distance towards the harbour's seaward entrance, where a seat beckoned. It was not a particularly comfortable seat, solidly constructed in concrete to withstand the ravages of coastal storms rather than to resist vandalism, I would think. However, it was such a lovely day and such a peaceful, serene and tranquil setting that we spent a considerable time here. For much of the time the silence was only disturbed by the splashing of the water against the harbour walls as a boat silently made its way out to the open sea.

Then, a number of tiny yachts with distinctive coloured emblems began to assemble some distance from the shore, making an attractive sight – perhaps it was some kind of competition! After a while I returned to the car to fetch some welcome refreshments. Midst this heavenly tranquillity one could not begin to imagine the scene that morning of 6 June 1944 – the hundreds of warships at sea, the hundreds of aircraft flying overhead, the incessant noise of gunfire and of bombs – simply a hell on earth. It must have been terrifying for those civilians who were not able to escape and many did not survive. Of course, for us at home these events prompted immense interest, excitement and optimism. Perhaps we could look forward to the end of the war, the restrictions, the rationing, the tyranny and destruction – that Europe could live in PEACE as ONE.

Eventually, we felt we should seek rather more physical exertion and we walked past the harbour on our right and the several fish restaurants on our left and turned left into Rue Aristide Briand in the direction of Centre Ville. This road is closed on market day (Tuesday?), but it is a pleasant walk today with very little traffic. Soon we spot the familiar sign of a Pharmacie (Pharmacie Besnard, 72 Rue Aristide Briand) and I immediately thought it may be an opportunity to purchase some dressings for my injured hand. Fortunately, it was open and on explaining the circumstances to the young lady she immediately decided that she should examine the wound. She did so with great care and exclaimed, "it is still bleeding". However, having cleaned and treated the wound she was happy to renew the dressing and I purchased a supply of dressings for future use. Again, there was no charge for the excellent attention I had received.

As the street broadens out, it reveals a village-like scene. Although of a character of bygone years, many buildings are of an elegantly smart and clean complexion. No doubt much rebuilding was carried out after 1945 and, in any case, these properties, sheltered and facing inland, have not become 'weathered' like those looking out to sea. It is as if the houses have been set back to accommodate this striking profusion of trees of different sizes, of shrubs and of varied plants providing a splendid display of colour – on windowsills, in tubs, on railings and on lamp standards, indeed, everywhere, it seems. What an attractive prospect. It is all the more remarkable considering that not far behind these houses enclosing such colour and warmth, are the buildings of a more austere appearance facing the varying weather and climatic conditions of the English Channel! We did not fail to notice one particular building – it was 'La P'tite Frincale Crêperie'. How opportune – a crêpe would be most welcome at this time. It was open and we were welcome.

We enjoyed the refreshment and, particularly, the opportunity to sit for a while and, not least, the inevitable conversation. Rather reluctantly we resumed our walk which soon took us to rejoin the Quai Crampon towards its eastern end. Although it was now late afternoon, the sun was maintaining a comfortable temperature as we walked slowly towards our hotel, while appreciating the totally different scenery than that which we had just left behind. On approaching Le Duguesclin, our thoughts soon turned to the prospect of our evening meal.

We have not only sojourned at Le DUGUESCLIN in the past, but we have driven along the seafront road on a number of occasions, always casting an envious eye up at the restaurant windows. Also, it was the first hotel at which we sought accommodation on our first family holiday in France – on 17 July 1979; unfortunately, there was only one room available! Perhaps it is not surprising, therefore, that we have had an interest in the history of this hotel.

In June 2010, when driving along the N88, midway between Mende and Langogne, over the higher regions of the Department of Lozère, in the deep south, in the Region of Auvergne (after 2016 – new Region of Occitanie) we passed close by Châteauneuf-de-Randon and we noticed on our map a reference to a 'Tour des Anglais'. We did not feel that we had sufficient time to make a worthwhile short detour, but we subsequently learned that the Battle of Châteauneuf-de-Randon took place in 1380, during the Hundred Years War. The English garrison commanded by De Ros was besieged by the French under, one Bertrand du Guesclin; the English surrendered on 4 July 1380. Is there a link with the hotel we know on the coast of Normandy?

With grateful thanks for information provided by Monsieur, le propriétaire, we now know that Bertrand du Guesclin was born at la Motte Broons near Dinan in Brittany in 1320. He was a distinguished warrior who became connétable – supreme commander of the French armies. He was the complete chevalier, a popular hero who incarnated one of the first patriotic manifestations of the kingdom of France. Bertrand du Guesclin came to Normandy and established his camp at Maisy; moreover, vestiges of his tower can still be seen. The Comte de Bayeux and Bertrand du Guesclin maintained a relationship which explains his sojourn at Maisy. Bertrand du Guesclin was engaged in several campaigns, but he contracted an illness during the siege of Châteauneuf-de-Randon and died on 13 July 1380; he was buried at Châteauneuf-de-Randon. (I have also read that his remains were interred in the tomb of the Kings of France at the Cathédrale de Saint-Denis in Paris and his heart at the Basilica of Saint-Sauveur at Dinan, but we have never visited these churches.) Apparently, everywhere he established a base, an establishment carries his name; this hotel has that distinction.

At the beginning of the 20th century Le Duguesclin was a Maison de Maître. In 1928 it became a

Hôtel-Restaurant-Dancing and in 1932 it appeared in the Guide Michelin for the first time.

The three-wheel walker has been a great asset today, but we must now hasten to return it to the car; then make a brief visit to our room before negotiating the many steps leading to our window table in the restaurant, with its splendid grandstand view of la mer. Splendid it is, indeed, at this time, as day slowly and reluctantly succumbs to night – the period of crépuscule (twilight). We enjoyed our meal last evening and felt that we could do little better than to repeat the order – except that we would advance to un filet de boeuf (French), which together with frites in a basket and mixed vegetables, followed by une glace, all accompanied by a small glass of red wine, completed an excellent repas. We did not have the celebratory atmosphere, the excitement, of yesterday, but it was certainly pleasant and friendly. As soon as we began to leave the restaurant Monsieur approached; he took Margaret's arm to help her down the stairs, across the car park and saw us safely inside our building. What a kind spontaneous gesture! Today has not been a particularly eventful one, more relaxed and somewhat restful, yet nonetheless memorable.

(Mileage – Nil)

Day 6 – Sunday, 20 September 2015

Dimanche – the second day of 'le week-end' and how different it is than that which is familiar en Angleterre. Again, it is a beautiful morning with the promise of a lovely day ahead. It is surely an opportunity to explore a little of an area we have not visited, the Parc Natural Régional des Marais du Cotentin et du Bessin.

Here, petit déjeuner is not to be regarded as a routine episode, but as an overture to a new day, a setting and atmosphere to be absorbed and appreciated and nourishment to be enjoyed, to be prepared in mind and body for the new day. As we left the restaurant, Madame came to us to say that they had realized that it was difficult for Margaret to frequently ascend and descend the flights of stairs in the detached building and, consequently, they would like to offer us a room in the hotel building. Although the charges for such rooms were higher, we would not be required to pay an additional sum. All we need do was, gather our belongings together in our room and a member of the staff would transfer them to room seven during the day. We expressed our appreciation for this gesture.

Although, at this time, we don't wish to give thought to our return journey to Poole, it has occurred to me that we should have made advance arrangements for the same service of personal assistance as we received on the outward crossing and that I should have contacted Brittany Ferries to do so. Madame offered me the use of her telephone and, in fact, established contact with the company offices in Cherbourg for me. I was then able to talk to a very helpful lady who, having established the relevant details, assured me that the full service for the disabled would be available for us on our arrival at the port. It was a great relief and comfort to know that we could look forward to this excellent service.

How irritating it is, how annoying, when one of those vital components of personal clothing fails to function when its services are urgently required, when it chooses to abandon its roots. I was not equipped to deal with a button falling off and, somehow, I will have to continue without it! That was not the only misfortune this morning, for shortly afterwards a shoelace broke – for this, I was prepared. Fortunately, these events did not delay us greatly, but because of the slow process of preparing ourselves and making other arrangements, etc., it was 12.50 when we left the hotel.

We set off from the car park by an exit which leads directly on to Rue Aristide Briand and then joined the D514 for Isigny-sur-Mer, from here the D5, the D11 and the D8 led us into St-JEAN-de-DAYE. We are familiar with this village of about 600 inhabitants, having driven through many times on the N174 towards St Lo, en route from Cherbourg to Vire. However, today we wondered if there might be a possibility of having something to eat here. We stopped, first on one side of the road, then the other, but there was little sign of life and all the premises appeared to be closed – until we left the car to look through the door of what might be a bar or a salon de thé; we could see two or three people sitting at a table. We ventured inside and asked if they could offer us some refreshment – the choice would be very limited, perhaps no more than un gateau – that, with a drink, would be very welcome, merci! It was evident that the premises were shortly to close and we thanked Madame for the hospitality.

Nearby is the CHATEAU de la RIVIERE, a building with an interesting history. Constructed from the 11th century, it was the possession of the grandson of Odon, Bishop of Bayeux (half-brother of William the Conqueror). It ceased to be inhabited in 1818. In 1944 it was seriously damaged by the Germans after using it for the storage of 'munitions'. However, it was subsequently acquired and used by several owners, but is now a sanctuary for cigognes (storks) and there is no access to the interior. It is now classified as 'ruinè'. In fact, some years ago we spent a night in this ancient building – a night which is remembered because the roof leaked and we had to move the bed to avoid getting wet!

Our Michelin map tells us that there is a 'viewpoint' in the region of the village of Graignes-Mesnil-Angot – a good place for a general view of the marais, we thought, and so we left St-Jean-de-Daye in a westward direction. We have since learned that, in 1944, there was an airfield in this area, operated by the US Army Air Force. It seems that the runway was the straight stretch of the road D389 towards Mesnil-Véneron. Perhaps we drove along that 'runway', but I cannot be certain! As we approached Graignes-Mesnil-Angot (merged in 2007) we were guided by a sign to the 'Memorial'. We did not know of the wartime events in the village of Graignes or the significance of the Memorial. As the road reached its highest point, there, above us, were the remains of a church and a cimetière all securely enclosed and surrounded by a substantial stone wall; but where is the 'view-point'?

We continued, but immediately the road began to descend; it was narrow and there was no immediate opportunity to turn around. Why not carry on and make a short circular tour of the marais? This we did; however, being on the same level, it was difficult to comprehend the extent and vastness of this natural region. When we reached the Memorial for the second time, we did not hesitate to park the car; we climbed the steps to enter the large cemetery. On the inside of the perimeter wall there is a continuous pathway loosely surfaced in fairly large gravel; it is a long distance to walk round and Margaret found it increasingly uncomfortable to do so on the uneven surface; however, being about halfway round, we had little choice but to continue. We are very glad we did so, as we eventually came to a gateway in the wall with access to an excellent viewing platform. Although I did so, Margaret did not feel able to climb down the short, but uneven, bank and up into the platform; however, she had a good view from inside the wall. Whereas, for the first part of this 'walk' we were looking down on to a typical rural scene of a farmstead, etc., here, before us, were spectacular views of the vast PARC REGIONAL DES MARAIS DU COTENTIN et du BESSIN – a peaceful expanse (1,480 square kilometres) of wetland, moors and hedgerows, full of birds and extending across the base of the peninsular; it is a protected nature park. We spent some time in the cemetery, contemplating on the scene – the tombstones, the memorials and the remains of the church. Well, we had found the viewpoint but, unfortunately, we left without being aware of the events which gave rise to the Memorial.

The BATTLE OF GRAIGNES is not very prominent in the history of the Normandy Campaign; however, it was a gruesome episode which left a permanent scar on the village. In the very early hours of Tuesday, 6 June 1944, 12 planeloads of American paratroopers were dropped some 15 miles from their drop zone, near Ste-Mère-Eglise, and thus scattered over the flooded marshes near Graignes. Many drowned by the weight of their equipment, but those who survived, scattered and isolated, identified in the moonlight, that most recognizable of village buildings – the parish church. Gradually, more and more reached this focal point and 48 hours later 14 officers and 168 men had struggled into the village. Commanded by Major Charles Johnson and being far inside enemy territory, they decided to establish themselves and to defend the village. On the morning of 7 June the Mayor, Alphonse Voydie, called a meeting which was attended by almost every man, woman and child of the village; it was unanimously agreed to assist the Americans, despite the inevitable consequences if caught – execution. Villagers searched the marshes to recover considerable quantities of weapons and equipment and to provide much needed food for the soldiers. From 8 June there were sporadic skirmishes with the enemy, mainly reconnaissance patrols, and several Germans were killed. However, during the course of the afternoon of Sunday, 11 June, Graignes was subject to a heavy bombardment and, in the evening, a final assault by some 2,000 men of the 17th SS Panzer Division. The Americans, with Major Johnson now dead, could hold out no longer – the battle had been lost. However, 150 paratroopers escaped and some civilians also. Subsequently, the Germans ransacked the village and carried out a merciless massacre of a number of American prisoners and many villagers, including the parish priest; they then destroyed most of the village, including the eight centuries old church.

Graignes is the third village we have visited which suffered an indiscriminate and brutal massacre and ruthless destruction following D-Day. The others are Oradour-sur-Glane, Haute-Vienne, near Saint-Junien (10 June 1944) and Maillé, Indre-et-Loire, near Chinon (25 August 1944).

We returned to Grandcamp-Maisy via Saint-Jean-de-Daye and Isigny-sur-Mer and reached Le Duguesclin at 17.40. We were pleased to remember that we had far fewer stairs to climb to reach our new room (No 7) and we managed well. Our belongings had been transferred as promised and we are now on the floor above the restaurant and we have a sea view – splendid! As 19.00 approached we made our way down to the restaurant; we spent little time studying the menu as we could not resist the opportunity to enjoy an identical meal to that which we had yesterday and at 'our' table. A fitting end to an interesting day!

(58 miles)

Day 7 – Monday, 21 September 2015

We are nearing the end of our stay at Le Duguesclin, but it will be a leisurely departure as it is a fairly short distance to the next destination on our journey; also, we will be spending another night here next week when returning to Cherbourg. In contrast to the past two days the weather this morning is somewhat overcast; however, it does not greatly detract from the panorama from the restaurant windows as we enjoy our petit déjeuner. In fact, it was 11.50 when we eventually left the hotel.

We soon re-joined the D514 which hugs the coast of Calvados; we passed the turning for the famous Pointe du Hoc, but at the little commune of Vierville-sur-Mer (population about 250) we drove down to the beach road – D517 – of OMAHA BEACH. We soon found a convenient spot to park and we sat in the car at this historic site for a considerable time. Nearby, and at the western end of Omaha Beach, is the National Guard Memorial. On D-Day Omaha was divided into two sections, DOG, where we are and EASY to the east. The plans were that an Infantry Regiment and supporting forces, of the United States 29th Division would establish a foothold on DOG and proceed to clear the area beyond the N13 and to Isigny to the west. A similar force of the 1st Division would embark on EASY and advance eastwards to link up with the British Army at Port-en-Bessin. By the end of 6 June it was expected that a bridgehead some 16 miles wide and five miles deep would have been established. In fact, by nightfall on that first day the bridgehead was barely the length of the beach and less than one mile deep. In unexpected storm conditions many soldiers failed to reach the beach; those who did so had to climb the cliff-like slopes overlooking the beach, negotiate the barbed wire and overcome the German defences. They suffered very heavy losses in doing so and for many of the young Americans their D-Day was very brief. Many were from a Pals Battalion and a small American town of 3,000 inhabitants lost 23 men on D-Day, including three sets of brothers. It was here on DOG Green that the heaviest casualties, perhaps of the entire invasion coastline, were suffered; it features in the film *'Saving Private Ryan'*.

Eventually, and slowly, we drove eastwards – the beach on our left and, on our right, attractive dwellings positioned on the low sea-facing cliffs – a peaceful scene now! At the end of Dog Green, Les Moulins, we parked in the spacious car park to view the impressive memorials and the fascinating sail-like structures and pillars rising out of the sand and of which I would like to know more. There are information panels which include a poem by Jean, which ends:

> *To those brave men*
> *A ship of iron,*
> *time – defying in our thoughts*
> *on each side, Hope and Fraternity*
> *and, central, Liberty dearly bought.*
> *In the whole, a breath of history*
> *murmurs, "Hold fast our Liberty".*

So far as I am aware, it was in this area that the second artificial harbour was erected, but it was severely damaged by a violent storm on 19 June and, unlike that at Arromanches, it could not be repaired – apparently vestiges are still visible at low tide.

We did not continue into EASY Red – we recall driving along the pebbles of this section of Omaha with George and Samuel some years ago and of climbing the cliffs to reach certain memorials – of course, we brought home some souvenir pebbles! Instead, we continued to rejoin the D514 at St-Laurent-sur-Mer (population 250).

It is just a short distance to Colleville-sur-Mer and the site of the NORMANDY AMERICAN CEMETERY. Situated high above Omaha Beach, where many of them died, it contains the graves of 9,387 soldiers and the names of 1,557, who have no known grave. We have visited this cemetery several times and one cannot pass by without recalling its grandeur and its emotional solemnity, its inspirational design, its expansive layout and, always, its immaculate presentation. In the car park there is a message for the visitor:

> *Look how many of them there were*
> *Look how young they were*
> *They died for your freedom*
> *Hold back your tears and be silent.*

Soon, we reach PORT-en-BESSIN, a pretty little harbour-village – Françoise Sagan described it as 'le petit Saint-Tropez Normand'. It was an important harbour in past centuries – at the time of the Romans and Normans – and Vauban built a tower here in 1694. It was an important harbour too and a key target for the Allies in 1944. However, it would have been suicidal to attack the heavily defended port from the sea. Therefore, on 6 June 1944 No 47 Royal Marine Commando, 420 mainly young men of 18 to 22 years of age, landed at Le Hamel east of Arromanches; they lost 76 men, as well as weapons, in reaching the shore, but the remainder, carrying some 90lb of weapons, etc., each, worked and fought their way some ten miles westward along the coast to attack Port-en-Bessin from inland. Towards the end of the next day they discovered an undefended pathway to the German port defences and in commando style, shouting and firing, they stormed the enemy bunker – the Germans surrendered. By nightfall on 7 June they had liberated the village – they had achieved their objective. This must have been one of the greatest feats of endurance, bravery and suffering of the entire Normandy Campaign. They had created a link between the British 50th Division on GOLD BEACH and the US First Division on OMAHA BEACH and, remarkably, within a week the port was handling more than 1,000 tons of vital supplies each day. Importantly, it was a vital stage in establishing PLUTO (Pipe Line Under The Ocean), the facility for supplying the armies with vital supplies of petrol from England. It is said that the idea of PLUTO was that of Lord Louis Mountbatten! Port-en-Bessin is now one of the most important and modern fishing ports of France. Since the 1940s the population has surprisingly risen and then fallen – 1946 – 1,314; 1975 – 2,388; 2008 – 2,080. In the past we have looked at the details of apartments being constructed here! Port-en-Bessin is well worth a visit!

Only about five kilometres further along the D514, through Commes, we come to Longues-sur-Mer and, at the traffic lights at the crossroads, we turn left to drive the short distance to the site of the Longues (le Chaos)

Battery – another section of Hitler's Atlantic Wall. This is not our first visit here and we decided not to attempt to walk to the actual battery, but we parked the car as there is a boutique and a convenient toilet nearby!

Back to the D514, then, as we leave Tracy-sur-Mer we meet the roundabout at the junction with the D516 for Bayeux. Turning left and descending gently, still on the D514, the familiar and nostalgic sight of the remains of the Mulberry Harbour emerges – it is Arromanches. Bearing right we continue to the car park on our left, where we have parked so many, many times – the first occasion being on 17 July 1979 – and on our right is the bureau de poste and the parking spaces for coaches. It is now 15.20 and we can think of nothing better at present than a visit to our favourite restaurant – Brasserie Au 6 Juin. The free car park is parallel with, and open to, the Boulevard Gilbert Longues which leads down to the seafront – on the opposite side is the convenient little supermarket and then l'école maternelle, where we have often watched the young children in their supervised activities. Leaving the car park, with the aid of the three-wheel walker, and crossing the road from the right, we join the pavement which, we are pleased to find, has been resurfaced since we were last here. There are then, on our right, one or two private dwellings, a small car repair workshop and a small military memorabilia store. Next is a favourite patisserie, before the wheelchair side entrance to the restaurant. AU 6 JUIN is a popular meeting and eating place of the many visitors of different nationalities who constantly visit Arromanches; the staff are efficient and friendly and it generates a wonderful atmosphere and we have enjoyed

SEPTEMBER – OCTOBER 2015

many hours here absorbing the animated conversation of the different languages and also, when at a window table, observing the seemingly endless stream of visitors along the pedestrianized rue Marechal Joffre. Often, we have exchanged comments and sometimes joined in conversation with visitors at nearby tables. It is an entire experience. I do not recall what we had to eat on this occasion, but quite probably it was ham, egg and chips or something of that nature.

The Maison Jeanne family enterprise was established in 1963 and in past years we have found a senior lady at the till, however, today we have not seen her, and a very courteous and friendly gentleman is accepting the payments. Has the business changed hands, or perhaps our lady has retired! It is now 17.35; we have enjoyed our meal and the couple of hours in which to revive and enhance our memories of this special place. Incidentally, the background of the chosen name of the restaurant is explained on a small leaflet which is presented with the receipt!

ARROMANCHES is now a small tourist town of about 600 inhabitants – in June 1944 it was the site of one of the two artificial harbours, codenamed Mulberry, and it is proudly referred to as Port Winston. However, Arromanches was not attacked from the sea, but was liberated on the afternoon of D-Day by men of the Royal Hampshire Regiment, commanded by General Sir Alexander Stanier, who had landed further east on Gold Beach and descended upon the German defenders from the heights of St Come. Consequently, there was very little damage to the buildings in the town, but six civilians died. Despite a severe storm on 19 June, which lasted three days, during the first 100 days of its operation the Mulberry Harbour had handled 2.5 million men, 500,000 vehicles and four million tons of materials. The conception and creation of the artificial harbour was an ingenious and incredible enterprise. Arromanches possesses two excellent museums – le Musee du Débarquement, on the seafront, and le Cinema Circulaire 360° up the hill at Come.

Over many years we have visited Arromanches very many times – with its easily accessible and free car park, the short pleasant walk down into the busy traffic free Rue Marechal Joffre offering restaurants, refreshment bars and shops, leading into the attractive compact open seafront with a further car park and many memorials, all enclosed by inviting hotels, restaurants and shops and, on its eastern side, the excellent museum; on the beach and out at sea are the permanent reminders of that momentous event in 1944 and, not least, its respectful and reverential atmosphere. Arromanches has long been a favourite place of ours.

Returning to the car park is an easy walk and we leave Arromanches in the direction of Ryes. On leaving Ryes we remember to take a left turn on to the D127, then to cross the D112 by the grain store, to turn right (towards Bayeux) on to D12 and, after a few hundred yards, to take the left turn signed for Vienne-en-Bessin. Soon we see the welcome sign 'Ferme des Châtaigniers' on our left. This access to the farm and to a number of private dwellings, we would describe as 'single track and not made up'. However, there is an easy entrance into an adequate parking area surrounded by the farm buildings and property. This is a journey of five miles and we rarely meet more than two or three other vehicles; in fact, later in the evening we are likely to see more rabbits than cars on the road! Although it is now raining, we are pleased to arrive at this peaceful Normandy haven again and we look forward to meeting the owner, Fabienne. Unfortunately, Fabienne is nowhere to be seen! However, we do not have to wait long before Fabienne arrives, explaining that she has joined a choir in Bayeux – perhaps we shall hear more about this! We receive the usual warm and friendly welcome and Fabienne assists us up the concrete staircase, along the passageway, with its unforgettable view of her fields and cows, and into the room, with its typical ceiling beams, which we have occupied in past years and which overlooks the parking area, etc. We feel at home!

(32 miles)

Day 8 – Tuesday, 22 September 2015

Ten to fifteen years ago we visited a number of gites in this Calvados Department with a view, in particular, to finding accommodation which would be suitable for us to give our grandsons an experience of France and French life. We found nothing better than a living farm, in a small village but, at the same time, adjacent to open farmland – we found la Ferme des Châtaigniers and we met Fabienne and her, then, very young daughter, Amandine. In addition, it was only five miles from one of the notable sites of the D-Day landings – Arromanches. The property offered not only a gite, but also chambre d'hôte. Since that time, we have enjoyed memorable weeks here with George and Samuel and made many visits ourselves. Now, we could not make what may well be our last visit to Normandy and France without spending a few days here in Vienne-en-Bessin.

LA FERME des CHATAIGNIERS comprises a number of stone-built buildings of a type traditional of the Bessin and which I believe are about 200 years old. The farmlands of 60 hectares (about 150 acres) are used for the breeding of (at present 24) Charolaise beef cattle and the production of, in addition to meat, wheat and maize.

The BESSIN is an extensive, peaceful and undulating region of rich pastures and marshlands with historical origins. It corresponds to the territory of the ancient tribe of Gaul, the Bajocasses, who gave their name to its chief town, Bayeux. The Bessin corresponds to the diocese of Bayeux, prior to the revolution. One of the features of the Bessin is the bocage, the hedgerow farmland which the allied armies had such difficulty in conquering in 1944.

Fabienne is very kind as she tolerates our late arrival for petit déjeuner – normally after other guests have left – for there is always a good selection of confitures on the turntable, cartons of juice and yoghurts still available, although we may have to wait for fresh coffee to be made. This morning we relax and linger at the large solid table in this spacious room with inviting bookcases and also with windows on each side and which is underneath our room. When Fabienne is free she joins us, and we have the opportunity of a long and interesting conversation. She well remembers the visits of George and Samuel and is interested to hear of their progress. We are pleased to learn of Amandine's progress at College (?), of her clarinet playing and to learn that she is now studying English and Chinese! Not surprisingly, we took the opportunity of asking if she has any recollections of personal family memories of the events of the 6 June 1944.

Yes, she does, and she told us that on that night/day her dad was at Longues-sur-Mer and only two kilometres from the sea. He has described the experience as, "The night was like day" and "The sea was black". Fabienne also recalls her aunt telling her of sitting on the knees of liberating British soldiers – no doubt there are photographs! That was a very interesting conversation and we still haven't heard more about the choir, but we must not take up more of her time this morning. Fabienne has many responsibilities, the management of the farm – she has an assistant – and the gite and chambre d'hôte; there are also rabbits, cats and a dog to be looked after and, not least, the care of her father who is about the same age as myself and who now lives with her. Our priority now is to renew the dressings on Margaret's ankle and my hand.

Early rain had cleared when we eventually set off from la ferme and we head, as we have so often done, across the open plains of Bessin in the direction of Arromanches. There is only one village between Vienne-en-Bessin and Arromanches – Ryes. RYES is a commune of about 500 inhabitants; in 1060 it was referred to as

Rigia, when it was the seat of Hubert, a vassal of the Duke of Normandy. From 1899 until 1932 a 60cm gauge railroad between Courseulles and Bayeux passed through Ryes with a branch from Ryes to Arromanches. Much of the church of Saint Martin is of the Roman style and dates from the early 12th century. It was classified as a Monument Historique in 1840.

We cannot resist pulling in at the entrance to this church to read again of the remarkable episode in the life of one of the outstanding characters of all history. He was born in 1027 and from the time that he succeeded his father, at the age of eight, William, Duke of Normandy faced opposition, in particular, from his uncles and cousins on the grounds of his illegitimacy. Early in 1047 and aged about 20 he was in Valonges, (where we were last week) when he had word of a plot to assassinate him. In the middle of a winter's night he fled southwards on horseback in an attempt to reach the safety of his castle at Falaise. It must have been a difficult, uncertain and perilous journey. His route took him through Asnelles and brought him here to Ryes – it became known as 'la Sente au Batard' (William the bastard's pathway). At Ryes he visited his friend Hubert, who had a fresh horse saddled for him and provided an escort to accompany him on the rest of his journey. He reached Falaise successfully and, subsequently, became WILLIAM the CONQUEROR and KING of ENGLAND. If the young William had not survived this determined plot, how differently our history would have been written!

When we have been in Normandy together, George and Samuel always welcomed the opportunity of visiting a salon de thé pour une tasse de thé. One day in the centre of Bayeux we were passing such an establishment – it was also a patisserie – and we decided to go in. It was quite small and there was only one other customer, a gentleman. As we discussed how to arrange four chairs around a table, he did not hesitate to speak to us – in English. Almost his first words were, "What part of England do you come from?". When we are asked such a question, particularly in France, we do not respond by saying Trowbridge or Radstock, but invariably the name of Bath is instantly recognized. Yes, he knew Bath. We then mentioned Radstock which, to our surprise, he also knew and, indeed, Midsomer Norton. In fact, he was quite familiar with our area, for his two sons, now in their forties, were educated at Downside School.

This was an introduction to a most interesting and friendly conversation. Our friend introduced himself as CHARLES HARGROVE. He told us that he had lived in Leeds, but he did not speak of that city with any great pride. He told us too that he now lives in France with a home in Paris and another nearby in, I suspect, Asnelles. His wife is French and her father was a contemporary of eminent French composers such as, I believe, Gabriel Faure. We learned that he had landed in France on D-Day, 6 June 1944. After the war he had been *The Times* correspondent in Paris. We gathered that, currently, he is active in French public life. It had been a most interesting meeting and conversation and a privilege to meet, so informally, such a distinguished yet friendly gentleman. We left the Salon de Thé at the same time and, being so absorbed in the conversation, I almost forget to pay for the cups of tea we had enjoyed.

As we were returning to the street, our friend, for that is what he had become, said, "By the way I have written a book – *A Gentleman of the Times* – but it is in French" and he added that we might be able to buy a copy at the nearby bookshop. We hastened to the shop but, unfortunately, they did not have a copy in stock. Needless to say, soon after our return home we were pleased to acquire a copy. Since that chance meeting we have seen Charles Hargrove on the television taking part in D-Day anniversary celebrations in Ste-Mere-Eglise and we have been interested to read more about his life and, sadly, of his death towards the end of 2014.

Charles Hargrove was born in Genoa in 1922 of a French mother and an English father. He was educated in Paris and became trilingual in English, French and Italian before gaining a degree at Cambridge. On enlisting in the army his language skills were to be of great value. In the early morning of 6 June 1944 he landed at Asnelles on 'Jig' sector of Gold Beach with 231st Infantry Brigade (known as the Malta Brigade) and alongside No 47 Royal Marine Commando. In the face of very fierce German defending he drove his jeep through shallow water on to the inhospitable and dangerous beach; he was transporting the brigade commander, Brigadier Alexander Stanier and Maurice Schumann, a close aide of Charles de Gaulle, who had become known as the 'Voice of France' for his BBC radio broadcasts. Maurice Schumann subsequently became French foreign minister. After his distinguished wartime service, Charles Hargrove married a French girl and they eventually made their home in Paris and Asnelles, where he was made an honorary citizen. He had had a distinguished journalistic career, as a foreign correspondent for *The Times* for 34 years, serving in Paris, Bonn, Berlin and Tokyo. Charles Hargrove wrote several books; in addition to *A Gentleman of the Times* he wrote two on Queen Elizabeth II. Unfortunately, his health had deteriorated following an attack in his Paris apartment in 2013, but he was still able to take part in the D-Day celebrations at Asnelles on 6 June 2014 when he dined with President Hollande.

Charles Hargrove, soldier, journalist and author: born Genoa 30 May 1922; OBE; Commandeur de la Legion d'Honneur; married; died Paris 19 September 2014.

On hearing the news of the death of Charles Hargrove, we resolved to visit his grave; today seemed to be a suitable opportunity! After a short visit to Arromanches, we re-joined the D514, climbed up and over St-Come before descending towards the beach at La Hamel, a hamlet of Asnelles. ASNELLES has a population of about 600 – the latin origin of its name apparently means 'little donkeys'. The village was severely damaged on 6 June 1944, but there were no civilian casualties. We decided we should head for the parish church and, from the D514 which becomes the Ave. de la Libération, we turned into Rue de Débarquement leading to Rue de l'Eglise Saint Martin. There was a convenient parking area nearby and just across the road there were quite steep steps up into the cimetière. As we entered and approached the church, we soon became conscious of a very strong and unpleasant wind blowing in from the sea. However, despite the weather conditions, often using, unwisely

I'm sure, old and unstable tomb stones for support, we searched the cemetery, but we could find no evidence of any recent inhumations. We were very disappointed – there must be another cemetery! The church itself was not open, but I took the opportunity of recording the following historical information displayed on the door.

ASNELLES – Le patrimoine religieux

The construction of Saint Martin's church dates back to the end of the 12th century. The building was modified in the 16th century and enlarged in the 19th century. The Romanesque style tower was built in 1856. The base of the spire shows the symbols of the Four Evangelists: the eagle, the man, the lion and the ox.

In the Middle Ages Sainte-Honorine chapel was built in a neighbouring field. The inhabitants of Asnelles and the surrounding area came in pilgrimage, to invoke the saint who cured fevers caused by the coastal marshes. It was destroyed by the protestants in the 16th Century.

The tithe barn, situated behind the church, was built in the 14th century. Farmers put a tenth of their harvest there, for the benefit of the abbey Saint Julien de Tours, the chief collector, for the Asnelles parish priest. Thus the abbots of Tours were authorized to display their coat of arms on the church; an escutcheon with an azure field, and a cross and four fleur de lys in silver.

There was nothing more we could do today and we returned to Arromanches, where we were pleased to find ourselves in the warmth and comfort of the restaurant Au 6 Juin. We had an enjoyable meal spending a couple of hours in the usual convivial atmosphere, leaving at, I see, 20.18 and returning by the very familiar route via Ryes to 'home' at la Ferme des Châtaigniers.

(18 miles)

Day 9 – Wednesday, 23 September 2015

Petit déjeuner chez la ferme – and an opportunity to relate to Fabienne the story of our meeting, about ten years ago, with Charles Hargrove; our interest in his life and our disappointment in not being able to visit his grave yesterday. "I will see what I can find out about it for you," said Fabienne. Soon, she returned after consulting the internet and was able to confirm that he is indeed buried at Asnelles, but in the current cimetière and she gave us directions for finding it. We will make a further foray to Asnelles today.

However, it would be sensible to first purchase some petrol. How habits quickly become established – whenever we have been in this area we have always purchased fuel at one particular petrol station and we will do so again today. On leaving the access road to la ferme we turn left until reaching the road from Creully, D126, then, turning right towards Bayeux. After passing the quarry on our left we arrive at the city's ring road. Driving clockwise, we pass, first, la gare and then the Campanile Hotel on our left before the road surface and layout prompts us to slow down in recognition and respect of, on our left, the Bayeux Commonwealth War Graves Commission Cemetery containing 4,648 graves; on our right is the Memorial to the Missing, recording 1,805 names. Continuing on the ring road and as it bears to the right the exit for Cherbourg is on our left. Soon we approach our immediate destination the Esso du Bessin. There are several petrol stations on the ring road, but this is the one we have patronized in the past. It does not present a spacious and grand appearance. In fact, the situation of the pumps does not make for particularly easy access and positioning – more of an intimate situation. The shop itself, although well stocked, is quite small and compact, but the service is friendly and we are greeted courteously in a way that suggests that we are recognized; perhaps we or the car are remembered and perhaps this is a family business. In any case we like this petrol station. For this record we purchased 53 litres of petrol which cost 71.02€; the time was 13.15.

Now we must set off on our second foray to Asnelles. Continuing on the ring road we soon reach the exit to Arromanches – a very pleasant journey of about five miles passing La Rosiere. From Arromanches, it's once again up and over St-Come and down to Asnelles. but today we leave the D514 (now Avenue de la Libération) at the right turn into Rue de Southampton; shortly, another right turn into Chemin du Magasin, then bearing left we are in a parking area and ahead of us is the entrance to the Cimetière De Cavigny. As we walk in we find a ceremony is taking place just inside. However, we were able to ask some bystanders if they could direct us to the grave of Charles Hargrove and they indicated that it was in the far corner of the cemetery. As we made our way respectfully past the tombs we realised that, ahead of us, were two standards, one bearing the Tricolour and the other, the Union Jack. We were first attracted to an established and impressive tomb – it was that of 'Maurice Schumann 1911–1998 Compagnon de la Libération' and 'Lucie Schumann 1929–2014'. Nearby, and beneath the furling Union Jack, was a somewhat insignificant grave with no more than two small trays and a single bowl of small plants standing above the level of the untended surrounding turf. No doubt it is intended to install a more appropriate and lasting memorial. Nevertheless, we are in no doubt that this is the resting place of Charles Hargrove. Gradually and slowly we retired from the surprisingly unkempt grave in the quiet extremity of the cemetery, but casting our eyes back as we did so – to the colourful concentration of tombstones, standing and lying, lovingly bedecked with plants, flowers and personal mementos and, at the rear, the flags of our two countries standing tall – for a final memory before passing through the gates and returning to our car. This is a very peaceful location with just a few dwellings some distance away across the field.

On all our journeys Margaret has maintained a daily record of varied and invaluable information and she has done so again on this journey. Sometimes it is relatively trivial, but it often revives the memory of a particular place or experience. Today, she has noted that while sitting in the car after leaving the cemetery, "We ate potato crisps at last" and that we left at 4.30pm.

We note that a section of the 'Sente au Batard' is close by the Cimetière. However, we returned along the Rue de Southampton and continued on to the Boulevard de la Mer where we lingered in contemplation, viewing the beach and sea – 'la belle plage entre mer et campagne'. It was not a beautiful beach on 6 June 1944 as tens of thousands of British soldiers poured on to the enemy occupied and defended territory. One of the first being Charles Hargrove – now he lies just a short distance from that very spot on which he drove ashore. One cannot fail to recognize the measure of gratitude permanently bestowed by the liberated on their liberators by the naming of streets – Libération, Débarquement, Southampton, The Dorset Regiment, The Devonshire Regiment and Major Martin. At 17.30 we continued, but paused again on the heights of St-Come to comprehend the vast extent of the vestiges of the Mulberry Harbour and to appreciate the seemingly advantageous position of the German defenders and the vulnerability of the attacking forces on D-Day.

From St-Come it is only a matter of minutes to the car park on Boulevard Gilbert Longues in Arromanches and in no time we are once again welcomed in the Au 6 Juin. After an enjoyable meal and a pleasant evening we left at 20.15 but, before returning to the car, we could not resist a short late evening stroll along to the seafront. The five-mile drive to Vienne-en-Bessin is a unique experience. It is now late evening and darkness has fallen; after leaving Arromanches there is no sign of personal human activity – only animals assert their presence – and the roads are not just quiet, they are virtually devoid of vehicles; after

Ryes, crossing the wide open plain – there is no bocage here – we feel very much alone, but not insecure. We reached 'home' at 21.00.

(24 miles)

Day 10 – Thursday, 24 September 2015

After petit déjeuner we spent more time in conversation with Fabienne – unfortunately our French has been neglected – and we were pleased to have the opportunity of taking some photographs – with the assistance of her 'farmhand'.

Once again it is time for the respective dressings to be renewed!

It was in April 2004 that we, and George and Samuel, spent our first week in the gite. One day we walked to the village church of Vienne-en-Bessin; we were not able to go inside but we spent some time in the adjacent cemetery and the boys were intrigued by the inscriptions on certain tombstones – the following, for instance – "A LA MEMOIRS DEM PAUL MORICE, DOCTEUR MEDECIN, 1818–1875, PRIEZ POUR LUI". Perhaps he was the village doctor!

It was well into the afternoon (14.40) when we left la ferme, but we decided that we would first make a brief visit to the church. L'EGLISE SAINT-PIERRE de Vienne-en-Bessin was constructed from the 11th Century and has been classified as a monument historique since 1974. A very interesting feature is the fishbone masonry of the nave, a building method used in Normandy until the 12th Century. Unfortunately, we were again not able to see the inside of the church, but here is a copy of the historical record displayed on the outside.

Eglise Saint-Pierre -XI- XVIII Centuries

> The estate belonged to the monks of Jumieges until the Scandinavian invasions and Duke William the Bastard gave the church to Saint-Pierre-de-Preaux (Eure). The 11th century building is famous for its fine gateway-belfry. The Romanesque nave exhibits opus spicatum or fishbone masonry an ancient construction technique often used in Normandy until the early 12th century. The cornice is supported by a magnificent collection of sculpted brackets. Most of the openings are 18th century modifications, but a magnificently embellished Romanesque doorway remains. The choir, sacristy the north and chapel to the south, were rebuilt in the 18th century.

We have driven along the D514 through the village of Longues-sur-Mer many times and, several times, have visited the famous Batterie, but otherwise we have not stopped in the village. It was the home of Fabienne's Dad and he was there in June 1944. The Batterie was a prime target for the RAF – I understand that, unfortunately, many bombs fell on the village instead of on the gun emplacements. Leaving Vienne-en-Bessin for Ryes where the D127 quickly takes us to Longues-sur-Mer. We are attracted by the signs to L'ABBAYE-SAINTE-MARIE – a Monument Historique. We were particularly interested to read that the Abbey's Foundation Charter was dated 1168 and was confirmed by Henry II and that in 1932 the American Senator, Charles Dewey, bought the Abbey site. We parked at the side of the road alongside the site where we had good views of the various buildings and, although Margaret decided not to do so, I walked into the site for a closer view of the exterior of the buildings and the activities going on. We recorded the following information.

Sainte-Marie Abbey

The Longues Abbey, dedicated to the Holy Virgin, was created by Hugues Wac, wealthy lord of the Bessin. Henry II Plantagenet King of England and Duke of Normandy confirmed the founding charter dated 1168, a short time later. The estate of the first Benedictine monks from Hambaye Abbey (Manche) was enriched with donations from local lords. When the Archbishop of Rouen, Eudes Rigault, visited in 1257, the community numbered twenty-two monks, possessed four priories and the patronage of some twenty parish churches across the Bessin. The 16th century was even more of a disaster than the Hundred Years' War. Conferment of abbey revenues in 1526 deprived the monks of a regular abbot and the community became obsolete.

Protestants ransacked the abbey in 1562, during the Wars of Religion. The decline continued and in 1760, the community counted only five members. After a lengthy procedure, the Bishop of Bayeux succeeded in having the abbey closed in 1782. The revenues (24,000 pounds) were then shared between the last abbot having benefited from conferment, who was also the Bishop of Lectoure (Gers), Louis Emmanuel de Cugnac, and the Bayeux seminary. Sold during the Revolution, the remaining buildings were saved from ruin by the American senator Charles Dewey who, in 1932, bought the whole complex and began work to safeguard the buildings. The Abbey, fortunately spared by the destruction in 1944, is undergoing renovation and its owners have opened it and its recreated gardens to visitors.

Well, it is only about five kilometres to Arromanches, but if we set off now we must be sure of a window table Au 6 Juin. Yes, a window seat it is, and we are able to observe all the activity both within and outside in the street. We had an enjoyable meal and as the time passed we entered into a long and interesting conversation with a couple at a nearby table. They were Lynn and Arthur, who were in Arromanches on their way home to Chichester after a cycling holiday in France. We did not leave the restaurant until 21.20 but were home safely at 21.50.

(19 miles)

THE PREPARATION OF THE RECORD OF THIS JOURNEY HAS BEEN SPREAD OVER A LONG PERIOD, MAINLY BECAUSE OF THE ATTENTION TO THE CARING NEEDS OF MARGARET. IT IS NOW NOVEMBER 2017 AND AT THIS POINT, SADLY, SHE PASSED AWAY AT

HOME ON 18 NOVEMBER 2017. ALTHOUGH SHE HAD BEEN ABLE TO READ THE EARLIER DAILY RECORDS, SHE WAS NOT WELL ENOUGH TO READ THE MORE RECENT ONES. HOWEVER, IT WAS HER CLEAR WISH THAT I SHOULD CONTINUE TO FINISH THE RECORD OF THIS JOURNEY, AND INDEED OF EARLIER JOURNEYS, MAKING USE OF HER DETAILED DAILY DIARIES.

Margaret was taken from us as I was in the stage of reliving and recording our final journey in France and, it so happened, at the time we were in Normandy, at La Ferme des Châtaigniers, the home of a special friend, Fabienne. At this point I must resume my 'recollections and reflections'.

Day 11 – Friday, 25 September 2015

We awake at la ferme for the last time – it is our final day here and we shall be in no hurry to leave. As usual we have no difficulty in spending excessive time enjoying our petit déjeuner and absorbing this, for us, unique situation and atmosphere. After a while Fabienne joins us and, during the course of the conversation, she decides that her dad may be able to join us also. Soon she returns with son père and clearly the thoughts of Monsieur turn immediately to the events of 6 June 1944. He proceeded to give us a vividly descriptive account of a British bomb exploding just 50 metres from him, how it extracted the air from his lungs – clearly a frightening and unforgettable experience. We already know that he described the scene as "The night was like day" and "The sea was black". We were so pleased to have this meeting, to learn personally of the memories and emotions of an innocent civilian as the mighty allied armies descended on the shores of France on the most momentous day in European history. We must now hasten to leave Vienne, but not before expressing our sincere thanks to Fabienne for the warm welcome and help. Our four days here have cost a modest €188. We finally leave La Ferme, with a fond farewell, at 13.30 and, as we are not likely to return, we promise to keep in touch.

Without any consideration we proceeded to drive directly to Arromanches. After parking in the usual park we take the three-wheel walker and passing Au 6 Juin, we continue along Rue Marechal Joffre until we find that to continue beyond the refreshment bar we have to step down to a lower level. It was obviously going to be a very difficult manoeuvre for Margaret to achieve – getting both her feet and the walker together on to the lower level. Suddenly, an English gentleman left his ice-cream and his wife and came to our assistance; with the walker on the lower level he simply lifted Margaret down to join it. What a kind spontaneous gesture! After which he told us that he was born in 1952, that he had worked in a residential home and, I think, that they came from Portsmouth. It would now be sensible to have a meal at this time and we returned to Au 6 Juin. Our visits to the restaurant earlier in the week have been later in the day and we have remarked on the absence of the familiar 'senior lady' at the till of past years. However, we realised with great joy that today she is at – for us – her usual station. We chose to have a croque-madam today – it was very enjoyable. We left the restaurant at 17.50 and Arromanches at 18.15 to drive to Bayeux. Our 'home' for the next four nights is the Campanile Hotel which we reached at 18.40. We were allocated Room 8 on the ground floor and facing inwards towards the restaurant and not, as we always hope, a room overlooking the meadow with views of the railway on the right and, to the left, a view of the splendid cathedral spires. However, we are familiar with this hotel and we shall be happy here. I must, of course, add the recorded observation that it had been 'a lovely day'.

(18 miles)

Day 12 – Saturday, 26 September 2015

There is one feature of the Campanile Hotel which we do not welcome – its petit déjeuner timetable. On weekdays it is available from, perhaps, 7.00 to 9.00. However, this is the weekend when breakfast is available until 10 o'clock. It is a very different regime than that we enjoyed with Fabienne!

When we read, in the directory of 'Special Places to Stay', of a property at St Germain-du-Pert of, "The solid beauty of the old fortified farmhouse and the serenity of the Marais lapping at the lawn", "of a luminous landscape of marshes and fields, watch storks nesting, the heron fishing in the pond", we could not resist making a reservation. On our initial arrival, quite late in the evening, I am not sure whether it was Paulette or Herve who led us up the 28 steps of the rope-handled stone spiral staircase to our room; unforgettably, there on the wall was a painting of the scene of the Battle of Bosworth! When, as we left after a later visit our hosts told us that we were, in fact, their final guests, that they were retiring to live in Bayeux; they added that if we were able to visit them in their new home, we would be very welcome. We accepted their invitation and we have made a number of visits and, with great pleasure, taken George and Samuel with us on some occasions.

Paulette and Herve know we are in Normandy at the present time and, on telephoning them, we are pleased to find that they would welcome us this afternoon. The Campanile is adjacent to the ring road at its western end and the home of Paulette and Herve is in a quiet street near the opposite end of the ring road. Equipped with the essential dictionary and atlas, we reached them at about 15.00 to a warm welcome. Although we have communicated electronically, we have not, in fact, met since the year 2011 and we soon find that our versatility and familiarity in the French language had clearly diminished. However, with mutual contributions and accompanied by lovely refreshments, we are able to create meaningful conversation. Paulette and Herve are always pleased to tell us of the places they have visited during their latest tour in France and of family members they have visited in different parts of the country. They are particularly pleased when, quite often, we can say that we have also visited those same sites. We mentioned that tomorrow, Sunday, we might plan a short drive around some of the pleasant villages of the Normandy countryside; wherewith Herve suggested that we might find a visit to Colombieres interesting. We have so many interests in common – family, travel, etc; we had had an enjoyable and rewarding afternoon, having, we think, acquitted ourselves quite well. Paulette and Herve were concerned for Margaret and her great difficulty in walking as we left them at about 17.30. Margaret's comment on the afternoon was that it was a "Wonderful visit".

We returned directly to the Campanile for a meal in the restaurant of ribeye steak and chips followed by fruit salad. It was not an inspiring meal!

(6 miles)

Day 13 – Sunday, 27 September 2015

There is always a very wide range of choices invitingly laid out for petit déjeuner at Campanile – it is a pity that the timetable does not appear to encourage wider selection to be enjoyed more leisurely. However, we are always content with the basic menu of cereals, croissants, bread, etc. Fortunately, we succeeded in reaching the restaurant soon after nine o'clock; nevertheless, we have not finished eating when staff begin clearing the restaurant and laying out the tables for lunch.

It is a lovely morning and the view from our parked car towards la Cathédrale is accompanied by the bells calling worshippers to morning messe – we wish we could join them, but it is not practicable. We must prepare ourselves for an afternoon drive and, hopefully, before staff arrive to carry out the daily service of our room – they are usually quite accommodating!

Our first family holiday in France – in July 1979 – was not as well prepared for as the present journey. We had not made any reservations and we were unable to find accommodation, first at Grandcamp Maisy, then in two other towns until reaching Le Molay Littry, where there were rooms for all four of us in the Hotel du Commerce.

The Campanile is situated at the junction of the ring road and the D5, the road for Le Molay Littry. Where better could we begin our nostalgic drive? We left the Hotel at 13.30 and, about 14km later, parked in the centre of Le MOLAY LITTRY. It is an attractive little town with a population of about 3,000, colourfully dressed with shrubs and flower beds and, being Sunday, no shops are open and it is virtually deserted. We are close to the 'Hotel' which is now described as a 'Cafe de Commerce'; also, overlooking, is the clock which regularly interrupted our sleep during that hot July 1979 night. Back in the 17th century it was a centre of coal mining and a wealthy town. There is an excellent mine museum nearby which we have visited. Outside the town the beautiful Château du Molay stands in 45 acres of magnificently wooded grounds – it was built in 1758 by Jacques-Jean le Coulteux du Molay, a wealthy young banker, and his wife Geneviéve-Sophie.

Taking the D10 and D13 we continue to BALLEROY (population about 900) where the rising road skirts the town's large car park. There was one other car and a couple enjoying a picnic. We sat for some while appreciating the scene, particularly the splendid building ahead of us – it is l'Hôtel de Ville and we admired the impressive War Memorial. The nearby Château de Balleroy dates from 1626 and was in the Balleroy family until 1970. From our earlier visit we recall that an annual Hot Air Balloon Festival took place at the Château. However, this was discontinued after 1999, but since 2007, by public demand, a festival has again been held at the village stadium.

We returned to L'Embranchement on the D13 and continued on that same road towards Cerisy-la-Forêt. Le FORET DE CERISY is a national nature reserve extending over more than 5,000 acres and comprising of mainly beech woodland; it is rich in fauna and flora. We cannot simply drive through the forest without more intimately savouring and absorbing its special features. It reminds us of our home at Camerton in the early days when there was a beech wood adjacent to us – in fact, we named our house 'The Beeches'. As soon as we see an opportunity to do so we drive off the road a very short distance into a small open area where, on one side and in front and behind us, we are seemingly quite deep in the forest. Now, we can open doors and windows and breath the fresh air and appreciate the distinctive and pleasing smells of the forest. What an appropriate time to enjoy a couple of Mr Kipling's Trifle Bakewells! In fact, we ate the boxful!!

Eventually, we drive on, leaving the forest and, at the same time, the Department of Calvados. CERISY-LA-FORET is in the Manche Department; it has a population of about 900. There are ruins of an oppidum nearby and the Romans built a fort here. When Christianity arrived early in the 6th century, Vigor built a monastery dedicated to St Peter and St Paul on a former Druid holy site. The Vikings invaded in the 9th century and destroyed the monastery. Under the Normans, Cerisy became an important market town; they built the Abbey of Saint-Vigor de Cerisy on the site of the former monastery – it consisted of 48 parishes, including Sherborne and Peterborough in England.

It would make a more interesting journey to continue on a somewhat circular route, heading now towards the coast and visiting Colombières in doing so. The first lords of COLOMBIERES (present population about 200) were three brothers – Guillaume, Raoul and Baudoin – friends of Guillaume le Conquérant. Subsequently, the town passed into the hands of the powerful Bacon du Molay family. During the course of the Hundred Years War the village and the château were ruined. On 9 June 1944 Colombières was liberated, following which General Omar Bradley established his headquarters in the château.

Our approach to le CHATEAU DE COLOMBIERES was well assisted by the direction signs. However, as we approached we found the gate closed. We left the car outside and we walked the quite long distance to the Château. At the door we were very courteously greeted by a very polite and friendly gentleman; we paid the entrance fee and we were invited inside. Almost straightaway our host explained that he had noticed that it had been difficult for Margaret to walk the distance from our parked car. He said that if we would like him to do so and that we would give him the keys, he would drive the car to just outside the door. He mentioned that it was a Saab car!!! We were very grateful for his offer and he invited us to sit in the stately dining room while he did so. Afterwards, we were invited into the medieval kitchen, with many pans hanging on the wall, and the chapel. The oldest parts of the present Château date from the end of the 14th century. After 1750 the Château came into the ownership of the Girardin family to which the present owners are linked.

We are very pleased to have been prompted to visit this Classified Historical Monument and privileged to be welcomed by Le Comte Charles on behalf of himself and the Comtesse de Maupeou d'Ableiges and their children. As we expressed our thanks and said au revoir to the Count, he told us that we had the distinction of being their last visitors for the season. Even so we lingered for quite a while to savour the exterior of this exceptional location and to photograph our Saab standing proudly near the entrance to the Château, before driving off in the direction of Trevieres. With our thoughts still focussed on what we had left behind we twice took a wrong turning in Trevieres before finding Formigny and eventually linking up with the D514 at St Laurent. Thenceforth we find the coast road to Arromanches very familiar. We had hoped that we might arrive in time to buy some food at our favourite patisserie – unfortunately, it had already closed. Never mind, we still have an assortment of nourishment bars and varied cartons of drinks in our 'larder'. We drive on to Bayeux arriving at the Campanile at 19.40. We have had a splendid journey of more than six hours, visiting places familiar and new, enjoying driving many miles along the peaceful roads of rural Normandy passing typical shuttered old houses. Now to enjoy our 'meal' accompanied with a welcome cup of coffee.

(60 miles)

Day 14 – Monday, 28 September 2015

After petit déjeuner our first priority is to renew our respective dressings. Margaret's comment on the weather is that it was "Il fait très beau mais il fait du vent".

It is 14.15 when we leave the Campanile, but this being our last day in Bayeux, we feel that we would like to make a final visit to its magnificent Cathédrale. The entrance on the north side is that most familiar to us, but we do not know of any parking facility nearby; it is in the medieval area of the city with pavements difficult to negotiate and, once inside la Cathédrale, there are many steps to descend. Consequently, the three-wheel walker will not be of practical help. Margaret will have to rely on her walking stick – and me – for support. We drive towards the entrance and we find some cars parked (and one or two spaces) in a small square – I think it may be Place Aux Bois – but I could not find any facility for purchasing a ticket – perhaps it's free. However, a visit to a nearby pharmacy revealed that there is a ticket machine, quite small and inconspicuous, hidden behind one of the cars. We can now happily leave the car and begin to walk down the ancient Rue des Chanoines. There is a narrow pavement, but the surface is very uneven and cars are parked indiscriminately. Nevertheless, I seized an opportunity of taking a photograph of the two spires soaring majestically above the city. It was a difficult exercise for us both, but eventually we reach the Cathedral entrance and with great care and caution we descend the steps safely. It was with relief and a feeling of accomplishment that we sat and relaxed for a while.

NOTRE DAME CATHEDRAL BAYEUX is the title of an excellent book produced by François Neveux, who is also the Cathedral Organist. It tells us that, "Construction of Bayeux Cathedral began in the Roman period, under Bishop Hugues, to continue under William the Conqueror's brother, Bishop Odo (11th century). Following serious fire damage during the 12th century, the Cathedral was rebuilt in Gothic style in the 13th century. Construction of the central tower began in the 15th century, under Bishop Louis d'Harcourt, to be completed only in the 19th century following major work by Eugène Flachet; this is one of France's finest cathedrals and an indisputable masterpiece of Norman Gothic art".

As we sat and observed this wonderful building, we took more photographs including, of course, the organ and we reminisced on earlier visits. We recall Samuel expressing his wish to "light a candle for Mr Mills" (our late neighbour at Trowbridge). On one Sunday morning in 2008 we visited shortly after the office had finished. Exceptionally, it had been the occasion of the celebration of the installation by Bishop Pierre Pican of a new archiprêtre, Laurent Berthout. There was a distinct atmosphere of excitement and hope. We were welcomed by a gentleman who also offered us a glass of wine. Regrettably. we did not accept his offer and I have never been sure why we declined the invitation. Eventually, we began to move around a little and independently. Soon I noticed Margaret in conversation with another elderly lady visitor. They were both using a walking stick and it became obvious that this was the subject of their conversation. As we converged, our new friend suggested that the three of us should sit down and we had an interesting conversation. Madame was, I think, 91 and Bayeux has been her lifelong home. She didn't hesitate to express her gratitude that on 7 June 1944 the British mercifully liberated her beloved city without causing any damage. She asked if I was there and I had to explain that I was too young to be involved. She was very interested to know from what part of England we came from. Of course, London was familiar and the West Country conveyed something to her. She appeared to have a recognition of Cornwall and perhaps in relation to a wedding. Eventually she decided that she should leave. Perhaps this is part of her daily routine of physical exercise and spiritual renewal. We then spent some time in the shop and, in addition to the book I have mentioned, we chose a selection of CDs of organ music played by Francois Neveux playing the Cavaille-Coll organ and also with trumpeters and a vocalist. (Sadly, after returning home and into the increasingly demanding routine associated with her general health, the CDs remained unopened – Margaret never heard the music she had chosen.) Before leaving the Cathédrale we had to note this Memorial:

"TO THE GLORY OF GOD AND TO THE MEMORY OF ONE MILLION DEAD OF THE

BRITISH EMPIRE WHO FELL IN THE GREAT WAR, 1914–1918, AND OF WHOM THE GREATER PART REST IN FRANCE".

A monumental fact!

Eventually, we began to climb the steps towards the door and then, out into the street, make our way carefully and cautiously back to our car. Our last day in Bayeux means that it is our final evening meal at Au 6 Juin in Arromanches. Once again, we spent an enjoyable couple of hours here as we have done so many times in past years. We enjoyed our meal and it was 19.53 when we left to return to our room at the Campanile. Another memorable day!

(17 miles)

Day 15 – Tuesday, 29 September 2015

Campanile Hotels are widespread in France; with their distinctive design and prominent locations they are readily recognized and easily found; all facilities, services and standards are identical. Although lacking a little of the personal attention and concern found in privately owned hotels, Logis de France for instance, they often provide very convenient accommodation. We have used them on a number of occasions, particularly that on the outskirts of Vire, in the south of Calvados, for our first night on many France journeys. We are pleased to have spent the last four nights here in Bayeux Campanile, but the time has come for us to leave for the very last time – it is 11.45!

Before leaving Bayeux, we return to Esso du Bessin to purchase petrol for our journey home – 35 litres for €46.91. It is now noon and we will make a final visit to Arromanches – at 12.30. Just one last walk down Boulevard Gilbert Longues and into Rue Marechal Joffre where we visited la Presse to buy one or two items, including a copy of that excellent daily regional newspaper *'Ouest France'* and two large table mats displaying historical information of 1944; then on to the seafront where, surprisingly, we found the sea very angry, which was a challenge to one brave lady. At 14.15 we reluctantly drove away from Arromanches. We travelled leisurely along the D514 until St Laurent-s-Mer where we decided to make a detour.

In the course of an identical journey on 6 October 2011 we reached this point only to find that the road ahead was closed, and we had to make a detour via Formigny. It revealed to us the site of the Battle of Formigny but, we did not have sufficient time to visit the whole area. Today our time is not limited.

The BATTLE of FORMIGNY was fought on 15 April 1450 between the English and French and ended in a decisive French victory. It was the penultimate battle of the Hundred Years' War. The opposing monarchs at this time were Henry VI of England and Charles VII of France. The final battle of the war was fought at Castillon in Gascony in 1453 – another decisive French victory.

When we reached the area of the Battle we found the Office de Tourisme open and a very helpful lady explained the various features of the site and directed us to interesting leaflets, etc. She advised us to visit the little chapel, dedicated to Saint-Louis, which we did. It was constructed in 1486 by the Comte de Clermont (also Charles I de Bourbon), commander of one of the French armies, to commemorate the victory. It is situated at the side of the road and Margaret was able to have a good view from the car. It appears to be in good condition, but I read that the bell tower is in danger of collapsing and there are appeals for donations; I was not able to go inside. Back near the Office we parked near the magnificent statue, created by the Norman sculptor, Arthur Le Duc; it was inaugurated in 1903 and is entered in the Inventory of Historic Monuments. It incorporates three bronze statues, one of which represents France pointing its sword at England symbolizing France's victory. The re-conquest of Normandy was finally achieved in the summer of 1450. Across to the other side of this rather busy road we were able to park alongside another memorial – to those who fell in the Great War – 'FORMIGNY A SES ENFANTS 1914–1918'. We are disappointed that in the course of moving from one position to another and being engrossed in what we had discovered we somehow failed to see the little Memorial which marks the actual battlefield. Nevertheless, it was a most interesting diversion!

We left Formigny to rejoin the D514 at St Laurent-s-Mer; we left the road and drove towards Pointe du Hoc, but it is not now possible to drive beyond the official car parks and, as we have visited the site several times in the past, we promptly returned to the D514. The approach to Grandcamp-Maisy from the east, where the road forks to the seafront, is unforgettable; there, salient, soaring, shining, sparkling is the spectacular "STATUE DE LA PAIX – WORLD PEACE STATUE" by Yao Yuan (Wen Yuan Yan) – "AU PEUPLE DE NORMANDIE". In this attractive garden there is a particular memorial:

> "In memory of Leonard G. Lomell DSO CO D. 2nd Ranger BN. WWII US ARMY RANGER. HALL OF FAME and the 225 American soldiers who, on 6 June 1944 assaulted and destroyed the 5 German guns at Pointe du Hoc. By the morning of 8 June, only 90 were still able to bear arms. They gave proof of their great courage. We will never forget them."

As we neared the seafront, we noticed a variety of temporary makeshift barriers which were, or had been, positioned at a number of accesses to the seafront. However, we found we could now drive on to the Quai Crampon and as we continued towards Le Duguesclin we were amazed to find so much debris across the road. There must have been a severe storm, but we had not experienced any of it. At the hotel entrance I was barely able to stay on my feet, the wind was so strong and when I eventually reached the door, it was locked! We drove on past the harbour, turning left into rue Aristide Briand then along the narrow route to the rear of the hotel – relieved, we parked the car. I climbed the stairs and found a lady at the desk. When I enquired what had happened, she said that it was une grande marée (a spring tide). It was a new experience for us! I returned to the car to accompany Margaret up to our room.

Even here we have not escaped the exceptional weather conditions, for the very strong wind was making an unbearable noise in forcing its way through the not tightly closed window. We could not tolerate that throughout the night! I called for the assistance of Monsieur who promptly applied sufficient physical strength to improve matters considerably. After an hour's relaxation we felt ready to make our way to the restaurant for we were looking forward to another enjoyable meal. Sitting at the table we occupied last week (I am sure) we did not hesitate to once again choose un filet de boeuf, with frites and mixed vegetables which, together with profiteroles and a small glass of wine, made an excellent and fitting final evening meal in France. On returning to our room we were pleased to find that the very strong wind had abated a little and was not likely to interrupt our night's sleep.

(36 miles)

Day 16 – Wednesday, 30 September 2015

Morning – and we have had a comfortable night. It was not inappropriate that we should spend our final night at Le Duguesclin, the hotel at which we hoped to spend our first night together in France some 36 years ago. We enjoyed a very leisurely petit déjeuner, appreciating for the last time the splendid 'sea view'. After thanking and saying au revoir to les propriétaires, we finally left the hotel at noon.

It is only about 50 miles to the ferry port of Cherbourg and our sailing time is not until 22.15 – we do not need to take the most direct route, via the N13. Instead, for the first part of the journey, we will take the road we used to use. Again, it's the D514, first to Osmanville and then Isigny-s-Mer, but continuing on the old road (D197A) to Carentan where we pass again the entrance to le gare. From Carentan we drive along the D913 to Vierville and Ste-Marie-du-Mont. STE-MARIE-du-MONT (pop. 800) was in the forefront of the actions on D-Day, being close to Utah Beach. Thousands of American soldiers were dropped in the area, scattered and finding themselves isolated in hostile territory, many were able to make use of their click-clack devices and congregate using the distinctive shape of the church steeple as a focal point. We are able to park near this same church and photograph it. The Church of Our Lady of the Assumption dates from the 11th century and has been a Listed Monument since 1840. In this same position we are close to the impressive war memorial and also the Hotel de Ville – it is evident that the village is eagerly looking forward to the privilege of being a 'GRAND DEPART du TOUR de FRANCE 2016' – 275 days from today.

As we sat in the car, we could see a direction sign – it conveniently took us along minor roads into Ste-Mere-Eglise. We parked at the church again and walked the short distance to La Libération for our lunch of croque-monsieur and Kit Kats. There is a useful toilet here – it has minimal space, situated under the stairs, but it is quite satisfactory. We could not leave this historic village without a final visit to the church; we spent some time inside in quiet contemplation. I looked at the organ (again) and I meant to record the inscription, but I think the instrument was donated by the British (?) Army. Close to the entrance is the figure of SAINTE ANTOINE de PADUA with child. We have found the figure of this saint in so many churches and he has been a favourite of Margaret; I had to take a photograph.

Sainte Antoine (1195–1231) was a Portuguese Franciscan priest who died in Padua, Italy. He was a powerful preacher, with a great knowledge of the scriptures; he had an undying love and devotion to the poor and the sick and he was one of the most quickly canonized saints in church history. He was proclaimed a Doctor of the Church in 1946. We returned to our car and after surveying the scene of the church and its effigy of John Steele, we set off at four o'clock to now join the N13 and drive directly to the ferry port. After entering the bypass of Cherbourg, I have to be particularly attentive on the descent as there are roads leading off to the right and we must ensure that we remain in the direction of the ferry-port. Often there are other vehicles and by their nature and appearance it is certain that they are heading for the same destination. However, the road is very quiet today, but we successfully reach the entrance to the Brittany Ferries terminal – it is now five o'clock.

We look forward to our first experience of an overnight crossing on this route. *BARFLEUR* was built in Finland and entered service in 1992. It has 72 four-berth cabins and 295 reclining seats.

Boarding for *Barfleur* will not begin for several hours and we find a convenient place to park near the refreshment hall; that is where we spend much of the time enjoying a snack and a drink in the company of a number of other travellers. Before the official time for boarding I moved our car to a position in front of the entrance gates and, in good time, we returned to the car to be among the first to pass through the ticket and passport checkpoint. However, when we reach the boarding queue we are held back to be, perhaps, the last vehicle to drive on board. The reason being that we had to be positioned with sufficient space for a member of the crew to assist Margaret from the car into a wheelchair. We were then taken to our outside large two-berth cabin with en suite facilities – No 8104. It was very compact, but comfortable and we soon established ourselves for the night. As the ship sailed at 22.15 we were a little disappointed to realize that, although we had an outside cabin, the superstructure of the ship obscured our view as we left Cherbourg and France for the last time. Also, we soon realized that with the ship moving we had to be exceptionally careful when moving about, particularly in getting in and out of the bathroom. Clearly the beds were the best and safest place to be and we quickly settled down for the 'night'. Our arrival time at Poole was 07.00 and we had not been given any advice that we should be ready to disembark at that time. In fact, before that time members of the crew were knocking on the door wishing to prepare the cabin for the next voyage. We were by no means ready to leave; it was a very hurried process and we had no time for breakfast. Soon a member of the crew returned with a wheelchair and he checked that together we were taking all our belongings with us. In no time we were back to our car. We had had a satisfactory night, but we should have observed the time reminders which were broadcast and prepared to leave the cabin much earlier. However, the assistance we had received was invaluable.

(55 miles)

Thursday, 1 October 2015

Driving off the ship at seven o'clock in the morning was an unfamiliar experience and we did not feel fully alert. However, there was a long delay at the customs checkpoint, and we had time to collect our thoughts. As we left the port at 07.10 and began to drive through the urban area, already with a considerable volume of traffic, we felt we had been plunged into a different world. Nevertheless, we successfully found our way through Hamworthy to Blandford. By now, the sun was very bright and quite low in the sky and with the considerable volume of traffic I was finding it difficult to read all the road signs correctly. Suddenly I realized we were heading towards the centre of Blandford. I am not familiar with the town and it took us quite a while to return to the A350 in the direction of Shaftesbury. Henceforth, we succeeded in negotiating the route successfully, but it was with relief that we reached Green Lane at 9.15.

(53 miles)

Our total mileage for the journey was 541.

Despite her physical condition and the progressive nature of her dementia, Margaret determinedly maintained a record of this journey as she had done for so many journeys in the past; I have since appreciated that it required a considerable effort for her to do so.

We had serious misgivings regarding the wisdom of undertaking this journey; however, it was an entire success and gave us much interest, pleasure, satisfaction and a feeling of accomplishment. We have no regrets!

Above all, we have been moved by the numerous instances of recognition and concern of our physical limitations and difficulties and we have been immensely grateful for all the help and support given to us on so many occasions. Those sixteen days left us with a permanent memory of so much kindness and goodwill.

In our cabin on the Barfleur, leaving Cherbourg and France for the very last time.
This is, indeed, the end of our *France – A Journey* and we are immensely grateful to have been able to accomplish this final stage at the ages of 82 and 85.

FRANCE – A JOURNEY

RECOLLECTIONS AND REFLECTIONS
AN EPILOGUE

We have reached the end of our *France – A Journey*, which began for Margaret and I more than 35 years earlier, although my introduction to France occurred in the early 1950's. It has been an abiding theme in our lives for many years; it has provided a constant interest from year to year, many, many hours studying the map and planning and preparing the next route to encompass places we wish to visit and friends we wish to see, as well as incorporating places and sites which might well be of interest; making reservations; most importantly, studying the language to enable us to read notices and information and, above all, to communicate with the people we meet. At the same time, it has presented a challenge and, subsequently, a sense of accomplishment.

Having completed plans and arrangements, we have left home confident that we could look forward to our planned tour, with no thoughts of when and how we would be returning; once on board the ferry or the train all stresses and strains seemed to evaporate. We allowed each 'adventure' to unfold, like turning the pages of a book. We have endeavoured to keep journey stages to a reasonable and comfortable length, thus allowing time to pause and reflect and, at the same time, giving us a feeling that the distance travelled was not as far as the number of miles recorded. Importantly, it created an impression that our many fond locations were not as distant as the map suggested; it produced an effect that this vast country was much more intimate than is indicated by its geography – a place which we came to regard as a 'second home'.

Of course, one can meet unanticipated circumstances, deviations, etc., when the route has to be modified. It is on such occasions that the navigator becomes invaluable. For many years we used the IGN France Grand Tourisme sheet maps, although excellent they were somewhat unwieldy to use while travelling in the car; in 2001 we bought a Michelin France Atlas which, although quite bulky, was much more practical.

Reliable navigating is an essential part of a journey; Margaret performed this role so reliably and well. In addition to constantly referring to the map, ensuring that we adhered to the planned route and advising me of our progress and drawing attention to interesting places and features as we went, she maintained a diary recording our progress as well as everyday and interesting information.

There are, naturally, many journeys, occasions and places which are prominent in the memory. Here are some which come to mind.

Firstly, the never to be forgotten journeys of discovery we enjoyed with Paul and Ian in 1979 and in the early 1980s.

AN EPILOGUE

1984 saw our last family holiday – with Ian – our Rhine Valley Holiday. It included a visit to Verdun and a deeply moving experience of the Ossuaire of Douaumont, overflowing with unbelievable history. Then a visit to historic Reims.

Weeks at Cap d'Agde, enjoying the Mediterranean sunshine and sea, with time for relaxation and rest and the opportunity to read and write.

Visiting all the templar and hospitaller sites on the Causse du Larzac.

Exploring the region, in the Languedoc, of the bitter and brutal conflict during the 12th and 14th centuries between the Cathars (the pure) and the Catholic Church which did not recognise their unorthodox Christianity.

Journeys into the Corbieres, the mountain region foothills of the Pyrenees which borders the Mediterranean.

Driving along the foot of the Pyrenees and a visit to Lourdes.

Travelling on the amazing Little Yellow Train to the heights of the mountains on two occasions and on another occasion driving a parallel route – a very strenuous journey – then walking across the frontier into Spain. The Little Yellow Train – one of the great railway journeys of the world – opened in 1909. The line rises through dramatic scenery from an altitude of 427 metres at its lower terminus at Villefranche de Conflent, to a summit at Bolquere Eyne at 1,592 metres.

It then drops down to a high Pyrenean valley, to its terminus at Latour de Carol. A total distance of about 39 miles. At Latour de Carol it connects with the French railway line from Toulouse and the Spanish line from Barcelona.

A total of ten weeks spent at Castelnau Montratier in the Department of Lot, exploring much of this region, becoming very fond of its chief town, Cahors, and establishing lasting friendships.

Some thirteen séjours at the Hôtel de France at Saint-Savin, Vienne, being so welcome there and always visiting its beautiful Abbey Church which has murals dating from the 11th and 12th centuries and exploring the interesting region.

Discovering the Correze Department and spending many happy stays with friends in Albussac and many hours sitting alongside the silent Dordogne at Argentat and Beaulieu-sur-Dordogne as well as visiting many interesting places in the area.

Visiting places which featured in the Wars of Religion in the latter part of the 16th century.

Tours of the Battlefields of the Somme, the Ypres Salient and standing where John McCrae wrote those immortal lines – '*In Flanders Fields*'.

Tours of the Region of Burgundy including visits to Cluny and to historic Vézelay, with its link with the Crusades.

Visiting the open-air display and record of the Battle of Poitiers (also Battle of Tours) in 732, overlooking the actual site, in which Charles Martel, leading the Frankish and Burgundian forces, was victorious over invasion forces of Umayyad Caliphate led by Abdul Rahman Al Ghafiqi – thus halting the advance of Islam into Northern Europe for centuries to come.

A train journey to Nice allowing visits to other places on the Cote d'Azur – Menton, Roquebrune and Antibes.

A visit to Albi and its dominating 13th century redbrick Cathedral – a Gothic landmark.

A weekend in Rouen by coach, which included a visit to the Gardens of Claude Monet at Giverny.

A journey into the Pays de la Loire Region, visiting Les Sables-d'Olonne and the Ile de Noirmoutier, using the bridge erected in 1971. The Passage du Gois, a paved-over sandbank with a length of 2.8 miles, is flooded twice a day! Inhabited since prehistoric times, Noirmoutier was subjected to a Viking raid in 799.

By train from St-Junien to the porcelain city of Limoges.

A day in Orléans – a city saved from the English siege by Jeanne d'Arc in 1429.

A memorable visit to remarkable Rocamadour; the buildings rise in stages up the side of a cliff, on the right bank of the Alzou, to the churches.

A visit to Caen with George and Samuel.

Visits to Perpignan with its extensive old centre which aligns its coloured houses in a series of picturesque streets and alleys. A 'City of Art and History'.

A privileged viewing of the skulls of Louis XI and of his wife, Charlotte, at the Basilica Notre-Dame at Clery-Saint-Andre.

Several visits to the magnificent cathedral of Chartres where Henri IV was crowned – the only king not to be crowned in Reims – and meeting the English guide, Malcolm Miller, who has been guiding visitors since 1958.

Discovering the tombs of two Kings of France who were not buried in the Cathedral of St Denis in Paris – Philip I at Saint-Benoit-sur-Loire and Louis XI at Clery-Saint-Andre.

Many crossings of the spectacular Viaduc de Millau, at 342 metres the tallest bridge in the world.

A most poignant and deeply moving visit to the preserved Martyr Village of Oradour-sur-Glane where, on 10 June 1944, 642 villagers were massacred – only six survived.

Many unforgettable welcomes at the Plantagenêt in Chinon.

Visiting 13 of the towns through which the River Vienne flows in the course of its 226-mile journey, reaching the view point near Candes-Saint-Martin to witness its confluence with the River Loire and then, eventually, reaching its source deep in the upper regions of the Plateau de Millevaches.

Arriving at the town of Saint-Junien, in the Haute-Vienne, as large crowds were excitedly celebrating the septennial ostensions ceremonies of worshipping the saints of the Limousin. The procession through the town, with flags, banners, decorations and costumed historical figures is a great occasion for the region. The camaraderie is remarkable as one gentleman put it to us. It was certainly a most memorable experience for us.

Visits to some 35 member villages of that exclusive association, of about 145 villages, of *Les Plus Beau Villages de France*.

The long drive up Mont Ventoux in Provence to its bare and windy summit at 1912m and the fantastic views.

Reaching the extensive site of the Battle of Alesia in 52 BC, where Julius Caesar finally defeated the Celts of Gaul (France), led by Vercingetorix, and which enabled his conquest of England.

Our meeting with Charles Hargrove in that café in Bayeux.

Discovering the vast natural region of the Camargue, the Rhone delta, (360 sq. miles) and its border towns.

Experiencing the remarkable volcanic region of the Auvergne.

An unforgettable visit to Puy-en-Velay, famous for its cathedral, for a kind of lentil, for its lacemaking and as a starting point for Le Chemin de St Jacques de Compostelle.

The mountainous Cevennes and, particularly, driving from Florac to Saint-Jean-du-Gard – the Corniche des Cevennes (D907) – a spectacular route of 53km built at the beginning of the 18th century.

A day in the southern city of Toulouse by train from Cahors. The fourth-largest city in France; it was founded by the Romans; has three UNESCO World Heritage Sites and is known for its unique architecture made of pinkish terracotta bricks.

A visit to Azincourt and to the traditional site of the Battle of Agincourt in 1415.

The Château de Chalus outside of which King Richard I was mortally wounded in 1199.

The wonders of the Gorges de l'Aveyron, Gorges du Lot, Gorges de la Dordogne and Gorges du Tarn.

Discovering some of the many natural regions – the Parc Naturel Régional des Marais du Cotenin et du Bessin, the Parc Naturel Régional de la Brenne and the Sologne in north-central France.

AN EPILOGUE

Many séjours at the farm at Vienne-en-Bessin in Normandy – visiting historic sites of the Battle of Normandy, enjoying the lovely countryside and the lasting friendships established there.

Discovering the spot, at the Chateau of Chinon, where Henry II died in 1189 and the spot, in Candes-Saint-Martin, where Saint Martin of Tours died in the year 397.

A visit to Rennes, the capital of Brittany.

Many visits to the beautiful historic city of Lille.

A number of visits by train to the wonderful city of Paris, including a memorable 70th birthday present from our family.

...and many, many more!

One of the man-made features of the land of France which has attracted our attention throughout our journey has been the seemingly innumerable war memorials. It may not be incorrect to state that every village, however small, every town and every city has its war memorial. The Great War (1914–18) occasioned the slaughter of the manhood of France on an appalling scale. In terms of figures an average of nearly 900 men were killed every day or a total of some 1.3 million. Little wonder that the cry came that the nation was bleeding to death. The memorials illustrate the depth of loss and grief suffered, by their size, their design, their elaborateness and detail. We have paused to view, to read and to photograph many memorials; to reflect on the number of names, the number of identical surnames and in relation to the size of the village or town is a very moving experience.

As we travelled and approached towns and villages, it was always a pleasure to meet the sign '*Ville-Fleurie*' – more effective than a speed limit!

A lasting impression and memory of the landscape of the country is of its vastness and of its spaciousness, contrasting with the intimacy of ancient villages. Its many features are on a grand scale – the immensity of the forests (one third of France is covered in trees) – the endless areas of fruit trees draped with netting, in the Perigord, for instance – the wonderfully neat and extensive vineyards, with a rose tree marking the end of each row, in Burgundy, the Corbières and around Chinon – the expansive cereal producing plains of the Touraine – the glorious sight of masses of the brilliant yellow tournesols – the amazing sight of the lavender fields of Provence, revealed when descending from Mont Ventoux – also, extensive fields of yellow rapeseed blossom and sweet corn plants.

Much of the history of Europe has been laid in France; the victory of Caesar over the Celts in 52 BC; the victory of Charles Martel in 732 over the Islamic forces; the Treaty of Saint-Clair-sur-Epte between Charles III of France and Rollo, leader of the Vikings in 911, thus establishing the Duchy of Normandy; the rise of William the Conqueror; the Hundred Years' War over the right to rule the Kingdom of France, during the 14th and

15th centuries; the Napoleonic Wars of the early 19th century; in the 20th century the focus of two horrendous World Wars.

Insignificant and unspectacular experiences, but nonetheless memorable, are –

Following a meal in the Hotel de France in Saint-Savin, the late evening strolls from the Abbey Church along the bank of the River Gartempe, sometimes spotting a heron on the opposite bank, to the bend in the river where the artist Joanna Carrington spent many hours painting, and then, in the ultimate of peace and tranquillity, sitting on the seat erected in her memory.

Sitting outside the home of our neighbours at La Taillade, Beatrice and Marc, in the silence of the darkness, listening to the owls as they gathered in the tall fir trees, remarkably responding to the calls of Marc.

Sitting at a pavement café on the busy central street of Boulevard Leon Gambetta in Cahors, enjoying a cup of coffee and allowing the world to pass by.

A delightful country walk with Beatrice, Marc and Tristan from the D32 near St Sauveur-la-Vallee (population 39) along a trail following a trickling stream which may have been the GR 46 (Grande Randonnée) and picking blackberries in an open field, which Beatrice later made into jam as a gift to us.

Margaret had suffered from an ankle ulcer for many years as well as arthritis in her feet and legs, which had made walking increasingly difficult and even painful. When, in 2013, she was diagnosed with Alzheimer's and Dementia we felt that our final journey to France had been in 2011. However, it was not to be so, and we have been very grateful that we were able to make a further three journeys after that time – in 2013, 2014 and finally, at the ages of 82 and 85, in 2015; the help and support we received from Eurostar, French Railways (SNCF) and Brittany Ferries was invaluable in completing these last journeys.

Throughout our 'journey' France comprised, administratively, of 22 metropolitan regions and, since 1790, of 96 departments. However, in 2016 the number of regions was reduced to 13. We traversed all the 22 regions and many of the departments. The region we had much fondness for, was the Limousin, one of the ancient Provinces. I think our favourite departments would be Calvados, in Normandy, the Lot and the Corrèze, both in the south-western part of the country and the Herault, bordering the Mediterranean.

We both had a basic knowledge and understanding of the French language and in 2003 we joined the French Group of the U3A in Trowbridge, which we thoroughly enjoyed and benefitted from greatly. The basis of the group was reading, understanding and conversation and our 'text-book' was the excellent bimonthly magazine *La Vie Outre-Manche*. This contains a wide variety of material, including grammar exercises, crosswords and descriptions of places and sites, several of which we have subsequently visited. The hosts for these sessions were, Joyce in Trowbridge, who

AN EPILOGUE

had taught French in a local school and Phyliss in Westbury. Phyliss, who had been the children's book editor for Faber and Faber for (I think) 27 years was a most excellent teacher who inspired us both. Sadly, both these ladies have since passed away.

For many years we have been interested in the local affairs of two departments of the country, in particular – Manche and Calvados in Normandy and Herault in Languedoc-Roussillon; especially by reading the daily local papers – *Ouest France* and *Midi Libre* – when in the area.

Since acquiring the means to receive all French Television channels, national and regional, in October 2002, we have enjoyed watching many programmes – entertaining, educational and for current affairs and news – *le journal at 20 heures* on France 2. We have taken an interest in the national affairs and the approach of France to international situations. We have watched the weekly broadcasts of the live celebrations of la messe, which have been broadcast regularly since 1949.

We have often experienced and appreciated the spontaneous and sincere concern, understanding, sympathetic and compassionate nature of French people on many occasions. Goodwill and kindness have been a lasting memory of our *France – A Journey*. From the exceptional efforts of Monsieur Cloarec to assist us in July 1979, to the extraordinary concern shown by that dear Lady organist of the Church of Valonges in September 2015 and the following attention I received from pharmacists, we have felt a permanent degree of security and care during our journeys.

Our *France – A Journey* has been both a physical journey and also a psychological journey.

I have to say that France thus became an integral part of our lives – a second home – which, of course, together with other aspects – family, friends and music – shed such gracious blessings on our joint lives throughout some 60 years.

Reviving the memories and reliving the experiences of our journeys and compiling these records retrospectively has been a work of great satisfaction and of pleasure, for any apprehensions and uncertainties we might have experienced originally no longer exist.

A DEDICATION

I dedicate these personal commentaries, journals and guides of our *France – A Journey*, to Margaret, who made these records possible by her enthusiasm, by navigating and throughout, by keeping an invaluable daily record and, not least, by being able to provide a refreshing Werther's Original on some of the longer driving stages. Margaret, I thank you!

Michael Clark

Lightning Source UK Ltd.
Milton Keynes UK
UKHW050251261021
392811UK00004B/198/J